SIMPLE PYTHON:
COMPUTER PROGRAMMIMG FOR BEGINNERS USING PYTHON 3

Dennis G. Pringle

Superfred Support Services

www.lulu.com

Simple Python

Edition 1.0
ISBN 978-1-291-22138-1
Copyright © 2012, Dennis G. Pringle.

Table Of Contents

Chapter 1. Introduction

This book explains how to write computer programs using the Python programming language. It is intended for absolute beginners and assumes no prior knowledge of programming. Although the book explains how to program using Python, many of the basic principles are common to all computer languages, so the reader should be able to make the transition to other languages relatively painlessly should he or she ever feel the need. However, given Python's versatility, most readers will probably never have any need to learn another language.

Approach

The best way to learn how to program is to do it. This book therefore provides numerous examples and exercises that you can attempt on your own. Copies of the examples and suggested solutions to the exercises are available for download from a website. These source code files are very small so the entire set should download very quickly even if you have a slow connection. Full instructions for downloading and extracting the files are provided in Chapter 2.

The examples are printed in full in the text so that you can read the book even when you may not have access to a computer, but it is strongly recommended that you run the programs on a computer and then experiment to establish what effect making various changes would have - even making deliberate mistakes can be instructive. Most of the examples are fairly short, so it is further suggested that you should type the source code rather than simply run a downloaded file. This may take slightly longer, but it will help to focus your attention on some of the details, especially if you try to understand what each line of code does as you enter it rather than just transcribe it unthinkingly.

It is also strongly recommended that you attempt each of the exercises before checking the suggested solution. Some solutions are more elegant than others, but if you can get your program to do what you intended then your answer is 'correct'. The answer files are primarily intended to allow you to compare your solution with mine. In some instances you may find that my solution is neater, but in other instances you will find that your solution is preferable. One of the best ways to learn any programming language is to explore other people's code, and then see if you can improve on it.

The material is sequenced to form a learning progression – i.e. the material in each chapter is intended to build upon the material presented in previous chapters. An attempt has also been made to organise the chapters thematically, although it is not always possible to provide an exhaustive coverage of each topic before moving on, as a full understanding of some topics is dependent upon a knowledge of material to be introduced later. Some topics are therefore introduced in the earlier chapters and then revisited in more detail later in the book. Readers who prefer a more formal (and more complete) description of each language component in a single place should consult the *Python Reference Manual* in the Official Python Website (http://docs.python.org/dev/reference/).

Why Program?

Back in old days, when even the new films on television were in black and white, if you wanted to use a computer you usually had little option but to write your own programs. Many computer users of a certain vintage (i.e. now old, grey and, if they have any sense, retired) consequently have a working knowledge of one or more of the older **procedural** programming languages, such as FORTRAN, BASIC or Pascal. Nowadays, however, pre-written application programs are available for just about every conceivable purpose, enabling almost anyone to use a computer with no programming skills whatsoever. Thanks to graphical user interfaces (GUIs), based on the now familiar WIMP (i.e. Windows, Icons, Menus, Pointer) technology, all you need to be able to do is aim your mouse pointer at the appropriate icon and click. GUIs did much to popularise computing and make it available to a much broader audience, but they also reduced the need to know how to program. Indeed the older languages were not very suitable for GUI development, so to write a program to take full advantage of WIMP technology, it became more or less essential to use one of the newer **object-orientated** languages, such as Visual Basic, C++, Java or C#. For many greybeards this was a learning curve too far.[1]

Although this book does not actually explain how to do it, programming GUI windows using Python is not very difficult. However, the present volume confines itself to procedural programming, which may be

---

[1] The term 'greybeard' is intended in a gender-neutral sense! Most early programmers were male and therefore probably now have grey hair sprouting out everywhere, except possibly the tops of their head, but the term is used to include women of a similar age. However, if you are female and actually do have a grey beard, you should probably consider seeing someone about it.

regarded both as an end in itself but also an essential pre-requisite for object-orientated programming (including GUI applications). A companion volume explains object-orientated programming, including how to program GUIs. Hopefully these books may tempt some of the greybeards out of (programming) retirement, as well as enable complete beginners of all ages to get started.

So, you may well ask: 'If knowing how to program is no longer essential, why write a book explaining how to do it?' Although ready-made software is available to do almost anything, it may be more accurate to say that it *almost* does almost anything – i.e. in many cases it does not quite do what you would ideally like it to. In such situations programming skills may enable you to fine tune existing applications to your specific needs. Also, whilst the software you need may be 'out there' somewhere, tracking it down (and then learning how to use it) may prove time consuming. With basic programming skills you can often write a simple program of your own in a fraction of the time that it takes to track down ready-made software written by someone else. However, although there are practical reasons for knowing how to program, the most persuasive reason (in my opinion) is that programming is fun. It provides a mental challenge, yet it is a challenge that can usually be achieved (which is good for the ego). It may take a couple of attempts, but you should eventually get your program to work. And if you get a complex program to work first time, the buzz is something similar to getting a hole in one in golf (or so I would imagine). If you like doing puzzles, you will love programming. This book will set you lots of 'puzzles' to help get you addicted.

There are also some less tangible reasons for learning how to program. To program it is important to be able to think logically, concisely and precisely (i.e. be able to break complex problems into simple steps, separate the essentials from the non-essentials, and to eliminate woolly thinking); it is also necessary to be imaginative and creative (i.e. to discover new and better ways to do things); and, if writing programs for other people to use, to be empathetic (i.e. be able to place yourself in the shoes of the end-user). Programming will help sharpen your skills in all these areas. These are qualities that we all like to think we have in abundance - but rarely do. Although you may fool yourself, you cannot fool a computer - if your skills are less perfect than you imagine, the computer will tell you. So, as an added bonus, programming will teach you humility as you develop a better appreciation of your deficiencies. These qualities are useful in all spheres of life, so (at the risk of possibly overstating the case) learning to program will make you a better person!

Computers And Programming Languages

Computers are comprised of all sorts of bibs and bobs, but the command centre of every computer is its **processor** or **central processing unit** (CPU).[2] The processor controls all the other components, but it requires instructions to tell it how to do this. These instructions must be in a form that the processor understands, known as **machine code**. Machine code is basically a series of electrical pulses that can be represented by a series of binary digits (i.e. 0s and 1s). Although machine code can be understood by the CPU, its binary representation is totally unintelligible to the average human. So, although it is theoretically possible to write programs directly in machine code, it is not very practical as one long string of 0s and 1s to a human looks very much the same as any other string of 0s and 1s. Most computer programs are therefore written using a programming language that is more intelligible to humans, but can be translated into machine code using special software.

Low And High Level Languages

These programming languages take many forms. Some languages, usually described as **low-level**, provide instructions broken down into fundamental steps and require a very detailed knowledge of the workings of the processor and other hardware components. The lowest level language is **assembly** language. Each type of processor (or family of related processors) has its own assembly language. Assembly languages use mnemonics as a shorthand notation for commands, usually followed by parameters to indicate data values or memory locations. Assembly language programs are translated by software, referred to as an **assembler**, into machine code that the processor can execute. The machine code can also be translated back into assembly code by another piece of software known as a **disassembler**. This provides a means for establishing the inner secrets of any piece of executable software, irrespective of the language it was originally written in. (However, in the case of copyrighted software, reverse engineering using a disassembler is generally illegal and could land you in a lot of trouble).

The mnemonics used in assembly language code are not much more intelligible to most people than machine code, so in practice most

---

[2] This section is not essential to knowing how to program in Python, so if you are eager to get started you could skip ahead to next section. However, it may be useful to be aware of the broader context. As the term 'bibs and bobs' will hopefully suggest, this section provides an extremely simplified outline.

programs are written using a **high-level** language. High-level languages use commands (mostly based on English language words), each of which may translate into several distinct steps at the machine code level. The use of English language words makes high level languages much easier to understand.

Some high level languages may be regarded as 'higher' or 'lower' than others. C, and its close relative C++, are sometimes described as 'medium level' languages. Although they are high level languages, they provide a greater degree of control over individual bits and bytes than most other high level languages. Programs written in these languages also run faster than programs written in most other high level languages. C and C++ are therefore the languages of choice for many professional software engineers. Python, in contrast, is sometimes described as a 'very high level' language because it uses a high level of abstraction, rather than directly dealing with the details. This makes it very suitable for beginners. Python programs do not run as fast as C or C++ programs, but unless you are doing something very complicated, the difference in performance is negligible.

Compilers And Interpreters

High-level languages can be divided into two broad categories depending upon whether they are normally translated using a compiler or an interpreter.

A **compiler** translates the entire program into machine code before attempting to run it. In fact, there are normally three steps involved:

1. **Compilation**. The high-level source code is translated into **object code** (i.e. machine code) required by a specific processor.

2. **Linkage**. The object code is linked with other pieces of machine code required for the program to run. These additional chunks include general-purpose functions or procedures previously translated to machine code. The linked program is referred to as an **executable**.

3. **Execution**. The executable is run.

Getting a program written in a compiler language to compile and link without errors can sometimes be a frustrating business, but once the code has been translated, the translated binaries can be saved either as object code or as executables. The executables can be run at any point in the future without further translation. Proprietary **application programs** are usually distributed as pre-compiled ready-to-run executables for a particular platform. This is not only more convenient for the end-user, but also helps to protect the source code from prying eyes.

Interpreters, in contrast, execute the source code one line at a time - i.e. they translate the first line, execute it, then translate the second line, execute it, and so forth. If the interpreter cannot translate or execute a particular statement, then the program stops running at the point where the error occurred. This makes it easier to develop new programs, because if a program breaks down you can often check the current values of its variables to get clues as to the nature of the problem. It is usually a simple matter to fix and re-run the program. The main problem with interpreted languages is that programs are translated every time they are run. They therefore take longer to execute than a compiled program.

The distinction between compiled and interpreted languages has become blurred in recent years because some languages now use a combination of both approaches.[3] Java, for example, was specifically designed to enable programs to be run on different platforms (e.g. Windows, Linux, Mac) over the Internet. The Java source code is initially compiled to produce an intermediate bytecode which can be distributed to end-users. The bytecode is subsequently interpreted (i.e. translated to machine code and executed) by a Java Virtual Machine (JVM) designed for the particular platform on which the program is run. This facilitates flexibility as the same bytecode can be distributed over the Internet, but can then be executed on any one of several different platforms.

Although generally thought of as an interpreted language, Python uses a somewhat similar two-stage process. The original source code is compiled into an intermediate bytecode which is then executed in a second stage by the interpreter. In some instances the bytecode is automatically saved for future use. Each time it is accessed, the Python interpreter checks if any changes have been made since it was run previously; if no changes have been made, the compilation stage is skipped and the saved bytecode is interpreted directly. This process is hidden from the end-user, but it reduces the total time taken to run a Python program.

---

[3] Strictly speaking a high level language is an abstraction which could be implemented using either an interpreter or a compiler, but *de facto* most high level languages are associated with one particular mode of implementation.

Procedural and Object-Orientated Paradigms

A distinction may be made between various programming paradigms, the two most important of which may be referred to as **procedural** (or **imperative**)[4] and **object-orientated**. Programs written in a procedural language provide instructions as a series of commands to be executed in a specific sequence; whereas programs written in an object-orientated language provide instructions on how objects should behave without necessarily specifying the sequence in which the actions should take place. Most of the older programming languages (e.g. FORTRAN, BASIC, COBOL, Pascal, C) adopt a procedural approach, whereas most of the more recent programming languages (including Visual Basic, C++, Delphi, Java and C#) utilise an object-orientated paradigm. Python is at heart an object-orientated language, but it is very flexible and can be used just as readily to write programs using a procedural approach. Indeed, as already noted, this book confines itself to procedural programming using Python.

In the early days of computing, programs required very limited user interaction – e.g. the user would specify at the beginning of the program what data were to be used and what operations were to be carried out (e.g. conduct a particular type of statistical analysis using a particular set of data), and the program would then be left to run on its own in **batch** mode (i.e. without further user intervention). This was in part a function of the input and output devices on the early computers – input was generally by punched cards or paper tape, and output was generally through a line printer, so there was little scope for ongoing interaction between user and machine – i.e. once the instructions had been specified they were not easily changed without replacing cards or re-punching a paper tape. **Procedural** programs were therefore designed to perform a specified series of operations in a well-defined sequence, which could be represented by a **flow diagram**. This sequence might contain branches and loops, but in many cases the program basically broke down into three main steps: read in the data; do something with it; and then output the results.

Certain operations might need to be performed several times within a sequential program. Rather than repeat the same instructions to perform

---

[4] The term 'imperative' is preferred by some authorities to 'procedural' to describe these languages because they are used to provide an ordered sequence of commands (or imperatives). However, the term 'procedural' is more common. Although the two terms mean something slightly different, the terms 'procedural' and 'imperative' will be used here interchangeably.

these operations each time they were required, the instructions could be written as a separate block of code variously referred to as a 'procedure', 'subroutine', or 'function' (depending upon the language), which could be called at any point in the main program – i.e. when required, the job could be 'subcontracted' to the procedure. The code for the procedure therefore only needed to be defined once but could be executed numerous times. Indeed, with careful planning, procedures written for one program could be saved in a library for reuse by other programs.

Whilst the procedural paradigm tends to think in terms of actions (e.g. procedures), the **object-orientated** approach (as the name suggests) tends to think in terms of objects. An **object** is basically a 'thing' (e.g. a car) that has various **properties** (e.g. current speed, an owner) and a number of **methods**, which may be thought of as procedures for changing a particular property. For example, a car object might have an accelerator method, a braking method, a change of ownership method, etc. Collections of similar objects form a **class**. Object-orientated programming entails defining the properties and methods for a particular class (e.g. a car class). The class may therefore be thought of as the blueprint for individual objects (i.e. specific cars). Having defined a class, you can create as many objects of that type as required, each with its own specific properties. In the same way that procedures can be reused in different programs, classes can be also be reused. Indeed, one of the main attractions of most object-orientated programming languages is that they usually come supplied with a large number of pre-defined classes which can be plugged together, a bit like a Lego set, making it possible to write sophisticated programs with minimal effort.

Object-orientated programming entails identifying the relationship between different types of object – e.g. car objects and driver objects. These relationships can be depicted using a **UML (Unified Modelling Language) diagram** showing the relationships between different classes of objects. A UML diagram may be thought of as the object-orientated equivalent of a flow diagram, except that it depicts relationships between different classes of objects rather than steps within a process.

The introduction in the 1970s of keyboards and monitors as the main input and output devices created the possibility of more **interactive programs** – i.e. the program could be instructed to pause at various points and display a text message on the monitor asking the user what to do next. The user could then respond by typing in an answer, and the program could be programmed to proceed in different ways depending upon the user's response. However, the approach was still basically sequential, so the older procedural languages could handle this without any need for major modifications.

New possibilities emerged in the 1980s with the introduction of graphics monitors as an output device, and the mouse as an input device. In particular, graphics monitors facilitated the introduction of graphical user interfaces utilising WIMP (Windows, Icons, Menus, Pointers) technology. Whilst in theory it would be possible to program a GUI (Graphical User Interface) using a procedural language, it is much more practical to treat each component of the GUI (i.e. each window, each button, etc.) as an object, with particular properties (e.g. dimensions, colour, captions) and methods (e.g. actions to be carried out if clicked). The newer object-orientated programming languages (such as Visual Basic, C++, Java, Delphi, C#) really came into their own as they provided major advantages for writing GUIs (e.g. by providing predefined classes for windows, buttons, etc.). The object-orientated philosophy also offered advantages in other areas.

GUI programs provide more scope for user interaction – i.e. instead of having to wait for the program to ask a question, the user can determine what to do next by clicking on an icon or selecting a menu option. The interface can also be reorganised to suit the user by opening, closing or moving windows. From a programming point of view, each of these objects (i.e. each icon, each menu option, each window) must be in a state of readiness to respond to the user's instructions. Each intervention by the user (e.g. moving a pointer, clicking on an object) is referred to as an **event**. Each object must be programmed so that it knows which events to respond to and what actions it should take. Event-driven programming clearly entails a different mindset to the strongly sequential procedural paradigm.

This book explains how to write standalone procedural programs that will run within a text window. It does not explain how to write object-orientated programs, nor does it explain how to program GUIs. These topics are covered in a companion volume that builds upon the material contained here. This book provides the essential pre-requisites for the second book, but it also stands on its own. I could of course have combined the books into a single larger volume, but for many readers procedural programming will satisfy all their needs, so they will have no need to read (or buy) the companion volume. By splitting the material between two books, readers can decide for themselves whether they wish to extend their skills to include object-orientated programming and graphical user interfaces.

Python

Python is an easy to learn, yet very flexible programming language suitable for the development of a wide range of software applications. Although essentially an object-orientated language, it is equally suited to procedural and object-orientated paradigms. Python was originally developed by a Dutch programmer, **Guido van Rossum**, who named it in honour of the BBC Monty Python television series. It was first released (as version 0.9.0) in 1991 and continues to be developed as an open source community project managed by the non-profit Python Software Foundation (PSF). Guido van Rossum retains a strong guiding influence, as reflected by his title within the Python community as BDFL (Benevolent Dictator For Life). The intellectual property rights are held by the PSF under an open source licence that makes Python freely available to all users, even for commercial purposes.

Implementations

There are several different **implementations** of Python. An implementation may be thought as the environment under which programs written in Python are run. Classic Python (or **CPython**) provides a compiler, an interpreter, and built-in functions and extension modules written in C. The compiler translates the Python source into an intermediate bytecode that is then executed by the interpreter.[5] CPython is the fastest and most complete Python implementation. It is also regarded as the reference implementation. **Jython** translates the Python source into Java bytecode that may then be run on any machine with a Java Virtual Machine. Jython provides an easy way to integrate modules pre-written in Java. The fact that it produces Java bytecode confers all the advantages of Java regarding transportability between different platforms. **IronPython** is designed to integrate into the Microsoft .NET framework. Written in C#, IronPython compiles the Python source into Common Intermediate Language (CIL) code which can be interpreted at runtime by Microsoft's Common Language Runtime (CLR). One of the main advantages of IronPython is that it provides access to the very extensive .NET framework library, including the Windows Forms library that provides access to native Microsoft Windows user interface elements. IronPython therefore provides a useful framework for writing applications to run on Microsoft Windows platforms. **Python for .NET** achieves somewhat similar ends but uses a different approach. Rather

---

[5] The compilation stage is generally hidden from the user, so it appears to the end user as if the Python source code is directly interpreted.

than generating CIL code, it integrates the Cpython engine within the CLR.

Further details of these and several other implementations are provided on the official Python website (http://www.python.org). However, as the objective of this book is to teach the basics of the Python language (which are common to all implementations), I will confine discussion to the CPython installation. As is common practice, this will be referred to throughout simply as Python

Version Numbers

Like most software, new versions of Python are identified by a version number. A distinction should be made between 'production' (or 'stable') releases (i.e. those that are tried and tested) and 'development' releases (i.e. works in progress). Python version numbers for production releases contain three digits separated by dots (e.g. 2.6.4): the first identifies the major version number; the second a minor version; and the third a point release. New point releases fix known bugs but add no new functionality, minor versions add new functionality but retain backward compatibility with previous releases, whilst major versions contain major changes, and do not necessarily retain backward compatibility (i.e. older programs may not necessarily run without modifications). Major versions provide an opportunity to remove 'deprecated' features (i.e. features that have become redundant or sub-optimal).

When new versions are being developed, alpha, beta and release candidate versions are released for testing and feedback. These development releases have numbers like 2.6a0, where the letters 'a', 'b' or 'rc' indicate alpha, beta or release candidate versions, followed by a digit (but no dot) starting at 0 (e.g. 2.6a0 is the first alpha release of version 2.6).

At the time of writing (2012), the Python Software Foundation is releasing new versions in both the 2.x and 3.x series. These will continue to co-exist for a transitional period, but the 2.x versions will eventually be superseded by the 3.x versions. As Python 3.0 introduced some new language features, and removed others, programs written using Python 2.x will generally not run under Python 3.x without alterations. Facilities are provided on the Python website to 'translate' Python 2.x programs into 3.x, but it makes more sense for beginners to learn Python 3 from the outset. This is the approach adopted in this book. However, readers may find useful 2.x programs published elsewhere that can be run with only minor modifications. The main differences between Python 2.x and 3.x are summarised in Appendix B.

Why Choose Python?

Given that there are so many programming languages you could learn, why choose Python? There are many reasons, but some of the more obvious include:

- **Python is easy to learn**. Every language has certain rules that must be adhered to and Python is no exception. However, Python has fewer rules. Furthermore, these rules are fairly intuitive and after a short while they become so natural you begin to wonder why anyone would want to do things any other way. Python has a restricted vocabulary and a simple syntax, so there is less to learn and fewer fiddly details that have to be remembered. For example, it uses less 'boilerplate' than most other languages (i.e. sections of standard code that must be included at certain places). It uses dynamic typing (i.e. variables are recognised as text, integer numbers, real numbers, etc. by their context), rather than having to be explicitly defined. Despite this, it is also a strongly typed language, so it will not allow you to do stupid things by mixing types inappropriately.

- **Python is easy to use**. Programs can be developed quickly using an interactive trial and error approach. In other words, you can write a section of code and test it immediately to see if it works. If it fails to work, Python provides reasonably intelligible error messages to help you identify where you went wrong. You can also use the interactive facilities (see Chapter 3) to display the current values of variables to check for logical errors.

- **Python code is easy to read**. One of the best ways to learn a computer language is to look at programs written by other programmers. Python programs tend to be very structured, whilst the rules governing indentation (which you will learn later) make Python programs very easy to follow. Programs written in Python are also considerably shorter (i.e. less verbose) than their equivalents in Java or C++.

- **Python is a multi-paradigm language**. Python is an object-orientated language that can be used to write object-orientated programs, but it is also equally suited for procedural programming (as this book will hopefully demonstrate). Other object-orientated languages may also be used to write procedural programs, but Python facilitates this in a more user-friendly manner than most.

- **Python is extendable**. Python is supplied with a large standard library containing facilities for almost everything imaginable, but if that is not enough you can easily integrate modules written in other languages (e.g. C, C++, Java or .NET languages), either written by yourself or (more likely if you are a beginner) by others. Python is often described as a good 'glue' language, suitable for integrating components written in different languages.

- **Python can be used as a scripting language by many proprietary applications**. Many application programs provide facilities to enable users to fine-tune the application using a scripting language (e.g. Visual Basic for Applications). Python is increasingly being adopted as a scripting language in some of the major applications software, so in addition to writing your own programs you may be able to use Python to fine-tune some of your favourite applications. The Wikipedia page on 'Python Software' provides a list of applications supporting Python scripting (http://en.wikipedia.org/wiki/Python_software). This list includes ArcGIS, Civilisation IV, GIMP, Autodesk Maya, Corel Paint Shop Pro, and SPSS amongst many others.

- **Python is multi-platform**. Python may be run on any of the major operating systems, including Windows, Linux, UNIX, Mac, Amiga and OS/2. Programs written on any one platform can be distributed and run on any of the other platforms without the need to alter the code, provided that Python is installed on the destination machine. You can use a tool called py2exe (www.py2exe.org) to convert your Python program into an .exe file that will run on any Windows machine even if Python is not installed. Also, as already mentioned, implementations of Python are available to produce Java or .NET bytecode.

- **Python is free (i.e. no cost)**. Strictly speaking every language is free, but the tools you need to compile and/or interpret the code may entail a licence fee. The tools required to write and run Python programs may be downloaded from the Python website completely free of charge. Third party enhancements are also available (many of which are also free), but you should find the basic tools to be more than adequate.

- **Python is free (i.e. open-source).** This is a different meaning of 'free' (more akin to 'free speech' than to 'free beer'). Python forms part of the free software movement. Free or open-source software means that the source code of the Python interpreter and other tools is freely available and that anyone can modify it without infringing copyright. This allows the software to be enhanced by anyone with the requisite skills. Proprietary software in contrast is normally provided for a fee under a licence that limits the number of copies a licence holder can make and which also prevents the user from making changes. The fact that Python is open-source does not actually make much practical difference to the average end-user (apart from the fact that it guarantees that it will remain free of charge), but the ethos of openness and giving freely for the benefit others, rather than for personal gain, is one that I hope you will agree deserves to promoted and supported. Indeed, when you have mastered how to program using Python, hopefully you will consider giving something back for the benefit of others.

- **Python programmers have access to a huge support base.** Support may not necessarily be available 24/7 at the end of a phone line (especially not mine!), but the official Python website (see below) provides information on just about everything you could possibly need.

Given its user-friendliness and suitability for beginners, one might assume that Python is not a serious mainstream language. It should therefore be noted that it is now widely used by many commercial companies, including some of the big players such as Goggle, You Tube, Yahoo, NASA and Air Canada. Python may be easy to learn, but do not underestimate its capabilities. If it can help navigate scientific instruments to the outer reaches of the solar system, it should be able to cope with cataloguing your DVD collection (or whatever other projects you may decide to use it for).

Python is not perfect – no language is perfect in every respect. So, you may wonder what its limitations are. The main one is that it is an interpreted language and therefore does not run as fast as a compiled C or C++ program. If you need to write computationally intense programs for a supercomputer then you may need to add C or C++ to your repertoire of skills. However, in most other circumstances, speed is not a serious consideration. Three further points might be noted:

- First, although not as fast as compiled C, Python is by no means a slow language. Python has a highly optimised byte compiler that translates your source into a bytecode that can be interpreted very quickly. Unless you have a very complex program that takes hours or even days to run, you will probably not notice any discernable difference in run times between a Python program and one written using one of the faster compiled languages.

- Second, because Python is easier to use and less verbose, and can be run interactively, the time taken to develop a Python program is usually considerably less than the time taken to get a program in one of the other languages up and running. Indeed, Python is often used by professional software engineers to develop prototypes, that can then be subsequently translated, or partly translated, if need be into C or other languages for greater speed.

- Third, work is currently in progress on compilers (e.g. Shed Skin) to translate Python into C++. These are still under development and cannot handle all Python programs, but they provide an easy way to reduce the run times of at least some Python programs in the unlikely event that speed does become an issue.

Do not be concerned if you do not understand all the details above – they will become clearer later on. The bottom line is that Python (in my opinion) comes close to being the ideal language for both beginners and more advanced programmers.

Rules And Conventions

Like all programming languages, there are a number of **rules** which must be obeyed otherwise your program will not work. However, in Python these are kept to a minimum. There are also a number of **conventions**. These are informal rules that most Python programmers adhere to, but which are not essential for the program to work. It is recommended that you follow the conventions as it results in a standard style, making it easier for other people to read your programs (and possibly offer suggestions if you run into difficulties) and also for you to read other people's programs and pick up useful tips.

To give an example, variable names may only contain letters, digits (0-9) and the underscore character (_).[6] The name may begin with either an

---

[6] Do not worry if you do not know what a variable is. This will be explained later.

underscore or a letter, but not with a digit. These are rules. If you attempt to use any other characters (including a space) within a name you will generate a syntax error. Thus, 'myVar' and 'my_var' are valid variable names, but 'my var' and 'myVar$' are not. Likewise, 'var2' is valid, but '2nd_var' is not. Note also that Python names are case sensitive, so although 'myVar' and 'MyVar' are both valid they refer to different variables.

Python programmers generally use lower case letters in variable names. This, however, is a convention rather than a rule. Names spelt with upper case letters are valid and work fine, but the convention is to use upper case letters sparingly. However, capitals are sometimes used to identify variables that have a fixed value (e.g. 'SPEED_OF_LIGHT' or PI). This provides a subliminal warning not to do anything that might change the value. If a name consists of two or more words, one option (sometimes referred to as 'camel case') is to begin each word with a capital (e.g. 'myVar' and 'currentSpeed'), although the convention in such situations is to begin the name with a lower case letter. However, the officially preferred alternative is to use lower case letters throughout, with underscores to represent spaces (e.g. 'my_var' and 'current_speed').[7]

This book will make a clear distinction between what is a rule and what is a convention.

The Official Web Site

I could provide lengthy lists of excellent books to read and links to web sites, but there is little point. The Official Python Website, hosted by the Python Software Foundation, contains an extensive list of links and suggested readings. It also provides FAQs (frequently asked questions), documentation, tutorials, sample code, and a wiki for its user community, among lots of other things. I would strongly recommend you pay the site a visit at the earliest opportunity, and spend some time browsing, if only to get a feel for what is available. The address is:

http://www.python.org/

---

[7] A comprehensive list of stylistic guidelines, referred to as PEP 8, is available on the Python website at http://www.python.org/dev/peps/pep-0008/. While most of this may not mean very much at this stage, you should read it sometime before you get too set in your ways.

Chapter 2. Setting Up

Before you can run Python programs, you must have Python (i.e. the interpreter, libraries etc.) installed on your computer. Depending on your operating system and software, you may find that a version of Python is already installed. However, if so, it is important to check the version number. Python 3.x is not backwards compatible with Python 2.x, so to run the programs discussed in this book it is essential to have a 3.x version installed. This chapter explains how to establish what versions (if any) of Python are installed on your computer and how to install the most recent 3.x version. The chapter assumes that you are running Windows, but Appendix A provides some additional information for users of other operating systems.

In addition to installing Python, you should also download a copy of the sample programs (or scripts) used in this book. Instructions are provided in the final section of this chapter.

Folder Organisation

It is a matter of personal preference where you install Python, and where you save the downloaded sample programs and the programs you write yourself. You could save everything in the same folder, but it is suggested that you at least separate the Python system files (i.e. interpreter etc.) from the program files.[8] The folder where you install Python (e.g. C:\Program Files\Python33) will be referred to here as the **installation** folder, whilst the folder for the sample program files (e.g. D:\My Documents\Python) will be referred to as the **programs** folder.[9] The 'programs' folder does not need to be a single location – you might, for example, decide to keep the programs you write yourself separate from the downloaded sample programs, or you may decide to keep programs for different projects in separate folders. Once Python has been

---

[8] I usually take this one step further by keeping folders containing data files on a different partition (e.g. D:) to the software (by default on C:). This makes it easier to make frequent backups of the data (including Python scripts) without having to back up the entire system. Data (including your own programs) may be difficult to recreate whereas, if the worst comes to the worst, Python system files can always be reinstalled.

[9] To change the location of My Documents from its default location on drive C, right click on the My Documents folder in Explorer and select Properties.

---

installed, Python programs can be run from any location on your computer.

To install Python you will need to download an installation file from the Python website. Unless you specify otherwise, this will be downloaded to the normal location for downloads on your computer (possibly your desktop). This location will be referred to as the **download** folder.

Checking For Python

To test whether a version of Python is currently installed on your computer, enter `python` at a command prompt.[10] If you get a message telling you that 'python' cannot be found, then the most likely explanation is that it is not installed. However, it is possible that it may be installed but cannot be located. To check this possibility, use the Search option on the Start menu to search for files or folders containing 'python' in their name. If the search fails to detect any files, then you can be certain that Python is not installed. However, if you do locate some files, then you may need to set the path (as explained below) and test again by entering `python` at a command prompt.

If Python is already installed, the `python` command should start the Python interpreter. This will consist of a few lines of text, ending with a >>> prompt. The first line will tell you which version is 'active'. The >>> prompt indicates that the Python interpreter is waiting for commands, but we will ignore that for now. Type `exit()`, or press CTRL+Z, followed by <ENTER> to exit the interpreter.

If you have a 2.x version installed you will need to install a 3.x version following the instructions in the following sections. However, do not delete the 2.x version, as you may find that other software installed on your system depends on having access to a 2.x version - if you did not put it there, then someone else probably did so for a reason. It is therefore safer to install a 3.x version into a second 'installation' folder, although this adds a few minor complications when specifying the search path (as explained below).

If you already have a 3.x version installed, you may wish to upgrade to a

---

[10] There are various ways to get a command prompt. One is to click the Start button, select Run on the popup menu, and then type cmd in the dialogue box. This will open a window with a command prompt. (N.B. Many commands can also be run by typing them directly into the Run dialogue box).

more recent release following the instructions below, although this is not really necessary as any version from 3.0 onwards should be okay for the purposes of this book.

Downloading Python

To install Python, the first thing you need to do is download an installation file. Go to the Official Python Website download page, currently http://www.python.org/download.

At the time of writing, you have the choice of downloading either 2.x or 3.x versions. You may also have a choice of different point releases. It is suggested that you select the current 3.x production version (i.e. the most recent stable 3.x version), rather than one of the development versions (even if it has a higher version number).

You may also need to choose between different versions of the same release. It does not matter which version of the Windows operating system you are using (i.e. 95, 98, NT, 2000, ME, XP, Vista, Windows 7, etc.), but there are different versions of Python depending upon whether you have a 32-bit or 64-bit processor. You need to select the Python installer suitable for your processor. If you have a 64-bit processor you should select the 64-bit installer; but if you have an Intel x86 processor (e.g. a Pentium), you should select the standard x86 installer. If in doubt, select the standard x86 version.

Finally, you may be offered a choice of format for the installation file. The easiest option for Windows is the msi (Microsoft Installer) format.

Having decided upon the appropriate combination of Python version, operating system and format, just click the appropriate link in the website. This will download the selected installation file to your selected 'download' folder. In case you are confused by the wide choice of options available by the website, note that you only need to download one installation file (assuming of course it is the correct one).

If you do not have access to the internet and need to use an Internet Café or some other public facility to download the installation file, you should note that the installation file typically requires about 10-15MB. It will therefore fit quite comfortably into a tiny corner of a flash memory stick. It is probably a good idea to download the sample programs (see below) on the same visit. The sample programs will occupy an even smaller corner of your memory stick. Once you have completed the two downloads you will not require Internet access again (although, needless to say, without it you will not have access to the resources on the official Python web site).

Installing Python

To install the Python msi installation file, Microsoft Installer 2.0 (or later) must be installed. Microsoft Installer will almost certainly be installed if you have XP or a more recent version of Windows, or if you have Microsoft Office or some other major Microsoft application already installed. It is also included in some Service Packs for Windows 2000. The simplest way to find out if Microsoft Installer is installed is to try installing Python to see what happens. Using Windows Explorer, open your 'download' folder and double click on the msi file to run it. If all is well, the installer will start asking you questions. If not, you will need to download Microsoft Installer from the Microsoft site and install it before continuing. If downloading Microsoft Installer, make sure to download the correct one for your version of Windows – installing the most recent Service Pack may be the easiest solution.

Once you have the installer working, you only need to answer a few simple questions. One requires you to specify a destination for Python. You can either select the default (a subfolder of the root directory on drive C:, for example C:\Python33), or else select an 'installation' folder of your choice. I prefer to keep all my software in subfolders of C:\Program Files (e.g. C:\Program Files\Python33) - but it does not matter where you install it. You will then be asked which features you want to install. Unless disc space is at a premium, just select them all.[11,12] The installer takes care of everything else from this point onwards.

When the installation has finished, you will find that a number of shortcuts have been added to the Programs section within the Start menu. If you wish to create a more accessible icon on your desktop, drag the shortcut for IDLE (you can ignore the others) from the Start menu onto the desktop - N.B. if you hold down the CTRL key when doing this the icon will be copied (rather than moved) onto the desktop, leaving the original on the Start menu.

---

[11] If disc space is at a premium, you could exclude the 'Test Suite' as it is unlikely that you will need to use it.

[12] If you do not have internet access, it may be worth noting that after installation the \Doc subfolder contains much of the documentation available on the Python website.

Double click on the IDLE icon to test the installation. If a window opens displaying some text before a >>> prompt, then everything is probably working. Further information on IDLE will be provided in Chapter 3, but for now you can close the window by typing `exit()` or pressing CTRL+D or CTRL+Q.

By default IDLE (a graphical integrated development environment for Python) will look for and save the Python programs (or scripts) that you write in the folder where you installed the software (i.e. the 'installation' folder). However, it is preferable to save your programs in a different folder (i.e. the 'programs' folder). To have IDLE open in the 'programs' folder by default, right click on the IDLE icon on the desktop, select Properties from the context menu, and then replace the path in the 'Start In' box by the path to your 'programs' folder.

You can now safely delete the msi file in the 'download' folder if you want to recover the disc space.

Setting The Search Path

If you intend to run Python from a command prompt (which you may wish to do sooner or later), it is useful to add the 'installation' folder (i.e. the folder into which the Python interpreter was installed – e.g. C:\Program Files\Python33) to the search path as this will save you repeatedly having to type the path explicitly later.

To do this, open System Properties (e.g. right click on My Computer and select Properties on the context menu) and then click on the Environment Variables button on the Advanced tab. You should see PATH listed in the system variables panel. If so, select PATH and click the Edit button; otherwise click the New button to create a new PATH variable. You need to add two folders to the existing path: the 'installation' folder, and a subfolder \Lib\idlelib of the 'installation' folder. Thus, for example, if you installed in C:\Program Files\Python33, you would add the following to the existing PATH:

```
;C:\Program Files\Python33;C:\Program Files\Python33\Lib\⤶
idlelib
```

(without the ⤶ symbol or any line feeds).[13] Note the semicolon at the

---

[13] The ⤶ symbol at the end of a line will be used where necessary to indicate that the following line should be appended without the insertion of either a line feed or a space. In other words, you should enter a single line ending ...\Lib\idlelib. (If a space character is required it will be shown immediately before the ⤶ symbol).

beginning – this is required to separate the two new items from the existing ones, but it should be omitted if you are creating a new path. If your 'installation' folder is not 'C:\Program Files\Python33' then modify the above accordingly.

The above additions to the path will enable Windows to find both the Python interpreter and IDLE, simply by typing `python` or `idle` at a command prompt (or in the Run option on the Start button).

To check whether the path includes the changes, just type:

```
> path
```

at a command prompt to display the current path.

Problems may arise if older versions of Python already exist on the system. If they are in folders located in the path before the new 'installation' folder, then the old versions will be used rather than the new one. One solution would be to edit PATH to remove the old location. However, the older version may be required by other applications on your system which may then cease to work if the older version cannot be located, so it is probably safer to leave the path to the older version. A reasonable compromise is to append the path to the new version to the end of the PATH environment variable (as described above), so that the old version is detected first, but then create a simple batch file called 'python3.bat' in the new 'installation' folder containing the full path to the python interpreter as a single line, for example:

```
C:\Program Files\Python33\Python.exe
```

You should now be able to start the new python by entering:

```
> python3
```

at a command prompt. However, if you omit the '3' the older version will be run. Your pre-existing applications will also default to the older version.

Downloading The Sample Programs

This book provides a number of sample programs. It is suggested that you type these yourself, especially the shorter ones in the early chapters, but for convenience copies of all the programs are available for download at

http://www.nuim.ie/dpringle/python

The sample programs have been saved as compressed archive files in three different formats (.zip, .tgz and .tar.bz2). Windows users should download the .zip file to their 'download' folder.

Some versions of Windows treat a zip file as if it were a folder. For example, in the absence of a specific zip utility program, zip files may be displayed in Explorer with a 'zipped folder' icon. Clicking on the icon will display the contents of the 'folder' without decompressing the archive. The files can even be run from within the archive without decompressing them. However, editing and saving files within an archive can be cumbersome, so it is suggested that you decompress (i.e. unzip) the files into your 'programs' folder. This can be done in Explorer by right clicking on the 'zipped folder' icon and selecting 'Extract All' from the context menu. Be careful where you extract to: by default Explorer will extract the files to a sub-folder of the folder containing the zip file (i.e. the 'download' folder), so make sure to specify your preferred 'programs' folder as the destination in the extraction wizard (e.g. D:\My Documents\Python). Once the files have been extracted, you can delete the zip file to avoid confusion - it can always be downloaded again if required.

If you have a decompression utility installed, the zip file will probably be represented by an icon indicative of that particular utility, rather than as a zipped folder. Most utilities allow you to run programs from within the archive but, as above, decompressing the zip file before use is preferable. Decompressing a zip file may simply require you to double click on its filename in Explorer to initiate the associated program. As before, be careful which folder you unzip into.

If you do not have a zip utility installed, and if Windows does not offer an 'Extract All' option, there are numerous options to choose from. WinZip is a tried and trusted option for Windows. You can download a free inspection copy (which will suffice for decompressing the sample file) from http://www.winzip.com/, but note that you are required to pay a small licence fee if you decide to retain it at the end of the evaluation period.

Useful alternatives to WinZip include Info-Zip (http://www.info-zip.org/) and IZArc (http://www.izarc.org/), both of which are completely free and provide both graphical and command line options. All downloads come with complete instructions.

What Next?

At this point you should have Python installed and your sample programs unzipped into your 'programs' folder. You are now ready to begin.

Chapter 3. Running Python

Now that everything is set up, we are ready to begin. This chapter explains the different ways to run a Python program. The instructions here are for Windows users, but they are much the same for other operating systems. Some minor variations for users of other operating systems are noted in Appendix A.

Python may be run in either of two modes: interactive or script. In **interactive** mode, Python code is entered one line at a time at an interpreter prompt (>>>). Each line is interpreted (i.e. executed) as it is entered. After each line has been executed, a new >>> prompt is displayed inviting the user to enter the next line of code, which is then executed immediately, followed by another prompt and so on. In contrast, in **script** mode all the lines that form a program (or script) are saved to a file (typically with a .py extension) using a text editor and then the script is run (i.e. executed) in a single step.[14]

In this chapter we will learn how to run Python interactively before looking at how to write and run scripts. You will also, in passing, write your first Python program. By tradition, the first program in any new language normally displays the message 'Hello world!'. Lacking the imagination to do anything different, that is exactly what we will do here.

Interactive Mode

The Python interpreter can be invoked either directly from a command prompt or indirectly from an integrated development environment, such as IDLE. This section outlines both approaches.

The Python Interpreter

The Python interpreter can be initiated in interactive mode by entering python (or possibly python3) at a command prompt.

Entering python at a command prompt should cause Python to burst into life and display a few lines indicating the version number and other

---

[14] The terms 'program' and 'script' are used here interchangeably, although the term 'script' sometimes has a more specific meaning in other contexts.

information, followed by a >>> prompt to indicate that it is open for business and expects you to enter some Python code (Figure 3.1).[15]

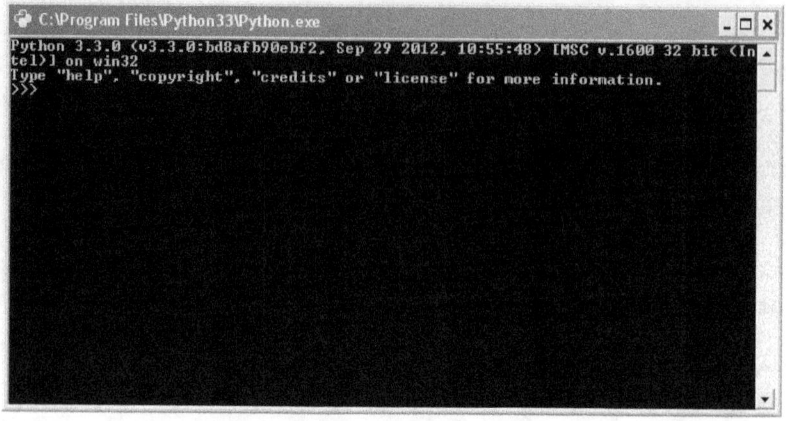

Figure 3.1. Python Interpreter Shell

If Python does not start as expected, the most likely explanation is that the Python installation folder is not listed in your search path. To remedy the problem, make sure the path includes the 'installation' folder as explained in the Chapter 2.

When you want to exit the interpreter, enter `exit()` at the >>> prompt, or press CTRL+Z followed by <ENTER> (Windows) or either CTRL+Z or CTRL+D (Linux).

The IDLE Development Environment

IDLE is the cross-platform Integrated Development Environment (IDE) supplied with Python. 'Why the extra 'L' in its name?' you may ask. It may be just to pick up the 'L' in DeveLopment to produce a catchier name but, given Guido van Rossum's obsession with Monty Python, and the fact that actor Eric Idle was a leading member of the Monty Python television team, the extra 'L' may be more than just a coincidence.

IDLE can be started from an icon either on the Start Menu or (if you followed my suggestion in Chapter 2) on the desktop. You can also start it by entering `idle` at a command prompt. If IDLE does not start from a

---

[15] In the following discussion the interpreter for convenience will simply be referred to as 'Python'. It should be obvious from the context whether 'Python' is used to refer to the interpreter (e.g. 'Python will provide a prompt to indicate it expects more input') or to the language (e.g. 'Python keywords must always be lower case').

command prompt, check that it is installed and that you have the path set up correctly as explained in Chapter 2.

IDLE by default opens in interactive mode in a window similar to Figure 2. This invites you to enter a Python statement at the >>> prompt.

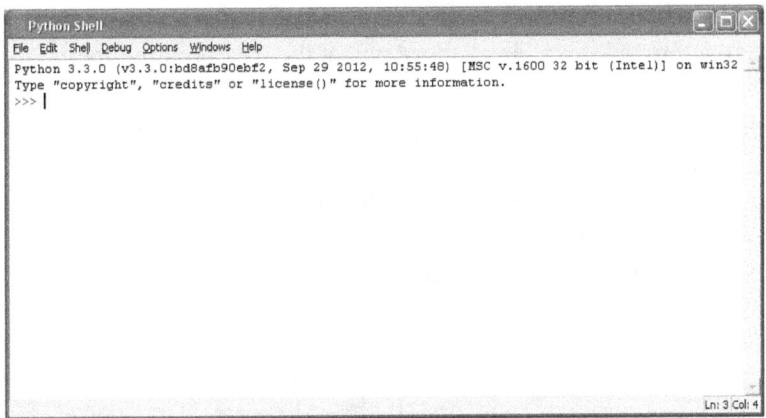

Figure 3.2. IDLE Interactive Window

IDLE behaves in much the same as the basic Python interpreter. However, there are a few additional features. One obvious difference is that the code that you type is colour coded. This makes it easier to distinguish between the different components within a program. A second feature is that popup messages are displayed as you enter code to provide reminders of the syntax.

It can be frustrating if you type a long line of code in interactive mode, only to discover that you have made a mistake. It is therefore worth noting that you can re-display the previous line for editing by pressing ALT+P (P for 'previous'). You can move further back, one line at a time, by repeatedly pressing ALT+P. If you overshoot, you can move in the opposite direction using ALT+N (N for 'next'). You can also redisplay any line entered previously, even if you need to scroll up to find it, by clicking on it and pressing the <ENTER> key. This will cause the entire line to be copied to the current prompt ready for editing.[16]

To edit a line, simply click at the point where you wish to insert, change or delete text, make the required changes, and then press the <ENTER> key to execute it.

---

[16] Mac users should use CTRL+P and CTRL+N instead of ALT+P and ALT+N.

To exit IDLE, select Exit on the File menu, or else press either CTRL+D or CTRL+Q.

Your First Program

So, let us now introduce ourselves to the world. Start Python or IDLE in interactive mode as explained above and at the >>> prompt type:

```
>>> print("Hello world!")
```

without any spaces between the prompt and the 'p' in 'print'.[17]

Press the <ENTER> key to send the line to the interpreter. The line you have just typed is Python code. If you have typed it correctly, Python should respond by printing your greeting to the world. Unfortunately, unless someone happens to be looking over your shoulder, this momentous event will probably pass totally unnoticed (a bit like a tree falling in a forest without making a noise if there is no-one around), but you have just written your first Python program. This makes you a Python programmer. We achieved what we set out to achieve so, as far as I am concerned, my work is done. Nevertheless, I will pad out the rest of the book with a few more details just to keep the publisher happy!

This line you typed is referred to as a **statement**. The word 'print' is a function call, but for now may be regarded simply as a command. Python commands (including built-in function names and other keywords) should always be written using only lower case letters. **This is a rule.** For example, if you type 'Print' (with a capital) you will generate a syntax error. Try it to see what happens!

The bit enclosed in parentheses is an **argument** telling Python what to print. In this case you are printing a **text string**, but it could have been a **number**, an **expression** (i.e. a piece of code that can be evaluated to produce a value, e.g. a formula), or any one of a number of other things. Text strings are a combination of letters, digits or other characters that you want to print. The string will be printed exactly as you have specified, and you can use both upper- and lowercase letters. The string, however, must be enclosed within quotes (which are not printed). It does not matter whether you use single quotes (e.g. 'Hello world!') or double quotes (e.g. "Hello world!"), but they must be matching (i.e. be the same

---

[17] The >>> prompt will be shown throughout to indicate when you should enter code in interactive, as opposed to script, mode. You should not type the prompt, nor should you leave a space after the prompt – the space is included to reflect how the line will appear on your screen, but it should never be typed as this will cause an error.

at the beginning and end of the text string.)

The statement should begin at the start of the line without any preceding spaces. **This is a rule**. Indentations (i.e. spaces or tabs at the beginning of a line), as we shall see later, are used to structure a program in Python. If you include any spaces before the word 'print', you will generate an error message. However, it does not matter how many spaces you leave between tokens (i.e. the basic building blocks of the statement - in this case between the 'print' command and the left parenthesis, or between the left parenthesis and the opening quote of the string) or even (in most cases) if you do not include any spaces at all (as in this example). Such spaces (known as white space) are simply ignored by the interpreter. Any spaces placed between the quotes, however, will form part of the string and will be faithfully reproduced in the output.

Experiment by entering the line with minor changes. You may generate errors messages, but you cannot cause any permanent damage. It is useful to include a few deliberate mistakes to get a feel for the type of error messages displayed by Python. If by some freakish occurrence you manage to put Python into an indefinite loop (i.e. where it appears either to hang or run out of control), note that pressing CTRL+C will return you to the >>> prompt.

It is useful to make a distinction between a physical line and a logical line. A **physical line** is a single line of code as it appears on the screen, whereas a **logical line** is an executable statement (or in some instances, as we shall see, a group of statements that function together as a single unit). In most instances a logical line will normally occupy a single physical line, but in some cases a logical line may be spread over several physical lines. Pressing <ENTER> at the end of a physical line will normally cause the line to be interpreted immediately, but if Python does not recognise the physical line as a logical line it will either issue a syntax error message or display a … prompt to indicate that it expects more code to complete a logical line. Python will only execute a logical line when all the required physical lines have been added. Once it executes the logical line, it will display a >>> prompt to indicate that it is ready to receive the next logical line.

There are several situations where Python will display a … prompt to indicate that it expects further input.[18] One is if a physical line contains an

---

[18] IDLE does not display a … prompt. However, it does not display a >>> either, so it is generally clear when it requires further input. The … prompt is displayed here for clarity.

opening left parenthesis '(', square bracket '[' or brace '{' without a matching (i.e. closing) right parenthesis, square bracket or brace. Another is if a line ends with a colon (signifying the beginning of a block of code known as a **suite** – see Chapter 9). A third situation is if using triple quoted string literals to display multiple lines of text (Chapter 5).

For example, if you enter:

```
>>> print(
```

Python would recognise that the logical line was incomplete and display a ... prompt to request more input. If you then enter:

```
... "Hello world!")
```

this would complete the logical line and Python will then proceed to interpret and execute it.

Much the same would happen if you omitted the final right parenthesis in the second line. However, if you were to enter:

```
>>> print("Hello
```

you will get an error message because the quotes have not been closed. Strings normally need to be entered on a single physical line. However, if it becomes necessary to split a string between lines (e.g. if it was too long to fit on the screen), you can split the string using a backslash (which is not printed). For example, you could enter:

```
>>> print("Hello \
... world!")
```

Python will display a ... prompt after the first line to indicate that it requires further input and then execute both lines after the second line has been entered.

Do not worry too much about these details - these situations will soon become familiar through experience. The main thing to remember for present is that a ... prompt indicates that Python requires more input.

On some occasions Python may display a ... prompt to invite you to enter more code when the logical line is in fact complete. This normally occurs when the logical line is actually complete, but where additional code could legitimately be added. In such situations you can terminate the logical line by pressing the <ENTER> key again (effectively entering a blank line). Python will then execute the code.

It is also possible to include more that one logical line on a physical line by separating the logical lines with semicolons. For example:

```
>>> print("Hello"); print("world!")
```

However, although this will work, placing more than one statement on a physical line is regarded as bad style (especially in a script) as it reduces readability, and should therefore be avoided.

Functions: A Brief Digression

Before we leave our first program, it may be useful to say a few words about functions.

As already noted, a function (e.g. `print()`) can be treated as a command that instructs Python to do something, but it is actually a defined set of instructions saved elsewhere that can be referred to by a name (in this case, 'print'). A function can accept input data (known as **arguments**). Functions are called using a statement which takes the form of the function name followed by the arguments expected by the function within parentheses. Thus, the `print()` function is called using its name ('print') followed by the arguments (i.e. the various items we want to print) enclosed in parentheses. When a function is called, the set of instructions referred to by its name are implemented, in this case causing the items passed as arguments to be printed.

After the function implements the instructions in the block of code, it returns one or more values to the calling statement. However, in the case of the `print()` function, the value returned is uninformative and can therefore generally be ignored (as in this case).

Many functions do not require any arguments, but their calling statement must always include parentheses even if they do not enclose any arguments. Thus, for example, the function `exit()` used to shut down the Python interpreter or to exit IDLE does not require any parameters, but the parentheses must still be included.

Python provides a number of built-in functions (or **BIFs**), such as `print()`, that can be called at any stage. In addition, many other functions are available through extensions referred to as **modules** which can be imported (i.e. made available) as required. You can also write your own functions to perform selected operations. We will see some examples of functions available from imported modules in later chapters, as well as discussing how you can add your own functions in Chapter 11.

Writing Scripts

Given that the Python interpreter retains a 'memory' of what it has done, including the results of calculations, you could in theory write a program by entering the code one line at a time in interactive mode. However, this is not very practical because if you wanted to run the program a second time you would need to type in the entire code a second time: this would obviously be very tedious, even using the ALT+P facility in IDLE. It clearly makes more sense to save the code in a file and then execute the file contents in a single step. The saved code (or script) can be re-run as many times as you wish. It may also, if necessary, be altered between runs. This section explains how to create and edit a program file, whilst the following section explains how to execute it.

Text Editors

Python source code is pure ASCII – i.e. it contains no special characters.[19] Python scripts may therefore be written and edited using any text editor (e.g. Notepad or Wordpad). However, it is advisable not to use a word processor (e.g. Microsoft Word) as files saved by word processors normally contain additional information (e.g. embedded formatting characters), which Python cannot interpret, unless you remember to save the file as text only. You may use any text editor you wish, but it makes sense to take advantage of the integrated features of IDLE. Python scripts can be saved using any extension, but the convention is to use a .py extension (e.g. my_program.py).

IDLE As A Text Editor

IDLE contains its own built-in text editor. As we have already seen, IDLE normally starts in interactive mode.[20] To start the edit mode, either select New Window from the File menu or else press CTRL+N. This will open a second window in edit mode. You can open as many additional edit mode windows as you want in a similar manner, but one is sufficient for now. The edit window behaves much the same way as any simple text editor. For example, you can cut and paste text, find and replace character

---

[19] Strictly speaking any UTF-8 Unicode encoding is permitted. However, ASCII is by far the most widely used sub-set of UTF-8 in the English-speaking world, so for simplicity I will refer to ASCII.

[20] You can in fact change the mode in which IDLE starts, plus many other features, from the Options menu, but we will assume the default settings for the present.

---

strings, and so on. A large number of editing functions can be initiated by keystroke combinations. To view (or change) these commands, select Configure IDLE from the Options menu and click on the Keys tab.

One difference between IDLE and most other text editors is that the code you enter is colour coded using the same colours as in interactive mode. This is useful for flagging possible problems. For example, if you were to accidentally type 'pint' instead of 'print', 'pint' would not be coloured alerting you to a possible problem.

So, let us save our first program. Start edit mode and enter:

```
print("Hello world!")
```

(or, if you are really lazy, you could cut and paste it from the interactive window).

When you press the <ENTER> key the cursor simply moves to the beginning of the next line, waiting for you to enter more code, rather than interpreting the code. In most cases you would then enter further lines of code in a similar manner, but one line of code is sufficient for our first script.

Before you can run the program, you must save it. You can save a program at any stage using either the Save option on the File menu or by pressing CTRL+S. Either way you need to indicate where you want to save the program and give it a filename. By default IDLE will offer to save the program in the Python installation folder, but (if like me) you prefer to keep your own programs in a separate folder then you will need to specify the location.[21] You can give the file any name you want, but the convention is to append a .py extension. So, in this case, you might call your file **'hello_world.py'**.[22]

If you need to edit a previously saved script, you can open the file by selecting Open from the File menu or by pressing CTRL+O. Alternatively if you right click on the file's name in Windows Explorer you should find an option to 'Edit with IDLE' in the context menu. Selecting this will open the script in an edit window.

---

[21] As noted in Chapter 2, you can change the default folder in Windows by setting the properties for the IDLE icon on the desktop.

[22] Filenames should conform to the normal conventions for your operating system, but there are no additional restrictions. For example, you do not need to begin the filename with a lower case character like you normally would for a variable name, although many Python programmers would appear to have a preference for lower case names.

Comments And Blank Lines

Our 'hello_world.py' program is obviously a very simple program that does not require much explanation. However, when you write more complex programs, it is useful to include some comments to explain what the program does, either for the benefit of others or for yourself in the future. This can be achieved very simply using a # (hash) character, followed by whatever comment you want to include. The # character may be at the beginning of a line (in which case the entire line will be treated as a comment), or it may follow an executable statement on the same line. The Python interpreter will ignore everything after a # character until the end of the physical line. It is good practice, to include one or more comment lines (each beginning with #) at the beginning of a program to indicate what the program does, and possibly who wrote it, the date it was written, and other relevant bits of information.

The sample program 'hello_world1.py' includes two comments to illustrate. Open it in an IDLE edit window to view.

Long programs can also be made more readable by the inclusion of blank lines to separate different sections of code. To insert a blank line, simply press the <ENTER> key at the beginning of a line – but do not enter any spaces. Blank lines are ignored by the interpreter.

Running Scripts

Once a script has been saved, it may be run either from within IDLE or externally as a standalone program. Running it within IDLE is preferable for testing and development purposes.

Running Scripts In IDLE

To run a script from an edit window within IDLE, either select the Run Module option on the Run menu or press the F5 key. All output and/or error messages will be displayed in the interactive window as your program is executed. If you have made any changes since the script was last saved, you will be prompted to save the file before the script is run. In fact, IDLE will not allow the script to be run until it has been saved. Given that saving a file will overwrite the previous version, it may be advisable if making major changes to a program to either make a backup copy of the program (e.g. using Explorer) before you begin, or use the Save As option in the IDLE File menu to give your program a new name. However, if you are simply making minor alterations, using F5 takes care of the need for you to remember to save your changes. Indeed, when I start a new program, I usually save an empty file with the name I intend to use before I enter any code at all. Then, any time I wish to test my changes, I simply press F5, followed by <ENTER> to accept the default answer to the question asking if I want to save the changes.

With your 'hello_world1.py' file open in the edit window, press F5 to confirm that it is working correctly. Then try making a few changes to the program (e.g. remove one of the quotes, change 'print' to 'pint') to see how the error messages are reported.

You will find that some changes generate a **syntax error**. When you close the pop-up dialogue, control will be returned to a point in the editor window close to where the error occurred. In other instances, the program may be syntactically correct, but generate a **run-time error**. This will produce several lines of traceback information in the interactive window indicating the nature of the error and how you got to the point where it occurred. Take a note of the last line number mentioned as this indicates where the error occurred. If you do not spot an error on the line indicated, check the previous line as the Python interpreter may overshoot slightly before it realises something is wrong.

If a program crashes, the Debug menu on the interactive window contains some useful options. For example, if you click on the line in the traceback information that specifies where the error occurred and then select the Go to File/Line option on the Debug menu, the edit window will open at the relevant line. The Stack Viewer option is also very useful if a program crashes: selecting it will display the current values of all the variables in the program (plus quite a few others that you never knew you had!). This may provide useful clues as to what may have gone wrong. Selecting the Auto-open Stack Viewer option causes this information to be displayed automatically each time a program crashes.

Make sure you have a working version of **hello_world1.py** before proceeding to the next section.

Running A Script From Windows

Python programs can also be run outside of IDLE provided that Python is installed on the machine. To run a Python program in Windows, assuming that it has a .py extension, simply double click on its filename in Windows Explorer. The program will run inside its own window. Indeed, you may find that your programs run slightly faster this way than they do within IDLE.

Try this with your saved '**hello_world1.py**' file. You may see a DOS / Command Prompt window flash on the screen and then disappear again before you have a chance to read its contents. The program has probably run okay, but the window has shut down and vanished before you have a chance to see what happened. However, there is a simple fix. What we need is a statement within the program that will cause it to pause until the user does something. This can be accomplished by using IDLE edit mode to add a line such as:

```
input("\nPress <ENTER> to finish")
```

at the end of our program. The `input()` function will be explained in more detail in Chapter 5, but basically it causes the program to wait until the user types something and then presses the <ENTER> key. In this case we do not actually need the user to type anything - the important thing is that they press the <ENTER> key. The argument in parentheses is a text string that will be displayed on the screen to tell the user what to do, otherwise they could spend some time staring at the screen waiting for something to happen.[23] You can change the text to anything you want. For example, in keeping with Windows logic (where you have to click the Start button when you want to stop), you could change your prompt to "Press <ENTER> to exit"!

The program **hello_world2.py** contains the suggested changes - try running it from Windows Explorer. Problem solved! It is suggested that you end all programs with an input statement along these lines, even if you normally run them from within IDLE.

Running Scripts From A Command Prompt

Python scripts can also be run from a command prompt – i.e. the prompt within a DOS or Command Prompt window in Windows or a Console or Terminal window in Linux.[24] A Command Prompt window can usually be opened in Windows from an icon on the Start button menu, or by the selecting Run command and entering 'cmd'.

To run a Python script, change to the folder containing the script and then enter its filename (including its extension) at the command prompt. For example, in Windows (assuming your programs folder is D:\My

---

[23] The \n at the beginning of the string will be explained in Chapter 5, but basically it tells Python to insert a blank line.

[24] See Appendix A for further details on running a script from a Terminal window in Linux.

Documents\Python), you could enter:

```
> d:
> cd \My Documents\Python
> hello_world.py
```

Make sure to include the .py extension as this identifies the file to the operating system as a Python script.

An alternative to changing to the folder containing the script is to enter the full path for the file. If the pathname contains spaces, enclose the entire command in quotes. For example, at the command prompt enter:

```
> "D:\My Documents\Python\hello_world.py"
```

Another alternative is to define an environment variable containing the path to your scripts folder. For example, you could define an environment variable called 'scripts' by entering:

```
> set scripts="D:\My Documents\Python\"
```

The program could then be run using:

```
> %scripts%hello_world.py
```

taking care to enclose the environment variable name (which can be almost any name you wish) between two percent signs. This option might be useful, for example, if you wish to run scripts that are stored in two or more folders – by creating an environment variable for each folder you easily switch from one folder to another as required.

Programs can also be run directly from the Run command on the Start menu, without opening a Command Prompt window, although you will probably need to specify the full path name or use an environment variable.

If a program does not run using any of the above methods, treating it as an argument to the Python interpreter should always work. For example:

```
> python "D:\My Documents\Python\hello_world.py"
```

or

```
> python3 "D:\My Documents\Python\hello_world.py"
```

Final Comments

You will probably do most of your work using edit mode. However, do not underestimate the usefulness of interactive mode. Interactive mode provides a very useful testbed. For example, if you are not too sure of the correct syntax for a statement when writing a large program, you can use interactive mode to test various alternatives until you get it right. The correct version can then be copied and pasted into the edit mode window. However, when copying, be careful not to pick up any surplus spaces at the beginning of a line (or even part of the >>> prompt), otherwise you will create a syntax error in edit mode.

Chapter 4. Numbers And Variables

Having well and truly introduced ourselves to the world, we are now ready to start learning a bit more about the Python language. We will begin by looking at some numeric data types before introducing the concept of a variable. It is suggested that you enter the examples using IDLE's interactive mode as you read. It is also suggested that you experiment by trying out your own variations to see what happens.

Numbers

Python recognises several numeric data types, but the two most common are referred to as **int** (integers) and **float** (floating point).[25] Integers are 'whole' numbers that do not contain a decimal point (e.g. 204), whereas floating point numbers are numbers that do contain a decimal point (e.g. 4.7). Floating point numbers are sometimes referred to in other contexts as 'real' numbers.

Although we will confine ourselves to the more familiar decimal (base 10) numbering system, it should be noted that Python allows integer numbers to be expressed in binary (base 2), octal (base 8) or hexadecimal (base 16) formats. Non-decimal numbers begin with a zero, followed by the letter b, o or x to indicate the base (i.e. binary, octal or hexadecimal respectively). For example, the number 20 could be written as 20 (decimal), 0b10100 (binary), 0o24 (octal) or 0x14 (hexadecimal). The letters indicating the base, and the hexadecimal digits A-F, may be written in either upper or lower case. For example, the decimal number 200 could be written 0xC8 or 0Xc8.

Floating point numbers can be entered using scientific notation. This is useful if the number is either very large or very small. Using scientific notation the number has two parts separated by the letter e: the first part, known as the signficand, is by convention a real number in the range 1 to just less than 10; the second part, known as the exponent, is an integer indicating the power of ten that the significand should be multiplied by. Thus, for example, 350 could be written 3.5e2 (i.e. 3.5×10^2 or 3.5x100). Negative exponents may be used for very small numbers. For example,

---

[25] Other types include **complex** (complex numbers). Complex numbers are mysterious beings, understood only by mathematicians. Unless you know what they are, you can probably forget about them.

7.3 millionths could be written 7.3e-6. The letter e may be either upper or lower case.

Calculations using integers are always completely accurate. Also, unlike many other languages, Python does not place any limit on the maximum size of an integer. However, floats have maximum and minimum permitted values. Although it is highly unlikely to arise in ordinary circumstances, an attempt to assign a float a value outside this range may result in an overflow error message. There may also be a loss of precision using floats. The degree of precision is variable, but estimates suggest floats are accurate to about 17 significant digits, which should be more than sufficient for most purposes. If more precision is required a more advanced data type called **decimal.Decimal** may be used.[26] However, we shall confine the discussion to ints and floats.

Type Assignment

Python is a strongly typed language – i.e. all data values have a type and Python will only allow you to carry out operations which are appropriate to that particular data type. This is a safety precaution. However, unlike many other languages, Python does not require the user to explicitly declare the data type in advance – Python automatically figures out the data type based upon the value of the data. In the case of numbers, if a number contains a decimal point then it is assumed to be a `float`; if there is no decimal place, then the number is assumed to be an `int`.

Arithmetic Operators

If you enter an **expression** (i.e. code that can be evaluated to produce a value, such as a 'formula') built from numbers and arithmetic operators at the >>> prompt, Python will evaluate the expression and display the answer. Permitted operators are listed in Table 4.1.[27]

For example, if you enter:

```
>>> print(5+3)
```

in interactive mode, Python will process the expression (i.e. 5+3) and display the answer (i.e. 8). Note that the expression is not enclosed in

---

[26] The two part name using 'dot' notation indicates that the type Decimal (with a capital) needs to be imported in a module called decimal (no capital). Modules will be explained in Chapter 11.

[27] There are actually a few other arithmetic operators, but we will ignore these.

quotes as it is not a string. If you were to enclose the expression within quotes, Python would treat it as a string and simply display 5+3. Try entering:

```
>>> print('5+3')
```

to see what happens.

+	Plus
-	Minus
*	Multiply
/	Divide
**	Exponent
//	Floor (truncated divide)
%	Modulo (remainder)

Table 4.1. Arithmetic Operators

If you enter an expression in interactive mode, Python will evaluate it and display the answer even if you do not include a `print()` command. This allows the Python interpreter to be used as a simple calculator. Thus, simply entering:

```
>>> 5+3
```

at the prompt will achieve exactly the same result as the previous command. However, if you wish to display the result of an expression within a program, a `print()` function is required – Python will do the calculation but it will not display the result unless it is specifically instructed to. The result of an expression is only displayed automatically in interactive mode.

Simple expressions can be built by inserting an operator between two numbers (e.g. 2+2). The first four operators in Table 4.1 are self-explanatory (although you should note that the multiply operator is * rather than x). The exponent operator raises the first number to the power of the second (i.e. the first number is multiplied by itself the second number of times), thus 3**2 gives 9 (i.e. 3x3) whilst 2**3 would give 8 (i.e. 2x2x2). Note that neither number needs to be an integer, hence 2.3**1.6, whilst difficult to get your head around, is a valid expression - type the expression into Python if you want to find out what it evaluates to.

The last two operators in Table 4.1 are associated with the division of one number by another. The floor or truncated divide operator truncates the result of a division by removing any digits to the right of the decimal place. For example, 7.5/3 would give 2.5, whereas 7.5//3 gives 2.0. If the numerator and denominator are both integers, then the answer will also be an integer. Thus, 7/4 gives 1.75, whereas 7//4 gives 1.

The modulo operator returns the remainder (i.e. the bit left over after the second number has been divided into the first a whole number of times). Thus, for example, 7.5%3 would be 1.5. Note that it is the remainder that is returned (i.e. 1.5), not the bit to the right of the decimal place if the answer was expressed as a decimal (which in this example would be 0.5). Note also that % operator has nothing to do with percentages.

Python assigns a data type to the answer of a calculation. The general rule is that if the two numbers in an expression are both integers, then the answer will be an integer, but if one or more of the numbers are floating points, then the answer will be a floating point number. The main exception is if you divide one integer by another integer - a floating point number is always returned, even if one number is exactly divisible by the other, because there is a possibility that the answer for a division could have decimal places (e.g. 6/2 gives 3.0).[28]

Try entering the following expressions:

```
>>> 7+2
>>> 7-2
>>> 7*2
>>> 7/2
```

In each case you should get the correct answer expressed as an integer, except for the last one, which returns a float. If you repeat the exercise using a float for one or both numbers (i.e. 7.0 or 2.0), the answers will always be returned as a float (even though the answer in the first three cases could be expressed as an integer).

Now try entering:

```
>>> 7/0
```

This produces an error message because any number divided by zero gives infinity. If writing programs involving division, it is often advisable to write code telling Python what to do if the denominator is zero. Methods for doing this will be discussed in Chapter 13.

---

[28] Older versions of Python (and many other computer languages) return a truncated integer. Thus 5/2 would be returned as 2 rather than 2.5. Integer division in Python 3 returns a real number. This might be disconcerting to those used to other languages, but it removes a potential pitfall for us lesser mortals.

Operator Precedence

More complicated expressions can be built using additional numbers and operators. For example:

```
>>> 2+4-3
>>> 2*3+5
```

In the first expression it would not matter if you did the addition or the subtraction first: either way the answer is 3 (i.e. 6-3 or 2+1). However, in the second expression if you did the multiplication first the answer would be 11 (i.e. 6+5), but if you did the addition first the answer would be 16 (i.e. 2x8). The sequence in which the operators are acted upon can clearly affect the result, therefore it is important to understand how Python decides which operators to process first.

The first general rule is that Python works from left to right, thus 2*3+5 gives 11 (i.e. 6+5). However, if you enter:

```
>>> 5+3*2
```

the answer is again 11, and not 16 as you might expect (i.e. 8x2). The reason is that Python prioritises some types of operator over others. Thus, a second rule (which overrides the first) is that exponentiations are carried out before multiplications, divisions and modulus operations, which in turn are carried out before additions and subtractions.

The sequence is summarised in Table 4.2. Operators towards the top of the table are processed before those closer to the bottom. If two operators are at the same level (e.g. multiply and divide) then rule 1 comes into play. Thus, 6/3*2 would give 4 (i.e. 2x2) rather than 1 (i.e. 6/6).

**	Exponent
+ -	Unary Operator
* / // %	Multiply, Divide, Floor, Modulo
+ -	Plus, Minus

Table 4.2. Operator Precedence (Simplified)

One exception to these rules is when you have an expression with two exponents. In such instances, the exponents are evaluated from right to left, not left to right as you might assume. Thus,

```
>>> 2**3**2
```

is 512 (i.e. 2^9) rather than 64 (i.e. 8^2).

Try to predict what the answer will be before you enter each of the following:

```
>>> 6/2+1*3
>>> 5-11%3**2
>>> 1+3-2**3
>>> 2*8%3**2
>>> -2**2
```

The chances are you got the last one wrong. You probably read it as 'minus two squared' (i.e. -2 x -2), which is +4, whereas Python has evaluated it as -4. The reason is that Python treats the minus in front of a number as a unary operator, so following the above rules of operator precedence, Python has calculated the square of +2, which is 4, before applying the minus sign, rather than calculating the square of minus 2.

It will be noted that + and – appear twice in Table 4.2. Higher precedence is given to – as a unary operator (i.e. when it is used to change the sign of a number rather than to subtract one number from another). In most cases treating – as minus will have the same effect as treating it as a unary operator, but there are a few situations where the difference may be significant. For example:

```
>>> 5--6//5
```

evaluates as 7 because the unary operator (the second minus) turns 6 into –6, so the line becomes 5-(-6//5). (-6//5) is -2 because -6 divided by 5 is –1.2, so rounding down gives –2. The line therefore becomes 5-(-2) which gives 7. On the other hand if the unary operator had been treated as a minus, // would be processed first and then 6//5 would evaluate as 1. The line would then become 5-(-1), which would evaluate to 6.

As you can see, trying to figure out operator precedence can sometimes be very confusing. Fortunately there is a third rule that makes it easier to specify exactly what sequence you require. The third rule (which overrides the first two) is that parts of an expression enclosed in parentheses (i.e. 'round brackets') are processed before the bits outside. For example:

```
>>> (6-3)**2
```

gives 9 (i.e. 3 squared), whereas

```
>>> 6-3**2
```

would give -3 (i.e. 6-9). If we wanted to calculate the square of minus 2, as above, we could write it as:

```
>>> (-2)**2
```

Parentheses can be nested within other parentheses. In such situations the innermost ones are evaluated first. Thus, for example:

```
6+(11-3**(7-5))*3
```

gives 12. The innermost parentheses (i.e. 7-5) give 2, so the outer parentheses would read (11-3**2). Given that the exponent takes precedence, this would evaluate as 2 (i.e. 11-9). The full expression would now read 6+2*3, which is 6+6, which gives us 12.

Please note that you must use parentheses () rather than either square brackets [] or braces {}. These have a totally different purpose in Python, as we shall see later.

Finally, remember that if you are writing an expression as part of a program in edit mode in IDLE, you can test out your expression in interactive mode using simple numbers to see if you get the expected answer. If things work as expected, you can copy and paste the expression from interactive mode into your program in the editor.

Variables

If writing a program containing a large number of numeric literals (i.e. 'raw numbers') it would be very easy to lose track of what each number refers to. It would clearly be less confusing if the numbers had names, hence **variables** are one of the cornerstones of every programming language. A variable may be thought of as the name for an item of data. For example, the name `length` might be used to refer to the length of the sides of a square. This name could then be used in place of the number indicating the actual length, hence the area of the square could be calculated by the expression:

```
>>> length**2
```

You can use any name (or **identifier**) you wish (subject to a few rules outlined below), so by choosing a name that indicates what the number refers to you can make your program more intelligible.

Before the area of the square could be calculated using the expression above, the variable `length` must be **initialised** (i.e. created) and **assigned** a starting value. A simple assignment statement taking the form:

```
>>> length = 5.75
```

does both jobs. This creates a new variable `length` and assigns to it a value of 5.75. This value would then be substituted for `length` if using the expression `length**2` to calculate the area of the square.

Variables can also be initialised by assigning them to an expression. For example, you could define a second variable called `area` using:

```
>>> area = length**2
```

The variable `area` would be initialised with the value calculated by evaluating the expression on the right hand side.

Python permits the assignment of more than one variable at a time. For example:

```
x, y, z = 123, 4.5, 6
```

would assign 123 to `x`, 4.5 to `y` and 6 to `z`, although many programmers prefer to keep the assignments separate in the interests of readability:

```
x = 123
y = 4.5
z = 6
```

One of the main benefits of using variables is that same name can be assigned different values at different points in the program – i.e. the values of a variable can vary (hence the name!). Thus, if we wanted to calculate the area of a square with sides of length 10.2, we could assign a new value to `length` using:

```
>>> length = 10.2
```

The new value (10.2) would be used instead of the previous value (5.75) in any statement in which the variable `length` is used subsequently.

Variables may be used anywhere that the value they represent could be used. Thus, you could use the statement:

```
print(area)
```

to display the area of the square. Of course, it would be better to print some additional text (e.g. 'Area of the square =') to explain what the number refers to, but we will come to that in Chapter 5.

Variables As Object References

Python operates slightly differently to other languages, so it may help to take a brief detour to consider what is happening 'behind the scenes'.

Many other languages require variables to be **declared** before use – i.e. you need specify the **type** of data that will be assigned to the variable. The declaration determines how much memory needs to be reserved (e.g. 1 byte for a character, 4 bytes for an integer, 5 bytes for a real number, etc.). This memory is then reserved and used as a 'container' for the data values. If the value of the variable is changed, the number stored in the 'container' is changed to the new value. However, although the values assigned to the variable can be changed, the type (i.e. which determines the amount of memory) and the location of the variable within memory remain fixed.

Python works in a different manner. Variable names in Python are actually **object references**. It is sometimes said that 'everything in Python is an object'. Object-orientated programming is discussed in much more depth in the companion volume, but a simple description here of some features may be useful to understanding how Python variables work.

As already mentioned in Chapter 1, an object may be regarded as a 'thing' that has various attributes or properties (including a data value and a type) and methods (i.e. built-in instructions for changing its properties and working with other objects). The type of object (e.g. int, float etc.) determines which methods are available, and hence the types of operation you can do with that particular data value.[29]

A variable name in Python is an **object reference** – i.e. it provides a 'pointer' to indicate where to find the data object (including its properties and methods) in memory. Thus, when you enter an assignment statement such as:

```
>>> length = 5.75
```

Python creates a float object with a value of 5.75. The identifier length can be thought of as a 'pointer' which tells Python where to find this object. The variable (or identifier) is said to be **bound** to that object.

When the value of a variable is changed (e.g. by a new assignment statement), the value of the original object is not changed as you might expect. Rather, a new object is created containing the new value and the value of the 'pointer' is changed to point to the new data object – i.e. the variable is unbound from the first object and is bound to the new one. The old object still exists and remains unchanged, but it is no longer referenced by a variable. This could obviously result in a build-up of redundant objects unnecessarily occupying memory, but Python recovers the memory used by unreferenced objects at intervals using a process

---

[29] Type, in object-orientated programming, is more formally referred to as a **class**. A class may be thought of as the blueprint used to instantiate or create objects of a particular type. Thus a class called int is used to create integer objects, whilst a class called float creates floating point objects.

---

referred to as **garbage collection**. This, however, occurs automatically behind the scenes, so you do not need to worry about it.

Because object references are basically pointers, Python variables do not actually have a type. This is why they do not need to be declared in Python. However, the data value (i.e. the object) that they reference does have a type, and it is this that determines what operations can legitimately be applied to the data value.

Given that a variable can be bound to new objects, the type associated with a variable may also change. This is referred to as **dynamic typing**. To illustrate, enter the following in interactive mode:

```
>>> length = 10
>>> area = length**2
>>> print(area)
>>> area=area+12.5
>>> print(area)
>>> area=area-12.5
>>> print(area)
```

The first `print()` function displays the value of `area` as an integer because it was calculated by taking the square of an integer, whereas the second `print()` function displays it as a float because `area` was calculated by adding an integer to a float (12.5).[30] Subtracting 12.5 does not change `area` back into an integer, even though the answer is a whole number (i.e. 100), because the subtraction involved two floats. If you now enter:

```
>>> area = 45
>>> area = area + 10
>>> print(area)
```

`area` is turned back into an integer because it is assigned to an integer object (i.e. 45) in the first line. Variables do not have a type; it is the objects that they are bound to that have a type.

The presence or absence of a decimal point in the above example indicates whether `area` at any given point is a `float` or an `int`. However, Python provides a `type()` function which may be used to determine the type of any object. Thus entering:

```
type(area)
```

at any stage in the above example will return either `int` or `float`.

---

[30] As noted previously, it is not necessary to use the `print()` function in interactive mode. Simply entering `area` instead of `print(area)` in above examples would achieve the same result.

It might also be noted in passing that the line:

```
>>> area = area + 10
```

means something different in computing than it does in mathematics. It does not mean that something is the same as itself plus 10 (which would of course be nonsense); rather it is an instruction telling Python to bind the object reference on the left hand side (i.e. `area`) to a new object containing the value of the object on the right hand side plus 10.

Variable Names

When creating a variable you can give it any name you wish, subject to a few **rules** that govern all object references:

1. The name may only contain letters, numeric digits and the underscore (_) symbol. Some other languages use special symbols to indicate the type of a variable (e.g. BASIC uses a $ suffix to indicate a string variable), but in Python any symbol other than _ will generate an error.

2. Variable names must start with either an underscore or a letter; they may not start with a numeric digit.

3. There are a small number of Python keywords you cannot use as variable names. The interpreter will return an error if you attempt to use one. These are listed in Appendix C.

There are also a number of **conventions** that most Python programmers adhere to:

1. Although variable names may begin with an underscore, this is generally best avoided as an underscore prefix has a special meaning in some situations.

2. Lower case letters are preferable to capitals. One exception is when capitals are used throughout to indicate a variable whose value should not be changed (e.g. PI, VAT_RATE).

3. Python programmers are divided whether to use underscores or capitals in compound names (e.g. my_favourite_animal or myFavouriteAnimal), but the official recommendation is to use lower case letters with underscores. If using capitals to separate words (sometimes known as 'camel case'), the convention is still to begin with a lower case letter (i.e. myVar rather than MyVar). (Although I

generally tend to adhere to the official recommendation, I sometimes use camel case in short names where in my opinion it improves readability).

4. Names may be as long or as short as you wish. Names should ideally be self-explanatory, but they should not be too long otherwise there is a risk of a spelling error. A balance therefore needs to be struck between too short and too long. A maximum of 15 characters is sometimes suggested as a rule of thumb. Single character names (e.g. x) are sometimes used for 'transient' variables that are discarded once they have served their purpose (e.g. a counter in a loop), but they are probably best avoided in other circumstances.

Whilst flaunting these conventions will not cause the interpreter to generate an error message, adherence to the conventions will make it easier for others to read your programs (and vice versa).

Although neither a rule nor a convention, it is best to avoid using the name of a built-in function for a variable. For example, if you enter:

```
>>> print = 5        # *** Not advised ***
>>> print(10)
```

Python will not object to you assigning the name print to a value in the first line, but the attempt to use the print() function in second line generates an error because print now references an int object rather than a function (i.e. a block of code). This is almost certainly not what you want.[31]

So how do you know if it is safe to use a particular name? One simple approach is to use the built-in type() function in interactive mode. As noted, the type() function identifies the class an object belongs to. If you place the name you wish to test in the parentheses, you will receive a message to indicate what type of object it is if it is already in use. Thus, for example,

```
>>> type(print)
```

identifies print as a 'builtin function or method'.

If the name is not already in use, the type() function will return an NameError message. For example,

---

[31] If you reassigned print, as in the example, you should reset IDLE to delete all the previously stored values. To do this in Windows, select the Restart Shell option on the Shell menu (or press CTRL+F6). However, this option does not appear to be available for all platforms, so you may need to shut IDLE down and restart it.

```
>>> type(myVar)
```

will return a message to say that 'myVar is not defined'. This means that it is safe for you to use.

Variables In Interactive Mode

Although lines are processed one at a time in interactive mode, the Python interpreter retains a memory of values previously assigned to variables in the same session. For example, the following line assigns a value to a variable called x:

```
>>> x = 10
```

This value is retained, so if you subsequently enter the line:

```
>>> x + 5
```

Python will evaluate the expression and display the answer no matter how many other lines had been entered in between, provided none of the intervening lines had assigned x a new value.

Python also uses a special variable in interactive mode called _ (a single underscore) to retain the result of the most recent expression not assigned to another variable. To illustrate, enter the following:

```
>>> 2+2
>>>
>>> 3+3
>>>
>>> _**2
>>>
>>> x=_-26
>>>
>>> print(x)
>>>
>>> x
>>>
```

To understand what is happening here, you need to remember that if you enter an expression in interactive mode Python will evaluate the expression and display the result. Entering a variable name by itself is treated as an expression, therefore entering x by itself resets the value represented by _. However, `print(x)` is a function (with x as an argument) rather than an expression, so it does not change the value of the variable _. Although x=_-26 involves an expression, the result is assigned to x and therefore does not change _.

Object Sharing

Two variables can be assigned to the same object. For example:

```
>>> a=5
>>> b=a
>>> print(a,b)
>>> a=a+3
>>> print(a,b)
```

The second line binds b to the same object as a, as confirmed by the first print() function. However, when the value of a is changed in the fourth line, a is bound to a new object containing the old value plus 3, whereas b remains bound to the original object, as confirmed in the second print() function.

You can track objects more clearly using a function called id() which returns the memory address of an object. For example:

```
>>> a=5
>>> b=5
>>> id(a)
>>> id(b)
>>> a=a+3
>>> id(a)
```

It will be noted that although b is not set equal to a in this example, the fact that they have the same value results in them sharing the same object. However, once the value of a is changed, it is bound to a different object.

Exchanging Values

Situations sometimes arise where you may wish to swap the values between two variables. For example, if

```
>>> a = 1
>>> b = 2
```

you might wish to assign a to 2 and b to 1.

The following piece of code would not work:

```
>>> a = b
>>> b = a
```

because after the first line both variables point to the same object and would have a value of 2; the second line would therefore produce no further change.

The exchange could be implemented with three lines of code using a third variable as a temporary store, viz:

```
>>> c = a
>>> a = b
>>> b = c
```

Variable c acts as a temporary 'storage space' for the value of a, enabling a to be assigned to the value of b, before assigning b to the old value of a stored in c.

Python, however, provides a neater method for exchanging values between two (or more) variables, viz:

```
>>> a,b = b,a
```

This in effect reassigns both variables simultaneously without the need for a temporary store.

Augmented Operators

The operators discussed in the first section are relatively intuitive. Even if you knew nothing about programming, you would probably have little difficulty figuring out what

```
>>> x = x + 10
```

meant. However, if you are new to programming you might struggle with:

```
>>> x += 10
```

As it happens, this does much the same thing but it uses an **augmented operator**. Augmented operators provide a more concise, although less intuitive, way to change the value of a variable. However, they sometimes operate in a slightly different manner behind the scenes, as we shall see in Chapter 6.

Operator	Example	Equivalent to
+=	x += 5	x = x + 5
-=	x -= 5	x = x - 5
*=	x *= 5	x = x * 5
/=	x /= 5	x = x / 5
**=	x **= 5	x = x**5
//=	x //= 5	x = x // 5
%=	x %= 5	x = x % 5

Table 4.3. Augmented Operators

Table 4.3 provides a list of some of the more common augmented operators. Each of these is the same as a plain arithmetic operator (as listed in Table 4.1) with an = sign appended. The variable, simply called x in the examples in Table 4.3, is only listed on the left hand side of an augmented operator. Although all the examples use an integer (i.e. 5), they could alternatively have used a float.

Augmented operators can only be used with variables that have already been assigned.

Other Data Types

Strings

The term **string** is used to describe text enclosed between a matching pair of either single or double quotes. We saw in Chapter 3 how strings could be displayed using the `print()` function. Strings are a data type, and like integers and floats they can be assigned to a variable.[32] For example, the statement:

```
>>> x = "Hello world!"
```

would assign the string 'Hello world!' to the variable x. In other words, the variable x would contain an object reference (or 'pointer') to a string object having the value 'Hello world!'. If the string is changed, x will point to a new string object containing the new text.

After assigning x as above, the 'Hello World' program in Chapter 3 could be reduced to:

```
>>> print(x)
```

or, in interactive mode, even more concisely to just:

```
>>> x
```

Strings may be concatenated (i.e. 'added' together) using a + operator. For, example:

```
>>> string1 = "Hello "
>>> string2 = "world!"
>>> string3 = string1 + string2
>>> print(string3)
```

will print 'Hello world!'. Note, that in this example string assigned to string1 includes a space at the end, otherwise the two words would run

---

[32] More formally, string objects are instantiated from a class called `str`.

into one another.

One can mix string variables and string literals. For example, replacing the third line above by:

```
>>> string3 = string1 + string2 + ", here I am."
```

would append a comma immediately after 'world!', followed by a space and 'here I am.'. Note also that if string1 did not contain a trailing space, it could have been inserted in the previous example as a string literal:

```
>>> string3 = string1 + " " + string2
```

The * operator can be used to used to concatenate a string multiple times. For example, entering:

```
>>> dash="-"
>>> 10*dash
```

would produce: '----------'.

It is also possible to use an augmented operator. For example, assuming string1 and string2 were initialised as above:

```
>>> string1 += string2
>>> print(string1)
```

would send our usual felicitations to the global community.

Boolean

Boolean variables and literals have only two possible values: True and False (each spelt with a capital followed by lower case letters). As one might guess, they are used in logical operations (as discussed in Chapters 9 and 10).

None

In some situations you may wish to create a variable but not allocate a value or specify a type. If you assigned the variable to 0 then it would have a value (zero) and be type int. Python therefore has a special predefined value None (with a capital N) which has no value or no type. For example:

```
>>> x = None
```

None is treated the same as False in logical operations.

Type Conversions

Although Python automatically handles data types, there may be situations where you will want to change from one type to another. There are a number of functions available to do the conversion (Table 4.4).

Function	Role
float(x)	Converts x to float number
int(x)	Converts x to int (rounding down)
round()	Converts x to int (rounding to nearest)
str(n)	Converts number n to a string

Table 4.4. Conversion Functions

The `float()` function may be used to convert from either an `int` or a `string` to a floating point number. For example:

```
>>> float(73)
>>> float("34.6")
>>> float("2.9e5")
```

When converting from a string, the argument must be the string representation of a valid number – i.e. it may not contain any characters which would be illegal in a number. The following would therefore generate an error:

```
>>> float("one")    # Generates an error
```

The `int()` function may be used to convert from either a floating point number or a string to an integer. For example, enter the following:

```
>>> int(34.0)
>>> int(34.3)
>>> int(34.9)
>>> int("34")
>>> int("34.0")     # Generates an error
```

It will be noted that the `int()` function truncates floating point numbers (i.e. they are in effect rounded down if positive, or up if negative). An alternative function `round()` may be used to round to the nearest integer:

```
>>> round(34.3)
>>> round(34.9)
>>> round(34.5)
```

Note that 34.5 is rounded down to 34.

The `int()` function can also handle strings, provided that the string is the representation of an integer (e.g. "34"). However, if the string represents a floating point number, even if there are no digits to the right of the decimal point (e.g. "34.0"), Python will generate an error message. If required, this conversion could be handled by embedding one function within another:

```
>>> int(float("34.0"))
```

The innermost function is processed first, and the value it returns is passed to the outer function. Thus the string is converted to a floating point number which in turn would provide the argument for the `int()` function.

Finally, integers and floating point numbers can be readily translated into strings using the `str()` function:

```
>>> str(325)
>>> str(34.2)
>>> str(3.2e7)
```

Literals were used in the above examples for the purposes of clarity, but the arguments could just as easily have been variables. Also, the values returned by the functions could be assigned to variables. The following snippet illustrates both points:

```
>>> x = '3.2e7'
>>> i = int(float(x))
>>> print(i)
```

The argument in each of the functions could also be an expression. The expression could include other functions. For example:

```
>>> int(float('2.7e2')/100)
```

evaluates to 2. The `float()` function returns a float value 270.0. When divided by 100, this gives a float value 2.7. The `int()` function truncates this to the integer value 2.

Exercises

(Answers are provided at the back of the book)

4.1. Setting x=10, evaluate the following expressions in your head, then enter the expressions into IDLE to check your answers:

```
1+2-3*4/5
1+(2-3*4)/5
12/2+4/2*6
12/(2+4)/(2*6)
```

```
x+x*x/x
-x**2+45*2
-2**3-5*3+x**2
```

4.2. Which of the following names are valid? Test your answers by assigning a value to each name (e.g. x=1, i%=1, etc.) using IDLE.

```
x
i%
ageOfMyWife
ElvisHasLeftTheBuilding
my_wife's_name
myName$
(subTotal)
2bRnt2b
KEEP_OFF_THE_GRASS
variable2
_NOT_OK
—
```

Which of these would be regarded as examples of good style?

4.3. What value do you think z would have after entering the following?

```
x,y,z = 1,2,3
x=y*z
x,y,z = y,z,x
```

Check you answer using IDLE.

4.4. What would happen if you entered the following:

```
20/((8+3)//4-2)
```

4.5. Rewrite the following using augmented operators. Assign a value to x, then check your answers using IDLE.

```
x = x + 10
x = x / 10
x = x * (10+5)
x = (15/3)*x
```

4.6. If x="Hello , " and y="What have we got here?", what would x*3+y evaluate as?

4.7. Predict what value would x and y have after you entered the following. Test using IDLE.

```
x = 3
y = x
x += 5
```

4.8. If x='2.3e2' and y=15, what would `round(int(float(x)-y)/20)` evaluate as? Test using IDLE.

4.9. What would you get if you entered the following into IDLE:

```
a)  0o12**0b10+0x10
b)  0o12**0b10+0x10+=10e2
```

Chapter 5. Basic Input And Output

We saw in the previous chapter how we could set the value of a variable using an assignment statement such as:

```
>>> length = 10
```

The variable `length` could then be used to represent 10 in numerous calculations throughout a program. If we wanted to perform the same type of calculation using a different value for `length`, then we could change the value assigned to `length` in the assignment statement and re-run the program. However, a better approach, which avoids the need to re-write the program each time we wanted to change the value of `length`, would be to get the program to ask the user what value they would like to use for `length`. This may be done using the `input()` function. We will look at the `input()` function later in this chapter, but first we will take a closer look at how we can get the program to display messages using the `print()` function as the prompts in `input()` follow the same syntactical rules as the output from `print()`.

Output

We have already used the `print()` function on several occasions in previous chapters, but we will explore it here in more detail.

The `print()` function takes the general form:

```
print(...)
```

where the bit in parentheses, represented by the ellipsis ... , is what we wish to have displayed. Older versions of Python did not require the parentheses, but they became mandatory in version 3.0 when the old `print` statement was replaced by a `print()` function. The output specified by the `print()` function is sent to the standard output stream (stdout) which, unless it has been specifically redefined, is normally your monitor screen. However, the output may also be redirected to a file (as we shall see in Chapter 15).

The bit in parentheses could be a string literal, a numeric literal, a variable of any type, or an expression. Thus the following would all be valid (assuming that the variable `length` has already been assigned a value):

```
>>> print("Hello")          #String
```

```
>>> print(34.7)          #Numeric literal
>>> print(length)        #Variable
>>> print(length**2)     #Expression
```

Note that variable names should not be enclosed in quotes, otherwise they would be treated as a string literal (i.e. the name of the variable rather than its value would be printed).

Multiple Arguments

The bit in parentheses may contain more than one item, separated by commas. These items may be different types. One very common use is to include some text to explain what the numeric output refers to. For example:

```
>>> length = 10
>>> print("Area of square =", length**2)
```

By default Python will insert a space between each item in the list - i.e. in this case it will insert a space between the equal sign and the calculated area. This space is inserted irrespective of whether there is a space after the comma in the print() arguments or not. Thus,

```
>>> print("Area of square =",length**2)
```

would produce exactly the same output as the previous line.

In some situations you may not want to have a space inserted. For example, suppose you wanted to separate numeric items by commas. The following line would insert a comma between the length and the area, but it would not look correct because the comma would be preceded by a space (generated by the comma after the variable length):

```
>>> print("Length =",length,", Area =",length**2)
```

To improve the punctuation, a special keyword called sep may be used to specify a different separator. We can use this to define the separator as a null string (i.e. no space), but we then need to add a space after the equal signs in each of the string literals to retain the previous spacing:

```
>>> print("Length = ",length,", Area = ",length**2,sep="")
```

An alternative to using the sep keyword in this example would be to use the str() function to convert the numeric items to strings. The strings can then be concatenated into a single string for printing:

```
print('Length = '+str(length)+', Area = '+str(length**2))
```

The print() function normally inserts a line feed at the end of whatever it prints so that the next output would begin on a new line. However, there may be situations where you want the next output to continue on the same line. This may be controlled within a script using another special keyword called `end` which specifies what characters should follow the specified text. By default, `end` is set to '\n' (meaning 'new line'), but if we change it to a null string then the line feed is omitted. Note, however, that in interactive mode `print()` will always force a line feed so that it can prompt for the next program statement, so to test, enter the following in edit mode, save it to a file (using any name you want), and run:

```
print("The man from Del Monte, he say ", end="")
print("'yes.'")
```

String Escape Sequences

When printing string literals, it does not matter whether you use single or double quotes, provided the start and end quotes are the same type. If quotes of the other type are embedded (as in the above example), they will be printed like any other character. This provides a convenient way to display apostrophes and quotation marks. For example:

```
>>> print("What's up?")
>>> print('And do not say "The opposite of down".')
```

Problems might arise if you wished to include an apostrophe within a quotation. For example,

```
>>> print('"So what's new?" said Mary')        #Error
```

would produce a syntax error because the apostrophe in "what's" would be treated as the end of the string literal, with the result that the interpreter would be unable to make any sense out of the rest of the line. However, this can be handled using a backslash to escape the apostrophe:

```
>>> print('"So what\'s new?" said Mary')
```

The backslash tells the interpreter than the apostrophe (single quote) following it is to be treated as a literal rather than as the matching pair of the single quote at the beginning of the argument. Backslashes may also be used to escape double quote marks in the same manner (i.e. \"). The backslash is not printed.

Because the backslash has a special meaning within a string, if you actually want to output a backslash character it is necessary to escape it with a second backslash. For example:

```
>>> print("c:\\Program Files\\Python")
```

Certain characters can be inserted in a string literal to control formatting (Table 5.1). Thus, for example, the letter 'n' may be inserted to indicate a line feed, whilst the letter 't' may be used to insert a tab. These need to be prefaced by a backslash to tell the interpreter not to print them as literals. For example:

```
>>> print("Names:\n\tEdgar\tAllan\tPoe")
```

In this example, \n forces a line feed in the output, whilst each \t inserts a tab.

Escape sequence	Effect
\\	Backslash \
\'	Single quote
\"	Double quote
\n	New line
\t	Tab

Table 5.1. Some Common Escape Sequences

If there is a large amount of text to be output, a string literal may be too long to fit on a single physical line. One solution is to break the string into a number of sub-strings separated by backslashes as the last character in each line. For example, if the following line was entered into IDLE in interactive mode:

```
>>> print("Mary had a little lamb,\n\
```

IDLE will wait for further continuation lines until it receives a quote and a right parenthesis, so continue entering the following:

```
Her father shot it dead,\n\
And now it goes to school with her,\n\
Between two lumps of bread.")
```

When the right parenthesis is entered, the sub-strings are concatenated (as if they were joined by + signs) and output. Note that in this case the \n insertions ensure that each sub-string is printed on a separate line. If they were not included, the four lines would be joined into a single line that stretched across the screen.

Triple Quoted Strings

An alternative, and possibly simpler, way to achieve the same end is to use a **long string**, sometimes referred to as a **triple quoted string**. A long string begins and ends with three matching quotes (either double or single). The text between the triple quotes is printed exactly as it is specified in the print() function. Thus, to repeat the above example:

```
>>> print("""
Mary had a little lamb,
Her father shot it dead,
And now it goes to school with her,
Between two lumps of bread.
""")
```

It will be noted that the above does not require any line feeds (\n) or continuation backslashes. Long strings provide an easy way to program text that might otherwise be difficult to format. To illustrate, load and run the sample program **big_hello.py**.

Raw Strings

Finally, as an alternative to using a long string or escape sequences, you can use a **raw string**. To do this, simply insert the letter r immediately in front of the string you wish to print and type the string exactly as you wish it to appear. For example:

```
>>> print(r"c:\Program Files\Python")
```

This format is especially useful when you have short strings that would require a lot of backslashes, but it is less useful when you need to insert line feeds or tabs as they just get printed out as \n or \t.

Input

Let us now look at how Python may be used to accept user input using the `input()` function. We have already seen an example of the `input()` function in the line that we added to scripts to prevent a window from closing automatically:

```
input("\nPress <ENTER> to finish")
```

The `input()` function accepts only one argument - a text string normally used to prompt the user. It is not absolutely essential to provide a prompt, but it makes sense to do so otherwise the user could spend a long time sitting around wondering what to do next! The same formatting rules (e.g. escape sequences etc.) apply to this string as for the `print()` function. It will be noted, for example, that the string begins with '\n' to insert a blank line.

The `input()` function accepts input from the user and makes it available to the program. Previously we were not interested in what the user entered as the objective was simply to create a delay until the user pressed the <ENTER> key (which they must do eventually no matter how many other keys they press to type something beforehand). Whatever the user typed (if anything) was therefore discarded. However, normally we are interested in what the user types. This input can be assigned to a variable.

For example, consider the following short script (**hello_you1.py**):

```
name = input("Please type in your name : ")
print("\tHello " + name)
input("\nPress <ENTER> To Finish")
```

The first line prompts the user to type in their name. Whatever the user types is assigned to the variable name. The print() function in the second line then uses name to say hello. (Okay, I know I seem to have a fixation with meeting and greeting, but we will move onto something a bit more interesting soon).

A Trap For The Unwary

It is important to stress that there is a pitfall waiting to trap the unwary. Consider the script (**input_problem.py**):

```
x=input("Enter a number : ")
y=input("Enter another number : ")
print("The sum of the numbers is:", x+y)
input("\nPress <ENTER> to finish")
```

It all seems straightforward enough. The program prompts for two numbers which are assigned to the variables x and y, and then it prints out the sum of the numbers. What could possibly go wrong? Run the program using two simple numbers (e.g. 3 and 4). See the problem?

Ironically the problem arises because of Python's flexibility. Unlike many other languages, Python does not insist that you declare a variable as a particular type (i.e. int, float, str, etc.). Rather, Python defines the type according to the value it is assigned. However, if you are assigning a value using the input() function, Python has no way of knowing whether what you enter is the number 3 or the string '3'. Given that anything you enter can be handled as a string, whereas letters and punctuation marks would be unintelligible if you tried to treat them as a number, Python treats all input as a string. Thus, instead of adding the numbers 3 and 4 together to get 7, the program assumes '3' and '4' are strings which it concatenates to get '34'. Not the type of error you would want to make if writing a program to assess how much you should pay the taxman!

This type of problem, which does not generate an error message or warning, but simply gives the wrong answer, is the most insidious to deal with. The only strategy is to be aware of the potential pitfalls and to take steps to prevent them arising.

The solution in this case is to use one of the conversion functions introduced in Chapter 4. We can re-write our program using `int()` functions to convert the input into integers (**int_input.py**):

```
x=int(input("Enter a number : "))
y=int(input("Enter another number : "))
print("The sum of the numbers is:", x+y)
input("\nPress <ENTER> to finish")
```

If you run this program using the numbers 3 and 4 you should now get the correct answer because the strings returned by the `input()` functions in the first two lines are used as arguments in `int()` functions and are converted into integers.

However, what would happen if you entered float numbers? If you run **int_input.py** using float numbers (e.g. 3.5 and 4.3), you will discover that you again run into problems. The reason is that the strings containing the float numbers are not in the correct format for the `int()` function. The simple solution is to use the `float()` functions instead of `int()` functions, as below (**float_input.py**):

```
x=float(input("Enter a number : "))
y=float(input("Enter another number : "))
print("The sum of the numbers is:", x+y)
input("\nPress <ENTER> to finish")
```

This will work with numbers containing decimal places. However, if you enter two integer numbers (e.g. 3 and 4), you will find that the program still works correctly, although the answer is expressed as a float (i.e. 7.0). If you do not specifically need your answer to be an integer, the `float()` function provides a more flexible option.

If you are writing a program for your own personal use, then the chances are you will quickly spot the problem if you enter the wrong type of data (e.g. a float number where an integer is expected). However, if you are writing the program for other people to use, then it is good practice to check the input and issue error or warning messages to inform the user if there are problems. Exception handling will be discussed in Chapter 13.

Exercises

5.1. Which of the following are valid:

```
print('My name's Marmaduke')
print(' "So what?" said Jemima')
print("My name's Marmaduke")
print("\"So what?\" said Jemima")
print('My name\'s Marmaduke')
print(" 'So what?" said Jemima ")
```

Enter each line into IDLE to check your answer.

5.2. Print the nursery rhyme 'Baa, baa black sheep' using a long string so that each line of the poem is displayed on a separate line. Repeat using line feeds but without triple quotes.

5.3. Write a program asking the user to enter his/her name. Then print 'Congratulations [name], you have just won millions of dollars in our on-line lottery.'

5.4. Write a program inviting the user to enter their first, middle and surnames as separate strings, then print a message to welcome the user using their full name.

5.5. Write a program requesting the user to enter three numbers. Calculate the average of the three numbers and output the answer as an integer rounded to the nearest whole number.

5.6. Write a program inviting the user to enter the radius (r) of a circle. Calculate and print the area ($\pi r2$) and the circumference ($2\pi r$) of the circle. (You can regard the value of π as 3.14159).

5.7. Latitudes and longitudes were traditionally expressed as degrees, minutes ($1/60^{th}$ of a degree) and seconds ($1/60^{th}$ of a second). These are usually converted to decimal degrees for computer use – i.e. latitudes and longitudes are expressed using a single decimal number, where the portion after the decimal place represents the minutes and seconds expressed as a fraction of a degree (e.g. 30 minutes is 0.5 degrees). Write a program to enable the user to enter a latitude or longitude expressed in degrees, minutes and seconds and then convert it to decimal degrees.

5.8. Write a program to convert a latitude or longitude entered in decimal degrees to degrees, minutes and seconds.

5.9. Write a program to draw a picture of a chessboard, similar to the figure below, using the letter 'W' to represent white squares and 'B' to represent black squares. There should be 8 rows and 8 columns.

```
----------------------------------------
: W : B : W : B : W : B : W : B :
----------------------------------------
: B : W : B : W : B : W : B : W :
----------------------------------------
: W : B : W : B : W : B : W : B :
----------------------------------------
: B : W : B : W : B : W : B : W :
----------------------------------------
: W : B : W : B : W : B : W : B :
----------------------------------------
: B : W : B : W : B : W : B : W :
----------------------------------------
: W : B : W : B : W : B : W : B :
----------------------------------------
: B : W : B : W : B : W : B : W :
----------------------------------------
```

Chapter 6. Sequences

We saw in Chapter 4 how variable names provide a convenient way to refer to individual data values. However, if you have several data items that are in some way related, it may be more convenient to refer to them using a single collective name, yet retain the capability to refer to and work with individual items. Python provides a number of built-in data types that can be used for working with **collections**. The next two chapters look at three such structures, collectively referred to as **sequences**, whilst two other types of collections will be discussed later in Chapter 12. The present chapter discusses some features common to all sequences, whilst the following chapter looks in more detail at features specific to each type of sequence.

A sequence is an ordered collection of data items in which each item can be specifically referenced using an index number. We have actually seen one type of sequence already, namely a **string** (which is actually an ordered collection of characters). Although until now we have only worked with strings as 'whole' entities, we shall see that it is also possible to manipulate the constituent items in a string (i.e. the individual characters).

Python provides several other types of sequence, but the two most widely used are **tuples** and **lists**. These are both ordered collections of data objects of any type – i.e. the individual items may be integers, floats, strings, or even other lists or tuples. Further, there is no requirement that the items in any given tuple or list should all be the same type – i.e. you can mix types any way you wish.[33] The main difference between a list and a tuple is that lists are **mutable**, whereas tuples are **immutable**. We shall begin by explaining these terms.

Mutability

The term 'mutable' means the value of a data object may be changed *in situ*; 'immutable' means that an object's data value is fixed. The numeric types `int` and `float` are both immutable. However, although they are immutable, we can change the value of an `int` or `float` variable using a

---

[33] The elements in lists and tuples are basically references to objects. It does not matter to the sequence what these objects are, so different types can be mixed in the same sequence. Items in a list can even be changed to items of a different type.

---

statement such as:

```
>>> x = x + 5
```

So how can we change the value of something that is fixed? The answer, as discussed previously, is that we are <u>not</u> changing the value of the data object (which remains unchanged), but replacing the object referred to by the variable x with a new object with the new value (and sometimes even a new type). The original object remains unchanged, but it is unbound and becomes available for garbage collection.

Tuples and strings are also immutable. Both types of objects contain object references (i.e. pointers to other objects); these references cannot be changed. For example, if x is assigned to the string 'Hello', the string object contains pointers to the objects containing the individual letters than make up the string. These pointers are immutable (i.e. they cannot be changed to point to different letters), but like integers and floats the value of the string variable x can be changed by binding x to a new string object. The same applies to tuples.

Lists, in contrast, are mutable. This means that it is possible to change their contents *in situ* – i.e. the pointers within a list object can be changed to point to new objects. It is therefore possible to change the values of individual items in a list, delete items, or even change the type of existing items. Lists are consequently much more flexible than tuples, but there are occasions where the stability of a tuple may be advantageous.

Initialisation

The methods for initialising and assigning values to strings, tuples, and lists are similar, but differ in detail. The general formats are:

```
name = 'abcde' or name = "abcde"          # String
name = ( itemA, itemB, itemC, itemD )     # Tuple
name = [ itemA, itemB, itemC, itemD ]     # List
```

where `name` is any valid variable name, `'abcde'` is a string of characters, and `itemX` is a data item of any type. Note that tuples use enclosing parentheses, whereas lists use square brackets. Strings, as we have seen, use matching single or double quotes. The items in tuples and lists are separated by commas, but there are no separators in a string (although you can of course include commas and spaces as normal text character items as part of the string).

The contents of a list, tuple or string can be displayed at any time by entering its name at the prompt in interactive mode or using its name as the argument to a `print()` function in a script. Python will display the contents in square brackets, parentheses or quotes to indicate the type of sequence (although the quotes are suppressed if using a `print()` function).

Tuples can also be assigned without using parentheses. If you assign a number of comma-separated items to a single variable, it will be assumed to be a tuple. For example, if you enter:

```
>>> x = 12, 34.6, 'marmalade'
>>> print(x)
```

the items will be displayed in parentheses indicating that *x* is a tuple. This is referred to as **sequence packing**.

Lists and tuples may also be initialised by converting another sequence using the `list()` or `tuple()` function:

```
aList = list(aTuple)
bList = list(aString)
aTuple = tuple(aList)
bTuple = tuple(aString)
```

Converting from a string to either a list or a tuple results in each character in the string being converted to a separate item.

An empty sequence can be defined by not placing anything between the enclosing delimiters:

```
>>> aString = ''
>>> aTuple = ()
>>> aList = []
```

This may be useful if you wish to initialise a sequence that will be built up by the addition of further items.

Indexing

First, a word of warning!

Computer scientists cannot count. Or, to be more precise, they can count, but they insist on counting from zero. The reasons for doing this are lost in the mists of time, but they are probably related to the way in which data in a computer's memory are referenced in machine code as offsets. However, having started to count in this peculiar manner, the habit would seem to have stuck and it is now found in most (although not all) high level computer languages, including Python. This peculiar method of counting causes no end of confusion for us lesser mortals more used to starting at 1, but it is something we just have to get used to. However, hang in there, you will get there eventually.

Unfortunately this is not the only quirky thing you will need to get used to in this chapter. If (like me) you find some of the rules counterintuitive, bear in mind that IDLE's interactive mode provides an invaluable resource for experimenting if you need to check whether you have the correct syntax when you are writing scripts.

Individual items in a sequence can be specified by enclosing an integer **index** number (or an expression that evaluates to an integer or a variable that references an integer) in square brackets. However, this is where the funny counting comes in. To refer to the ith item you need to set the index to i-1. Thus, for example, if:

```
>>> aString = 'Hello'
```

then

```
>>> aString[1]
```

in interactive mode will print the second letter 'e' and not 'H' as you might expect. The maximum possible index number is n-1, where n is the number of items. Note also that square brackets are used for indexing all sequences including strings and tuples, even though these use quotes and parentheses for assignment and display).

Sequence Item	Item1	Item2	Item3	Item4	Item5
Positive Index	0	1	2	3	4
Negative Index	-5	-4	-3	-2	-1

Figure 6.1. Alternative Indices In A Five Element Sequence

As if counting from zero was not confusing enough, you can also use a negative index (Figure 6.1). This is used to count from the end of the list backwards – i.e. `name[-1]` returns the last item in the sequence, `name[-2]` the second last and so forth. Thus, every item has two possible indices. The sum of their absolute values (i.e. ignoring negative signs) will be equal to n, where n is the number of elements. (Knowing this may help. But, then again, it may not!)

The following script (**day_of_the_week1.py**) illustrates the use of an index, plus a couple of other features discussed previously. The program requests the user to enter a number (nDays) and the program then identifies what day of the week it will be in nDays time, assuming that today is a Monday:

```
days =('Monday','Tuesday','Wednesday','Thursday','Friday',
       'Saturday','Sunday')
nDays = int(input("Enter number of days : "))
index = nDays%7                          #Discard whole weeks
print("In", nDays, "days time it will be",days[index])
input("\nPress <ENTER> to finish")
```

Note that when we initialise the tuple day, we can split the items between physical lines. Python will treat the following physical lines as part of the same logical line until it reaches a closing parenthesis.

The first line creates a tuple with seven elements in which each item is a string containing the name of a day of the week. The second (logical) line prompts the user to input the number of days. Note that the input is converted to an integer (nDays) using the int() function. The third line divides this number by 7 and assigns the remainder to the variable index, which must have a value in the range 0 to 6 – this removes whole weeks (i.e. multiples of 7). The variable index is then used as an index to select the appropriate item from the tuple days, which is then printed to the screen. Note that if nDays is an exact multiple of 7, then index would be evaluated as 0 indicating the first item in the tuple. The funny counting therefore works out quite nicely in this instance, so perhaps there is method to the computer scientists' madness after all!

Slicing

You can also specify a range of items using two indices separated by a colon, where the first index indicates the first item to be included and the second item indicates the first item *after* the items to be included. This is referred to as **slicing**. Thus, for example, if :

```
>>> aList = [1, 2, 3, 4, 5]
```

then:

```
>>> aList[2:4]
```

would return [3, 4]. Note the square brackets in the output indicate that the items form a list. Had aList been a tuple with the same items, the output would be enclosed in parentheses - i.e. (3, 4). Requesting aString[1:4] would return the selected characters in quotes – i.e. if aString was 'Hello', aString[1:4] would select 'ell'.

One might expect the second index to indicate the last item to be included, so it is important to stress that it indicates the first item **after** the slice – i.e. [2:4] does not mean 'from 2 to 4 inclusive' but rather 'from 2 to just before 4'. An alternative way to think of index numbers for slices is to think of them referring to the divides between items rather than to the containers of items (Figure 6.2). If the divides are numbered from 0, then [2:4] could be interpreted as 'all the containers between divide 2 and divide 4' (i.e. the containers indexed 2 and 3).[34]

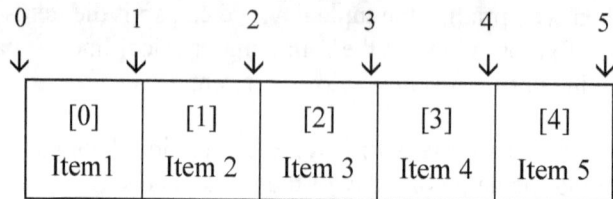

Figure 6.2. Index Numbers Used To Number Divides In A Sequence

In the older versions of Python, specifying an index that was outside the valid range generated an error message, but now the index is simply truncated to the maximum value allowed – i.e.

```
>>> aList[2:500]
```

would return [3, 4, 5]. However, a simpler approach is simply to specify no value. Thus:

```
>>> aList[2:]
```

would return [3, 4, 5]. You can also select from the beginning of the sequence by omitting the first index. Thus:

```
>>> aList[:2]
```

would return [1, 2].

In some instances you may wish to select items at some regular interval. This is referred to as **striding** and may be achieved by specifying an increment as a third term. Thus:

```
>>> aList[0:5:2]
```

would return [1, 3, 5], as indeed would `aList[::2]`.

The increment term may also be used to extract the items in reverse order by using a negative value. Thus, for example:

---

[34] Unfortunately this rule does not work if you are extracting the items in reverse order (as described below).

```
>>> aList[4:1:-1]
```

would return [5, 4, 3]. Note that the first (beginning) index needs to be higher that the second (end) index if the third one is negative. Note also that this does not simply return the same elements in reverse order as:

```
>>> aList[1:4:1]
```

because of the 'from to just before' nature of the specification. To get [3, 4, 5] you would need to enter:

```
>>> aList[2:5:1]
```

or, more simply:

```
>>> aList[2:]
```

As before, you can specify the first or last item by omitting the relevant index. Thus:

```
>>> aList[::-1]
```

will return all the terms in the sequence in reverse order.

Still hanging in? Good! I think we are now over the worst. You could attempt exercises 6.1 to 6.3 at this point if you are feeling brave.

Addition

Sequences of the same type can be added together using a plus sign. In the case of strings, this is what we referred to in Chapter 4 as concatenation. For example:

```
>>> s1="Goodbye "
>>> s2="cruel world"
>>> s1=s1+s2
>>> print(s1)
```

would display "Goodbye cruel world". Likewise:

```
>>> aList=[1,2,3]
>>> bList=[4,5,6]
>>> aList=aList+bList
>>> print(aList)
```

displays [1, 2, 3, 4, 5, 6] and

```
>>> aTuple=(1,2,3)
>>> bTuple=(4,5,6)
>>> aTuple=aTuple+bTuple
>>> print(aTuple)
```

produces (1, 2, 3, 4, 5, 6).

These examples, where we change a sequence into a larger sequence may sound a bit like squeezing a quart into a pint pot, but when we specify a=a+b, the a after the operation points to a different (and larger) object in memory than the a before – even if a is a mutable list.

The object pointed to by a before the operation is not destroyed. To illustrate enter the following:

```
>>> aList=[1,2,3]
>>> bList=[4,5,6]
>>> cList=aList
>>> aList=aList+bList
>>> print(aList)
>>> print(cList)
```

You will find that a now contains [1, 2, 3, 4, 5, 6] whilst cList contains [1, 2, 3]. In the third line cList was set equal to aList. This does not result in the creation of a new object; rather, cList is bound to the object already bound to by aList. This is an example of a **shared reference**. Following the addition in the fourth line, aList was set to point to a new object containing the new list, but cList remained unchanged. Consequently it continued to point to the list which had originally been bound to aList. This object would only become available for garbage collection if the binding for cList was changed.

Unfortunately (at least in terms of understanding things) augmented operators behave slightly differently behind the scenes, as you will see if you enter the following:

```
>>> aList=[1,2,3]
>>> bList=[4,5,6]
>>> cList=aList
>>> aList += bList
>>> print(aList)
>>> print(cList)
```

cList now refers to the same list object as aList – i.e. [1, 2, 3, 4, 5, 6]. The reason is that augmented operators, such as aList+=bList, change the contents of a **mutable** object, such as a list, *in situ* without changing its location, whereas aList=aList+bList binds aList to a newly created list object. Thus, in this example, the augmented operator does not change the location of the list object, so aList and cList still point at the same object. However, because the value of this object has changed, cList takes on the new value of aList even though cList was not directly changed. The id() function could be used with the above example to confirm that the locations of aList and cList remain unchanged throughout.

This only applies to mutable objects. The values of **immutable** objects, such as tuples and strings (or indeed ints and floats), cannot be changed, therefore when you add two objects together, irrespective of whether or not you use an augmented operator, you always create a new object, so any shared references will be broken. If you repeat the above example using tuples (i.e. using parentheses instead of square brackets in the first two lines), you would find that `cList` retains the original value of `aList`.

It is possible to test whether two identifiers refer to the same object using the `is` operator. Thus, to test if `aList` and `cList` in the above snippet refer to the same object we could enter:

```
>>> aList is cList
```

This would return `True` because the two identifiers refer to the same object. We could also test whether they refer to different objects using `is not`:

```
>>> aList is not cList
```

This would return `False`.

Multiplication

All sequences support multiplication by an integer number, either as a literal or an integer variable. This causes the sequence to be repeated the specified number of times. Thus, for example:

```
>>> aList=[1,2,3,4]
>>> b=3
>>> cList=aList*b
```

would set `cList` equal to [1, 2, 3, 4, 1, 2, 3, 4, 1, 2, 3, 4].

You need to be careful when multiplying a tuple containing only one item. A list containing only one item will work as you would expect. For example:

```
>>> [6]*3
```

evaluates to [6, 6, 6], but

```
>>> (6)*3
```

evaluates to 18. The reason is Python treats `(6)` as a number in parentheses rather than as a tuple. However, if you add a comma i.e. `(6,)`, then Python knows to treat it as a tuple. Thus:

```
>>> (6,)*3
```

evaluates to (6, 6, 6).

Membership

Python provides a simple way of testing whether a particular item is present in a sequence using the in operator. This returns a Boolean value (i.e. True or False). For example:

```
>>> aList = [123, 456, 789]
>>> 456 in aList
```

would return the value True, but

```
>>> 345 in aList
```

would return False. The Boolean value can be assigned to a variable if required. For example:

```
>>> is_present = 345 in aList
```

would assign the value False to the Boolean variable is_present.

The in operator is illustrated in the following simple program (**id_check1.py**) which tests whether the userid entered by a user is valid:

```
valid_ids = ["Jim", "Joe", "Janet", "Jezebel"]
id = input("Enter your userid : ")
print(id in valid_ids)
input("\nPress <ENTER> to finish")
```

The first line defines a list of valid userids; the second line asks the user to enter their userid; and the third line tests whether the userid entered is in the list of acceptable userids and then prints either True or False depending upon the outcome. We will see in Chapter 9 how this test could be used to determine an appropriate action (e.g. whether to allow the user entry into the system or to lock them out).

It is also possible to test for the absence of a particular item using not in. The not prefix reverses the result of the test. For example:

```
>>> aList = [2,4,6,8]
>>> 7 not in aList
```

would return True.

The in operator works with tuples exactly the same as with lists. However, it behaves slightly differently with strings. Consider the following example:

```
>>> aString = "abcdef"
>>> "c" in aString
>>> "cde" in aString
```

The first line creates a string with 6 elements (i.e. 6 characters). The second tests if one of the elements is 'c' and returns True as expected. One might expect the third line to return False because none of the elements (which are each only one character long) could be "cde". However, Python actually checks whether the sequence of characters 'cde' appears anywhere within aString and in this case returns True. Thus, in may be used to test whether any string is a substring of another. However, there are situations where using in to test the contents of a string might not be appropriate. For example, if testing if a userid was valid, we would want to ensure that the user entered a complete userid and not simply get access by guessing one or two characters within an acceptable userid.

You should be able to attempt exercises 6.4 to 6.7 at this point.

Functions

There are a number of built-in functions that can be used with all sequences (Table 6.1).

Function	Use	Sample Syntax
len()	Returns number of items	n = len(aSeq)
min()	Returns the minimum value	item = min(aSeq)
max()	Returns the maximum value	item = max(aSeq)
sorted()	Returns a sorted list	bSeq = sorted(aSeq)

Table 6.1. Some Functions That May Be Used With Sequences

Let us define five sequences for the following examples:

```
>>> aTuple = (28,45,24,84,34)
>>> aList = [38,28,90,'ABC']
>>> bList = [3, 7, 2.5, 9.3]
>>> cList = ['abc','DEF','XYZ']
>>> aString = '[}.,abcDEF'
```

len()

The len() function may be used to measure the length of a sequence (i.e. to count the number of items). Thus:

```
>>> len(aTuple)
>>> len(aList)
>>> len(aString)
```

will return the integer values 5, 4 and 10 respectively. Note that `len()` counts from 1.

min()

The `min()` function identifies which item has the lowest value. Thus, in this example:

```
>>> min(aTuple)
```

returns the number 24. However:

```
>>> min(aList)
```

produces an error message. Although a list (or a tuple) can contain a mix of numeric and string data types, the `min()` function can not compare numbers and strings. However:

```
>>> min(bList)
```

works fine and returns the float 2.5. Although `bList` contains a mix of `int` and `float` numbers, `min()` is able to compare them because they are all numeric. Likewise:

```
>>> min(cList)
```

also works fine because all the items are strings. This, however, raises the question as what is meant by 'minimum'. Basically `min()` compares the ASCII values of the first character in each string (and then, in the event of a tie, the ASCII values of the second characters). The fact that 'DEF' is identified as the minimum value in `cList` might seem odd, but uppercase letters have lower ASCII values than lowercase letters, therefore 'DEF' precedes 'abc'.

Comparisons within strings use a similar approach, except the comparisons are between individual characters. Thus:

```
>>> min(aString)
```

will return the character ',' as it has the lowest ASCII value.

max()

The `max()` function is very similar, except it records the item with the highest value. Thus:

```
>>> max(aTuple)
>>> max(bList)
>>> max(cList)
>>> max(aString)
```

will return 84, 9.3, 'abc' and '}' respectively. Note that `min(aString)` and `max(aString)` in these examples both returned punctuation characters. Unless you are very familiar with ASCII codes, the results can sometimes appear strange, but they are correct.

sorted()

The `sorted()` function can also be used to compare items in a sequence. As its name might suggest, this compares all the items in a sequence and rearranges the items in order. Thus:

```
>>> sorted(aTuple)
>>> sorted(bList)
>>> sorted(cList)
>>> sorted(aString)
```

would return the following:

```
[24, 28, 34, 45, 84]
[2.5, 3, 7, 9.3]
['DEF', 'XYZ', 'abc']
[',', '.', 'D', 'E', 'F', '[', 'a', 'b', 'c', '}']
```

The two sorted lists are as one might expect, but look again at the sorted tuple and the sorted string. Both have been returned as lists rather than as a tuple or a string. The reason is that tuples and strings are immutable (i.e. cannot be changed) so the `sorted()` function sorts the items within a list and always returns the results as a list. However, if required, a sorted tuple can be converted back into a tuple using the `tuple()` function. For example:

```
>>> aTuple = tuple(sorted(aTuple))
```

You should now be able to do exercises 6.8 to 6.11.

Nested sequences

A sequence may be an item within another list or tuple. This is referred to as a **nested sequence**. One very common situation is when a list contains strings as items – each string item is itself a sequence nesting within the list. The embedded sequences may themselves contain other sequences. Thus, for example:

```
>>> nested = [1, 2, (3, ['string1', 'string2'])]
```

defines two strings within a list within a tuple within another list – a total of 4 'levels'. As noted previously, the items at any one 'level' do not need to be the same type, nor do the sequences at each 'level' need to contain the same number of items. This provides enormous flexibility.

There are situations, however, where one might prefer more symmetry.

Many forms of statistical analysis organise the data to be analysed into a **data matrix** – i.e. a rectangular array of data values in which each row represents a case (e.g. a person, a household, a geographical area) and each column represents a variable attribute (e.g. age, number of children, total population). The value of a variable for any particular case is stored in the cell at the intersection of the relevant row and column. A **relation** within a relational database is similar and is normally envisaged as a rectangular table containing rows and columns: each row contains the data for an entity of a particular type and each column contains the information on some attribute.[35] Thus, by reading across a row one can read all the characteristics for a particular entity, whilst by reading down a column one can see how a particular attribute varies between different entities.

In computing, a rectangular data structure of this type is sometimes referred to as a two dimensional **array**. An array may also have three or more dimensions. For example, a three dimensional array might be used to store data for different periods in time – i.e. it could be envisaged as a cube in which each 'slice' in the third dimension provides a two dimensional array (of variable attributes and cases) for a particular time period. Four dimensional arrays are more difficult to conceptualise, but cause no additional computational difficulties (apart, possibly, from storage issues if they are very large).

A data matrix can be handled in Python using a nested sequence with the same number of items within each second level sequence.[36] For example, if we had information on the name, age and sex of a number of people, we could create a nested list along the following lines:

```
>>> people=[
        ['Herminone', 34, 'F'],
        ['Horatio', 52,'M'],
        ['Giovanni', 23, 'M'],
        ['Priscilla', 21, 'F']
        ]
```

The lines above were separated during input using the <ENTER> key to preserve the matrix appearance, but the information could have been

---

[35] A row within a relation (i.e. 'table') in a relational database is formally referred to as a 'tuple', but it does not have the same meaning as a tuple in Python.

[36] Although multidimensional arrays (such as a data matrix) can be handled using Python lists, there are better alternatives. For example, the array module provides an array data object, as does the third party NumPy extension (http://numpy.scipy.org). However, the following discussion may help illuminate some important points.

entered as a single line. Having entered the data, we can retrieve the details for Giovanni (item 3) using:

```
>>> people[2]
```

If we only wanted to print Giovanni's age, we could use a double index:

```
>>> people[2][1]
```

An alternative approach would be to define each row in the matrix as a separate list, and then include them in the main list:

```
>>> Hermione = ['Hermione',34, 'F']
>>> Horatio = ['Horatio',52, 'M']
>>> Giovanni = ['Giovanni',23, 'M']
>>> Priscilla = ['Priscilla',21, 'F']
>>> people = [Hermione, Horatio, Giovanni, Priscilla]
```

Priscilla's age could then be retrieved using either of the following:

```
>>> people[3][1]                 or
>>> Priscilla[1]
```

Note that if we had to update Hermione's age, the value in the nested sequence is automatically updated. Thus, if Hermione had a birthday which decremented her age by one (which curiously seems to happen to some women once they get to a certain age), we could edit using:

```
>>> Hermione[1]=33
```

and

```
>>> people[0][1]
```

would display 33.

Remembering which 'column' corresponds to which attribute could become problematic, but a simple solution is to assign variable names to the column index numbers. For example:

```
>>> age=1
>>> sex=2
```

The details for each individual can now be retrieved using these easier to remember names. For example:

```
>>> Giovani[sex]
```

The nested sequence structure allows all the details for a 'row' (i.e. a person) to be extracted easily. It is not quite so easy to extract all the information in a 'column' (e.g. all the ages), but the following would do the job, although it utilises features that will only be introduced in Chapter 10:

```
>>> for person in people:
        print(person[age])
```

Another Trap For The Unwary

One needs to be careful when initialising an array. One might decide to define a default set of characteristics for each new person to be added to the matrix. For example:

```
>>> default = [None,None,None]
```

In this case the fields are all set to None, which we saw in Chapter 4 is a null value, but in practice they might be set to more meaningful defaults which may or may not need to be changed (e.g. 'F' might be defined as the default value for sex, requiring us only to reset the values for males).

Having defined our defaults, we might then create two new people using the default values and add them to the matrix:

```
>>> people = []
>>> Joe = default
>>> people += [Joe]
>>> Fred = default
>>> people += [Fred]
```

We might then decide to change the default details for specific people:

```
>>> Joe[0]='Joe'
>>> Joe[1]='Male'
>>> Joe[2]= 34
>>> Fred[0]='Fred'
>>> Fred[1]='Male'
>>> Fred[2]=67
```

However, if you now check the details for Joe using either:

```
>>> Joe
```

or

```
>>> people[0]
```

you will discover that Joe has been renamed 'Fred' and aged dramatically. What has gone wrong? (Take a few minutes to see if you can identify the problem by yourself, based on what was said previously, before reading on).

The problem arises when we define Joe=default and Fred=default. We are not copying the current values of default into two new lists (as one might assume), but simply changing the object references of Joe and

Fred to point to the same list as default. Consequently, when we make any changes to the object bound to Fred, we are also changing the object bound to both default and Joe. Furthermore, any new people created using default will also be called 'Fred'. This is not really what we want!

The solution is to initialise the lists for Joe and Fred using:

```
>>> Joe=default[:]
>>> Fred=default[:]
```

Each of these lines creates a new list object containing a slice (containing every item) copied from default. These lists have a separate existence from default, so changes made to any of these lists will affect only that list.

Unfortunately things get even more complicated when working with higher dimensional data arrays. Attempts to copy a two dimensional slice using:

```
>>> people2 = people[:][:]          #Does not work
```

simply copies the object references contained in the lists corresponding to the 'rows' (i.e. each person) rather than the data values, so any changes subsequently made to any of the attributes in either people or people2 will also change the corresponding values in the other list (i.e. the two lists are not independent, but refer to the same objects). One solution, in such situations, is to use a method called copy.deepcopy() in the built-in copy module, but we are getting into deeper water than we really need for the present.

To summarise, although nested sequences *can* be used for working with two or higher dimensional data matrices, they need to be used with considerable caution.

You should now attempt the remaining exercises.

Exercises

6.1. If aList = [1, 2, 3, 4, 5, 6, 7, 8, 9, 10], what would be selected if you entered the following?

```
aList[5]
aList[0]
aList[-1]
aList[-5]
aList[1:3]
aList[:6]
aList[6:]
```

```
aList[:]
aList[-6:]
aList[1:7:2]
aList[-6::-1]
```

Check your answers using IDLE.

6.2. If aList = [1, 2, 3, 4, 5, 6, 7, 8, 9, 10], what would you need to enter to select the following? Check your answers using IDLE.

```
[1]
[10]
[2,3,4]
[7,8,9,10]
[1,3,5,7]
[7,5,3,1]
[10,7,4]
```

6.3. Modify **day_of_the_week1.py** by asking the user to indicate what day it is today. Print out what day it is today and what day it will be in the user-specified number of days. (Hint: Consider using a triple quoted string when asking what day it is today).

6.4. What do each of the following evaluate to? Check your answers using IDLE.

```
3*[6+3]
3*(6+3)
3*(6+3,)
456 in [123, 456, 789]
12 in [123, 456, 789]
'c' in 'abcdef'
'def' in 'abc, def'
'ab' in 'abc, def'
'ab' in ['abc', 'def']
'cde' in 'abc, def'
```

6.5. If a=(1,2,3) and A=[1,2,3], what would a, b, c and A, B, C evaluate to after the following lines were entered in sequence:

```
b = a
a *= 2
c = b * 3
B = A
A *= 2
C = B * 3
```

Check your answers using IDLE. Why does C have more elements than c?

6.6. After running the following snippet of code, would d be equal to

---

88

'New York'?

```
a=('New',)
b=('York',)
c=a
a+=b
d=(a[0]+' '+c[1])
```

6.7. If a=[1,2,3,4,5], b='12345' and c='1,2,3,4,5', which of the following would evaluate as `True`? Check your answers using IDLE.

```
3 in a
'3' in b
'3' in c
[2,3] in a
'23' in b
'2,3' in  b
'23' in c
'2,3' in  c
3 in b
'2,3' in a
```

6.8. If aList=[1,2,3,4,5,6], what would the following evaluate as?

```
aList[len(aList)-1] is not aList[-1]
```

6.9. If a=[1,2,3,4,5], why does a[len(a)] produce an error message?

6.10. What would be returned by each of the following? Check your answers using IDLE.

```
len('12345')
len(['12345'])
min(['ABC', 'abc', '123'])
max(['ABC', 'abc', '123'])
max(['a','AA','aaa'])
min(['a','AA','aaa'])
sorted(['abc','def','G','The end'])
sorted((3,2.5,2,11))
sorted([1,34,23,'abc'])
```

6.11. If aList = [1,2,3,4,5], what would you need to enter to initialise a new sequence s equal to:

```
a)  [1,2,3,4,5,6,7,8]
b)  (1,2,3,4,5)
c)  [1,3,5]
d)  [1, 2, 3, 4, 5, 1, 2, 3, 4, 5, 1, 2, 3, 4, 5]
e)  [5,4,3,2,1]
f)  (5,3,1)
```

6.12. John, Susan, Mohammed and Elizabeth are aged 34, 19, 45 and 63 respectively. John and Susan are single, Mohammed is married and Elizabeth is divorced. Create a data matrix called `matrix` containing one row for each person, in the sequence listed above, having columns for their name, age, sex and marstat in that order. What values would the following display:

```
matrix[2]
matrix[1][3]
matrix[0][0]
matrix[3][3]
```

6.13. Write a program to accept user entry of day, month and year (e.g. 25, 12, 2011) and display the information spelling out the month, e.g. 25 December, 2009.

6.14. The Slombovian secret service has devised a fiendishly cunning method of encrypting messages to prevent them from being read by prying eyes. To encrypt a message, they create three strings taking every third character (including spaces and punctuation) beginning at the first character, then every third character starting at the second character, and then every third character starting at the third character. The three strings are then joined together. Thus, the string 'ABC123abc' would become 'A1aB2bC3c'. Write a program to enter a message and encrypt it. Test it on the message: 'The eagle has flown the coup' (with no quotes or a full stop).

Chapter 7. Tuples, Lists And Strings

Having looked at sequences in general in the previous chapter, this chapter focuses upon features that are specific to tuples, lists and strings. There is in fact very little that needs to said about tuples that has not already been covered, but Python provides considerable functionality for manipulating lists and strings using 'methods'. The chapter begins by a short introduction to methods in general, before discussing the options available for each of the three main types of sequence.

Methods

Each tuple, list or string is an object, which like all objects inherits various features from the class to which it belongs. These features include **methods**, which may be thought of built-in code to perform certain operations on a particular type of object. They are similar in many respects to functions.

The most immediate difference between a method and a function is how they are called. Methods are called using **dot notation**: i.e. the method name is preceded by the name of the object to which it belongs, separated by a dot (i.e. full stop or period). Thus, whilst the general form of a function call is:

```
results = functionName(arguments)
```

the general form for a method is:

```
results = objectName.methodName(arguments)
```

This can be read as 'the method named `methodName` within the object named `objectName`'. As with a function, various values can be passed to a method as arguments enclosed within parentheses. Even if no arguments are required, the parentheses must always be included. Also, like a function, a method may return some values which can be assigned to a variable (or variables), represented above as `results`. However, many methods directly work upon (i.e. change) the object which called them, so the '`result =`' portion of the call statement may not be required.

Like functions, methods can be **chained** – i.e. the output of one can be used as the input of another. However, the general syntax is different:

```
results = function3(function2(function1()))
```

```
results = objectName.method1().method2().method3()
```

The sequence in which the functions are processed in line 1 is determined by the nesting of the parentheses – i.e. function1 is processed first and its output is used as the input for function2, whose output is in turn used as the input for function 3. The sequence is from right to left. The methods in line 2, in contrast, are processed from left to right. Note, however, that methods can only be chained if they return a result – most list methods, for example, change the list object *in situ* rather than returning a result, therefore attempts to chain them will produce an error message.

Tuples

A tuple is an immutable sequence. In other words, the items in the sequence can neither be changed nor deleted. Attempts to do so will generate an error message.

As noted in the previous chapter, it is possible to add additional items to a tuple using either addition or multiplication. For example:

```
>>> aTuple = (1,2,3)
>>> bTuple = (4,5,6)
>>> aTuple = aTuple + bTuple
>>> print(aTuple)
>>> aTuple *= 3
>>> print(aTuple)
```

Although it may appear that lines 3 and 5 change the contents of `aTuple`, they only do so by binding the name `aTuple` to new tuple objects. This can be confirmed by inserting an `id(aTuple)` statement after lines 1, 3 and 5.

There are no methods for manipulating tuples, so they can only be manipulated using the general procedures discussed in Chapter 6. However, if need be, a tuple can be converted to a list using the `list()` function, processed, and then converted back to a tuple using the `tuple()` function. For example, you could sort a tuple using the following:

```
>>> aTuple = 1,5,3,4,2
>>> aTuple = tuple(sorted(list(aTuple)))
>>> aTuple
```

The first line defines a tuple called `aTuple` (remembering that it is not essential to enclose the items in parenthesis). The second line, working from the inside outward, converts the tuple to a list (although in this case it is not necessary as the `sorted()` function does this automatically), the `sorted()` function then sorts the items in the list, and the `tuple()` function creates a new tuple object with the sorted values, freeing the original tuple object for data collection.

Lists are mutable which means you can change and delete items within a list. Lists, as we shall see, also provide several special methods that are not available for tuples, so they are much more versatile. So, given that you can do just about anything with a list that you can do with a tuple, plus a lot more besides, why use tuples at all? There are a few reasons. In some situations it may be advantageous to ensure that the contents of a sequence cannot accidentally be changed (e.g. when listing the days of the week). In other situations the Python language may specifically require you to use a tuple (e.g. when passing parameters to a function - see Chapter 11). However, in the majority of cases you will probably find yourself using a list rather than a tuple.

Lists

Lists, as we have seen, can be initiated by assigning a name to a comma separated list of items enclosed in square brackets:

```
>>> aList = [1,2,3,'text']
```

They may also be initiated by converting another sequence using the list() function:

```
>>> aList = list(aTuple)
>>> bList = list(aString)
```

assuming aTuple and aString were defined previously.

List Changes Using Indices

Lists are mutable, so it is also possible to change, insert or delete items in the list *in situ* (i.e. without creating a new list with the same name). The value of a single item can be changed using its index. Thus:

```
>>> aList = [1,2,3,4,5]
>>> aList[2] = 33
```

changes the 3 in the list to 33 to give [1, 2, 33, 4, 5]. An item can be replaced by a tuple, string or another list in a similar manner. For example:

```
>>> aList[3]=(9,8,7)
```

changes the list to [1, 2, 33, (9, 8, 7), 5]. Note that if the replacement sequence replaces a single item it is added as a single item, but if it replaces a slice it is 'unpacked' and each of its items are added as separate items.

Items can be deleted using the `del` statement. Thus:

```
>>> del aList[1]
```

would remove 2 to leave [1, 33, (9, 8, 7), 5]. Notice that everything to the right of the deleted item is shifted one place to the left (i.e. the index for the number 5 was previously 4 but is now 3).

Slices may be used to replace one or more items by one or more other items. For example:

```
>>> aList[2:4] = [44,55]
```

would replace the last two items to give [1, 33, 44, 55]. Note that the slice must be replaced by a sequence - e.g. [44, 55], otherwise you will generate a syntax error. The sequence does not necessarily need to be a list, but if the replacement sequence is a tuple or a string it will be converted into list items. Two or more comma separated numbers without parentheses will be treated as a tuple, but will be converted to list items. Thus:

```
>>> aList[2:3] = 34,23,12
```

would produce [1, 33, 34, 23, 12, 55].

You cannot replace a slice by a single standalone number, but a single number followed by a comma is okay as it is treated as a tuple. For example:

```
>>> aList[1:2] = 98,
```

gives [1, 98, 34, 23, 12, 55]

Each item in an inserted sequence is added as separate item. For example, each character in a string is added to the list as a separate item. If you want to add a sequence as a single item (e.g. as a tuple or a string), you need to enclose it in an extra pair of square brackets. To illustrate these points, try to anticipate what each of the following lines will do as you enter them in interactive mode:

```
>>> x = [1,2,3,4,5]
>>> x
>>> x [3:4] = 'text'        # Add text characters
>>> x                       # Characters are separate items
>>> x[1:2] = (6,7,8)        # Add items from a tuple
>>> x
>>> x[3] /= 2               # Modify a value from the tuple
>>> x                       # Item was converted to a float
>>> x[2:3] =  9,10,11       # Insert comma separated values
>>> x
>>> x[4:5] = ['one','two']  # Add two strings items
>>> x                       # Strings but separate items
```

```
>>> x[3:4] = [[1,2,3]]        # Add a list as a single item
>>> x
>>> x[1:2] =[('age', 45)]     # Add a tuple as a single item
>>> x
>>> x[1:2] = 7                # Error - not a sequence
>>> x[1:2] = [7]              # Replace one item by another
>>> x
>>> x[1:2] = 8,               # Ditto using a tuple:
>>> x
```

The slices in each of the above examples were only a single item wide, but they could be any length. Also, as the examples illustrate, there is no requirement for the slice and its replacement to be the same size – i.e. the insertion may be as large or as small as you want. This makes it possible to decrease the size of the list by removing more items than you insert, or increase the size of the list by inserting more items than you replace. Indeed, there is no need to replace any items at all. For example:

```
>>> aList[2:2] = [123,456]
```

would insert two items (123 and 456) before the third item (i.e. index 2). Reference to Figure 6.2 in Chapter 6 may clarify why this is the location of the insert.

It is also possible to delete items by replacing them with an empty list (represented by matching square brackets with nothing in between - not even a space). For example:

```
aList[1:4] = []
```

would delete the 2nd, 3rd and 4th items in the list.

List Methods

Table 7.1 lists methods provided by list objects. The third column indicates the possible syntax of a calling statement. Note that some methods return a value which would generally be assigned to a variable of some sort. With the exception of count() and index() they each modify *in situ* the list from which they are called.

append()

The append() method appends an item, supplied as the argument, to the end of a list. For example:

```
>>> days = ['Monday','Tuesday','Wednesday']
>>> days.append('Thursday')
```

would change days to ['Monday', 'Tuesday', 'Wednesday', 'Thursday'].

Method	Use	Sample Syntax
append()	Adds 1 item at end of list	aList.append(item)
extend()	Adds multiple items at end of list	aList.extend(sequence)
insert()	Inserts 1 item at specified position	aList.insert(pos,item)
remove()	Removes first occurrence of specified item	aList.remove(item)
pop()	Removes and returns item at specified position	var = aList.pop(pos)
sort()	Sorts the items *in situ*	aList.sort()
reverse()	Reverse the sequence of items in a list in situ	aList.reverse()
count()	Counts number of occurrences of item	n = aList.count(item)
index()	Finds first occurrence of item	n = aList.index(item)

Table 7.1. List Methods

You can only append a single item. This could be a single number, or it could be a sequence. For example:

```
>>> aList = [1,2,3]
>>> aList.append(4)
>>> aList.append([5,6])
```

The second line appends the integer 4 – note that it does not need to be 'disguised' as a sequence by enclosing it in square brackets or appending a comma. The third line appends a list containing [5,6] as a single item, leaving aList set equal to [1, 2, 3, 4, [5,6]].

extend()

The extend() method allows you to add several items supplied as a sequence. Thus:

```
>>> aList = [1,2,3]
>>> aList.extend([4,5])
```

sets aList equal to [1, 2, 3, 4, 5]. Note that, in contrast to append(), the items in the list [4,5] are added as individual items and not as a list. The extend() method is similar to concatenation using an augmented operator - i.e. the original list is modified rather than replaced. For example:

```
>>> aList = [1,2,3]
>>> bList = [4,5]
>>> cList=aList
>>> aList.extend(b)
```

produces the same outcome as `aList += bList` (i.e. `cList` is also modified).

insert()

The `insert()` method may be used to insert an item at a specified position. The method takes two arguments. The first is an index indicating where the insertion is to be made, whilst the second is the item to be inserted. If a list is supplied as the second argument, it will be inserted as a single item. For example:

```
>>> aList = [1,2,3,4,5]
>>> aList.insert(3,'3a')
```

changes `aList` to [1, 2, 3, '3a', 4, 5]. The `insert()` method has much the same effect as `aList[3:3]=['3a']`, but differs from `aList[3:3]='3a'` which would insert '3' and 'a' as two separate characters.

remove()

The `remove()` method removes the first occurrence of the item passed as the parameter. Two examples:

```
>>> aList = [1,2,3,4,5]
>>> aList.remove(3)
```

sets `aList` to [1, 2, 4, 5], whilst

```
>>> bList = ["That's ", "one", "small", "step", "for",⏎
"a", "man"]
>>> bList.remove{"a")
```

sets `bList` to ["That's ", "one", "small", "step", "for", "man"]. If you are confused by index numbers, you may find the `remove()` method preferable to setting a slice equal to []. However, you should note that if the specified item does not exist, `remove()` will generate an error message.

pop()

The `pop()` method also removes an item from the list, but the item is specified by its index number. The removed item is also returned and can be assigned to a variable. If no index number is specified, the last item in the list will be removed. Thus:

```
>>> aList = [1,2,3,4,5]
>>> var = aList.pop()
>>> var -= aList.pop(2)
```

would leave the variable `var` equal to 2 and `aList` equal to [1,2,4]. The first pop removes the 5, whilst the second removes the 3 and subtracts it from the 5. If you were now to enter:

```
>>> aList.pop()
```

the last item (i.e. 4) will be removed and displayed in interactive mode because it is not assigned to a variable.

sort()

The `sort()` method sorts the items in a list in ascending order. For example:

```
>>> aList = [5, 3, 4, 1, 2]
>>> aList.sort()
```

would leave `aList` equal to [1, 2, 3, 4, 5]. The `sort()` method does not have any arguments, nor does it return anything – i.e. the sorting is done *in situ*. This is potentially dangerous because once a list is sorted it cannot be unsorted. If you are likely to need the unsorted version later on, it would be preferable to save the sorted version in a new list and leave the original intact. However, you **cannot** do this directly using the `sort()` method.[37] Instead you should use the `sorted()` function, as discussed earlier. For example:

```
>>> bList = sorted(aList)
```

would be a safer option.

reverse()

The `reverse()` method is somewhat similar, except it reverses the sequence of the items *in situ*. Like `sort()`, it does not have any arguments. Thus:

```
>>> aList = [5, 3, 4, 1, 2]
>>> aList.reverse()
```

would leave `aList` equal to [2, 1, 4, 3, 5]. However, the effects of the `reverse()` method can be undone, if necessary, simply by running it a second time.

---

[37] You could of course copy the original list before sorting using `unsorted=aList[:]`. Note, however, that `unsorted=aList` would not provide a solution as it would simply bind `unsorted` to the same object as `aList` rather than preserving an unsorted copy.

---

count()

The `count()` method counts the number of occurrences of a specified item in a list. For example:

```
>>> aList = ["e", "i", "e", "i", "o"]
>>> oldMcDonald = aList.count("e")
```

would set the variable `oldMcDonald` to 2.

index()

The `index()` method is somewhat similar, except that it returns the index of the first occurrence of the specified item. Thus, using the same list as in the previous example:

```
>>> position = aList.index("i")
```

would set `position` equal to 1. Note, however, that like the `remove()` method, the `index()` method will generate an error message if the item is not found.

Neither the `count()` or `index()` methods change the list in any way.

You should now be able to attempt exercises 7.1 to 7.5.

Strings

Strings can be assigned using matching single or double quotes. For example:

```
>>> aString = "Some text"
```

They may also be initialised using the `str()` function. We previously saw how the `str()` function could be used to convert a number into a string. However, it may be used to convert any object, including lists and tuples, into a printable string representation. For example:

```
>>> aList = [123, 456, 789]
>>> aString = str(aList)
```

would set `aString` equal to '[123, 456, 789]'.

String Methods

Although strings are immutable (i.e. cannot be changed *in situ*), Python provides a large number of methods which allows them to be 'changed' by creating a new string. However, unless assigned to a new variable, the new string is temporary. Thus, if you were to enter the following sequence of commands:

```
>>> aString = "Some text"
>>> aString.upper()
>>> aString
```

the value of `aString` at the end is the same as it was at the beginning. The `upper()` method in the second line causes the string to be displayed on screen in upper case (see below), but because the output is not assigned to a variable it is not saved. The third line confirms that the original string remains unchanged. However,

```
>>> aString = "Some text"
>>> bString = aString.upper()
>>> aString
>>> bString
```

copies the changes from the `upper()` method into `bString` (so nothing is displayed on screen when the second line is entered). The output from the third line shows that the original string is unchanged, but the final line confirms that `bString` now contains an upper case version.

If you wanted to simulate an *in situ* change, you can assign the string's identifier to the changed version of itself. For example:

```
>>> aString = aString.upper()
>>> aString
```

As in similar situations, you are not actually changing the contents of `aString`, but pointing the `aString` variable to the new string object created by the string method, thereby freeing the original for garbage collection.

This section considers only a relatively small subset of the available string methods, as listed in Table 7.2. The Python website provides information on a much more comprehensive list of string methods.

upper()

The `upper()` method converts every character in a string to upper case. For example:

```
>>> aString = "Now is the winter of our discontent."
>>> aString = aString.upper()
>>> aString
```

There is an email convention whereby capital letters indicate shouting, so now you sound like a real actor! Note that the method does not require any arguments. If the string contains non-alphabetic characters they are left unchanged.

Method	Use	Sample Syntax
upper()	Converts all characters in string 'in' to upper case	out=in.upper()
lower()	Converts all characters to lower case	out=in.lower()
capitalize()	First letter is capitalized	out=in.capitalize()
title()	First letter in each word is capitalized	out=in.title()
swapcase()	Swaps case of all characters	out=in.swapcase()
strip()	Removes white spaces at beginning and end	out=in.strip()
find()	Returns index of first occurrence of substring 's'	index=in.find('s')
startswith()	Tests whether the string begins with substring 's'	in.startswith('s')
endswith()	Tests whether the string ends with substring 's'	in.endswith('s')
replace()	Replace 'old' string by 'new'	out=in.replace('old', 'new')
join()	Joins strings in sequence using delimiter 'delim'	out=delim.join(sequence)
split()	Splits a string using a separator sep or whitespace	out=in.split('sep') out=in.split()

Table 7.2. Selected String Methods

lower()

The `lower()` method converts every character to lower case:

```
>>> aString = aString.lower()
>>> aString
```

Now you are whispering. Note, however, that `lower()` does not quite reverse the effects of `upper()` as the letter at the beginning has also been converted to lower case.

capitalize()

The `capitalize()` method capitalises the first character in a string – note the method name is spelt with a 'z'. Thus:

```
>>> aString = aString.capitalize()
>>> aString
```

completes the conversion of `aString` back to the original.

title()

The `title()` method is somewhat similar, except it converts the first letter of each word to a capital, as in a book title:

```
>>> aString = aString.title()
>>> aString
```

swapcase()

The `swapcase()` method toggles the case of every character in the string – i.e. capitals become lower case and vice versa:

```
>>> aString = aString.swapcase()
>>> aString
```

There must be lots of situations where this is useful, although I am hard pressed to think of any just now.

strip()

The `strip()` method removes surplus white space (e.g. spaces) at the beginning and end of a string, but not from within the string. For example:

```
>>> bString = "    Some    text    "
>>> bString.strip()
```

If the 'spaces' in the first line are each three characters wide, the second line produces "Some   text". The surplus space at the beginning and end is removed, but the surplus spaces between "Some" and "text" remain.

Earlier we looked at a program to compare the userid entered by a user with a list of acceptable userids (**id_check1.py**). If the user accidentally includes one or more surplus spaces at the end of what they entered, their userid would be rejected, resulting in unnecessary frustration. The following program (**id_check2.py**) solves this particular problem:

```
valid = ["Jim", "Joe", "Janet", "Jezebel"]
id = input("Enter your userid : ")
print(id.strip() in valid)
input("\nPress <ENTER> to finish")
```

The program is the same as **id_check1.py** except that the `strip()` method has been added to the third line to remove any surplus white space at the beginning or end of the entered text that might upset the membership test.

find()

The `find()` method may be used to search for a substring, entered as a parameter, within a string. If the substring is found, the method returns the index of the first character within the string. If the substring is not found, the method returns −1. For example:

```
>>> cString = "To be or not to be …"
>>> cString.find("too")
>>> cString.find("to")
```

The first find returns −1 because "too" does not appear in the string (unless your spelling is even worse than mine). The second find returns 13. You might have expected it to return 0, indicating the first occurrence of the word "to", but the search is case sensitive so "To" fails the test.

If you want to check for the occurrence of "to", irrespective of case, you could enter:

```
>>> cString.lower().find("to")
```

This returns 0. What happens is that `cString` is converted to a new temporary lower case string, and then its `find` method is used to search for "to". As noted previously, the methods are processed from left to right.

You can also specify optional start and end points for the search as additional parameters. The start parameter indicates the index of the first character to be searched, whilst the end parameter indicates the first character after the search range (i.e. similar to defining a slice). The substring must be completely contained within the specified range. Thus:

```
>>> cString.find("to",0,15)
```

would return 13, but

```
>>> cString.find("to",0,14)
```

would return −1 because although the "t" is within the search range (0 to 14) the "o" is not.

startswith()

This is somewhat similar to the `find()` method, except it checks whether the string begins with the search substring. If it does, it returns the

Boolean value `True`, otherwise it returns `False`.

endswith()

This is similar to `startswith()`, except it checks whether the string terminates with the search substring. This might be used, for example, to text whether a file was a particular type:

```
>>> filename = 'c:\\My Documents\Python\my_prog.py'
>>> filename.endswith('.py')
```

The `startswith()` and `endswith()` methods are often used in conjunction with an `if` statement (see Chapter 9).

replace()

The `replace()` method replaces all occurrences of a substring, specified by the first parameter, by the substring specified by the second parameter. For example:

```
>>> dString = "Too be or not too be …"
>>> dString.replace('too', 'to')
```

would replace the second occurrence of 'too', but not the first because it begins with a capital. However,

```
>>> d.lower().replace('too','to').capitalize()
```

would provide the intended result. (Remember, the methods are processed from left to right).

join()

The `join()` method is arguably less intuitive because the object making the call is a string containing a delimiter to be used to join other strings stored in a list or tuple. The list or tuple containing the strings to be joined is passed as an argument. An example may help:

```
>>> path = ['My documents', 'python', 'scripts']
>>> print('~/' + '/'.join(path))
>>> print('d:\\' + '\\'.join(path))
```

The first line defines a list containing the three strings to be joined. The second line prints out the three items joined together in a Linux path format (where ~/ represents the user's home directory). The string containing the method is the literal '/'. Its `join()` method is called to join the three items in the list `path` using '/' as the joining text. This produces 'My documents/python/scripts'; this is then prefixed by '~/' to complete the path.

The third line does something similar, except the path is displayed in Windows format. Note that a double backslash must be used because a single backslash would be treated by `print()` as an escape character. When printed, the double backslashes are displayed as a single backslashes to give: 'd:\My documents\python\scripts'. Because Linux uses forward slashes, which are not treated as escape characters, the forward slash characters in the second line do not need to be doubled.

split()

The `split()` method can be thought of as the reverse of `join()`. Using a string argument as a separator, it splits a string into a number of entities which are returned in a list. For example:

```
>>> aPath = "documents/python/scripts"
>>> aList = aPath.split('/')
```

`aList` will contain three items: ['documents', 'python', 'scripts']. If the path was in Windows format, then the separator would need to be defined as a double backslash:

```
>>> bPath = "d:\My Documents\python\scripts"
>>> bList = bPath.split('\\')
```

If no arguments are provided, then each single or run of consecutive whitespace (e.g. space, tab, linefeed etc.) is treated as a separator. Thus:

```
>>> aString = "Top of the   morning to you"
>>> aString.split()
```

will return this well-known Hollywood salutation as a list with six items. Note that the surplus spaces before 'morning' cause no difficulties.

You could use `split()` and `join()` in conjunction if you wished to standardise the spacing between words in a piece of text:

```
>>> dirty = "Why do some   people insist  on inserting  ↵
      extra spaces between   words?"
>>> aList = dirty.split()
>>> clean = ' '.join(aList)
```

or, more concisely (cutting out the `aList` 'middle man'):

```
>>> dirty = "Why do some   people insist  on inserting↵
      extra spaces between   words?"
>>> clean = ' '.join(dirty.split())
```

Beginners may find it daunting to deconstruct the second line. As with expressions, the secret is to start at the innermost parentheses and work your way out. Note also that Python is generally much easier to write than to read – which is one very good reason for the liberal inclusion of comments in your scripts.

You should now attempt the remaining exercises.

Pep Talk

New programmers may have found Chapters 6 and 7 tough going. There is a lot of stuff to learn, much of which may appear confusing and counterintuitive. Also, by discussing sequences in abstract, rather than in an applied context, there may appear to be little gain for the effort expended. However, if you feel demoralised or disillusioned, resist the temptation to give up just yet. Once we discuss program control in the Chapters 9 and 10, many of the pieces should start to fall into place.

Bear in mind that it is not essential to remember all the details. As long as you are broadly aware of what is possible, you can always refer back to this chapter (or to Appendix D which provides a copy of the tables) if you need to check up on the specifics.

Exercises

7.1. What would be returned by each of the following?

```
sorted(tuple('Monday'))
list('Tuesday')[2:4]
list('Wednesday').count('e')
sorted(list('Thursday')).index('r')
sorted('Thursday').index('r')
list('Thursday').sort().index('r')
```

Check your answers using IDLE.

7.2. If aList=[5,2,3,4,1], try to predict what it would be equal to after the following had been entered in sequence:

```
aList.pop(1)
aList.insert(3,2)
aList.append(len(aList))
aList.sort()
aList.pop()
aList.reverse()
```

Check your answer using IDLE.

7.3. If aList=[1,2,3], what would you enter to change aList to:

a) [1,2,3,4,5,6]

b) `[1,2,3,[4,5,6]]`

7.4. If aList=[1,2,3,4,5,6,7,8,9], remove each of the even numbers (i.e. 2, 4, 6 and 8) one at a time using four different methods.

7.5. Would value would d have after entering the following in sequence?

```
a=[5,3,1,2,4]
b=a[:]
c=a
a.sort()
c.reverse()
d = b[3] is c[3]
```

7.6. Set aString = "The rain in Spain falls mainly on the plain." What would aString equal after entering these lines in the following order:

```
aString.title()
aString.swapcase()
aString.split()
' '.join(aString)
aString.replace('sPAIN','bAHRAIN')
aString.capitalize()
aString.replace('b','B')
```

Check your answer using IDLE.

7.7. If aString=" one two three four ", enter one line of code that would set aString equal to "four one three two". (Hint: the desired sequence places the items in alphabetical order).

7.8. Convert the letters in the sentence 'The quick brown fox jumps over the lazy dog' to upper case, sort them in alphabetical order and print them as a string with the spaces removed.

7.9. Starting with the sentence in exercise 7.8, change it so that the quick brown dog jumps over the lazy fox.

7.10. Write a program to store the name and population of a number of a number of countries. (Four is sufficient for demonstration purposes). Print out the name and population of the nth largest, where n is a number supplied by the user.

Chapter 8. Random Numbers

So far our programs have had a simple linear structure: i.e. the interpreter reads the first line in the script and processes it, then reads the second line and processes it, then the third line, and so on, until it gets to the last line. However, there are situations where it may be useful to either skip over a section of code, or to repeat a particular section multiple times, depending upon whether a particular condition is true or false. The following two chapters will look at **branches** and **loops** respectively, but the examples are more interesting if we do not know in advance whether the conditions are true or false. So, in this chapter we will take a small digression to look at how we can introduce randomness into our programs using random numbers..

Python provides a number of functions which may be used to generate random numbers. These, however, are not provided by the core Python language, but are made available by importing additional code referred to as a **module**. Modules will be discussed in more detail in Chapter 11, but before discussing random numbers we will take another short digression to consider briefly what we mean by a module.

Modules

The core Python language is extremely versatile, but it would become unwieldy if it included every function that might conceivably be required. A large number of more specialised functions are therefore provided as 'optional extras' in extensions called modules. Each module contains a number of related functions (and other things) that can be called upon (or 'imported') as required. The basic Python installation provides a number of such modules, collectively referred to the **standard library**, but it is also possible to import modules from third party sources or even import modules that you have written yourself (see Chapter 11).

Before you can use the functions within a module, the module must be explicitly imported into your program, or interactive session, using an `import` command. The format, in its simplest form, is:

```
import moduleName
```

where `moduleName` is the name of the specific module you wish to use. If the module is not part of the standard library, you will also need to tell Python where to find it by providing details of its path (see Chapter 11).

You may import two or more modules using a separate command line for each, or by placing them as a comma separated list on the same line:

```
import moduleName1, moduleName2
```

To access a particular function, you obviously need to know its name. The Python website provides this information for the modules in the standard library; similar documentation should be provided by third party sources for other modules. Because functions within different modules could possibly have the same name, to avoid ambiguity it is necessary to prefix the function name with the module name using a dot notation when calling a function. The general form is:

```
moduleName.functionName()
```

where the parentheses would contain any parameters that need to be passed. If the function returns some output, this may be assigned to a variable in the normal manner:

```
result = moduleName.functionName()
```

Random Numbers

The Python standard library contains a module called random which provides a number of functions to generate random numbers. These functions use an algorithm called a Mersenne Twister to generate pseudo random numbers. The numbers generated by the algorithm are completely deterministic and can be replicated if one knows the starting point, referred to as the **seed**. However, if the seed is unknown the numbers generated give the appearance of being totally random. By default Python assigns a seed value based on the time on the computer's system clock, so the algorithm will generate a different set of numbers every time it is called. However, it is possible to override this to provide your own seed. If the seed is set to a fixed value, the algorithm will generate the same series of numbers each time it is run. This may be useful for testing purposes.

Before calling any of the functions, you must import the module (either at the beginning of a program or in an interactive session) by entering:

```
import random
```

Once the module has been imported, it does not need to be imported again in the same program or interactive session, irrespective of the number of function calls.

Function	Use	Sample Syntax
random.random()	Generates a float number r in range 0.0 to just less than 1.0.	r = random.random()
random.uniform()	Generates a float number r in the range min to just less than max.	r = random.uniform(min,max)
random.randrange()	Generates an integer i in range 0 to max-1, where max is an integer parameter.	i = random.randrange(max)
random.randint()	Generates an integer i in range min to max, where min and max are integer parameters.	i = random.randint(min,max)
random.gauss()	Selects a float number r drawn from a normal distribution with a specified mean and standard deviation passed as parameters.	r = random.gauss(mean,sdev)
random.choice()	Randomly selects one item x from a sequence.	x = random.choice(seq)
random.sample()	Draw a sample of size n from a population without replacement.	aList=random.sample(seq,n)
random.shuffle()	Randomly reorganise items in a list in situ	random.shuffle(aList)
random.seed()	Set the seed used by the generator to specified number x.	random.seed(x)

Table 8.1. Selected Functions In The Random Module

The `random` module provides a wide choice of functions. Some of the more common are listed in Table 8.1 and described below.

random.random()

This can be thought of as the basic function. It returns a float number r in the range $0 \le r < 1$ (i.e. from 0.0 to just less than 1.0). Note that r could be zero, but will always be less than 1.0. The other functions modify the results of `random.random()` to produce pseudo random numbers with specific properties.

random.uniform()

This is similar to `random.random()` except one can specify the minimum and maximum values permitted as two parameters. As before, the value specified as the maximum is not included in the possible values to be selected.

random.randrange()

This is similar to `random.random()` except it returns an integer number. It requires at least one parameter, but may take up to three. If there is only one parameter, this defines the maximum possible value plus one – i.e. `random.randrange(10)` will return an integer between 0 and 9. This parameter may be prefaced by another parameter specifying the minimum possible value, and followed by another parameter specifying a step. Thus, `random.randrange(1,10,3)` would return 1, 4 or 7.

random.randint()

This is similar to `random.randrange()` except that it always takes two parameters which specify the minimum and maximum permitted values. Note that the value specified by the second parameter falls within the range of values that could be selected – i.e. `random.randint(min, max)` is equivalent to `random.randrange(min, max+1)`.

random.gauss()

The functions listed so far, whether float or integer, select numbers in the target range with equal probability. However, there are situations where you may wish the probability of selecting some numbers to be higher than that for other numbers. One common situation is where you wish to select numbers as if they were drawn from a Gaussian (or normal) distribution. This may be achieved using the `random.gauss()` function which takes two parameters – the first is the mean and the second is the standard deviation of the distribution you wish to simulate. (Note that 'Gauss' in the function name is spelt with a lower case 'g').[38]

Python also provides functions, not discussed here, for simulating other statistical distributions. If you think these could be useful check out the documentation on the standard library on the official Python website.

random.choice()

This function selects one item from a sequence whose name is passed as a parameter. For example:

```
aList = [1,3,5,7,9,11,13,15,17,19]
random.choice(aList)
```

The first line defines a population of odd numbers less than 20, and the second tells Python to randomly select one of these numbers.

The list in this case contained numbers, but it could be any type of sequence. For example:

```
aList=['Matthew','Mark','Luke','John','Hamish']
random.choice(aList)
```

would select a random name from the list.

random.sample()

This function is may be used to select a sample from a larger population without replacement – i.e. each item in the population can only be selected once. It requires two parameters. The first is a sequence defining a population from which you wish to draw a sample. The second is an integer identifying the size of the sample you wish to draw. For example:

```
aList = [1,3,5,7,9,11,13,15,17,19]
random.sample(aList,3)
```

The second line tells Python to select a random sample of 3 different numbers and return them as a list. If you enter the second line again, it will select three more numbers (which may or may not contain overlaps with the first selection). Note that the selected items are listed in a random order.

random.shuffle()

This function randomly reorganises the items in a list (analogous to shuffling a deck of cards). The items are reorganised *in situ* - i.e. the order of the items in the list is changed rather than creating a new list.

---

[38] The normal distribution is widely used in statistical modelling. However, if you do not know what it is, then the likelihood is you will never need to, so you can ignore this function.

Once shuffled, the items cannot be restored to their original sequence.

random.seed()

This function may be used to set the seed used by the random number generator. For example, enter the following lines:

```
>>> random.seed(123)
>>> random.random()
>>> random.random()
>>> random.seed(123)
>>> random.random()
>>> random.random()
```

The first line sets the seed equal to 123. The second line generates a 'random' number, which is in fact totally predictable if you know the seed. The third line generates another 'random' number. If you continued entering `random.random()` you would get a new number each time. However, in this case, we reset the seed to 123 in the fourth line. It will be noted that the numbers generated by the fifth and sixth lines are exactly the same as those generated by the second and third lines.

If you do not specify a parameter in the `random.seed()` function, Python will use the system clock to set the seed. If you enter:

```
>>> random.seed()
>>> random.random()
>>> random.seed()
>>> random.random()
```

the numbers generated by the second and fourth lines will be different because the seeds assigned by the first and third lines will be different as the clock will have changed in the interim.

Generally speaking the only situation where you are likely to want to set the seed is if you wish to replicate pseudo random numbers in the same sequence when testing a program during development. In most instances you will require unpredictable numbers, in which case the simplest approach is simply to avoid using the `random.seed()` function and allow Python to assign a default seed using the system clock when the random module is first imported.

A Simple Example

The following short script (**dice.py**) shows how the random number generator could be used to simulate the throw of two dice:

```
import random
```

```
die1 = random.randrange(6)+1
die2 = random.randint(1,6)
print('The two dice came up',die1,'and',die2)
input('\nPress <ENTER> to finish')
```

Having imported the random module, the second and third lines simulate the two throws of the dice. The `random.randrange(6)` call in line 2 generates an integer number in the range 0 to 5, but as we want values in the range 1 to 6 inclusive we need to add 1 to the number generated. Line 4 uses a different approach to achieve the same ends. The `random.randint(1,6)` generates a random number in the range between the two parameter – i.e. between 1 and 6 inclusive.

Other than that the script is fairly straightforward.

It would of course be more interesting to have repeated throws of the dice. We will see how to do that using a loop in Chapter 10.

You should now attempt the exercises.

Exercises

8.1. A sample of Slombovian schoolchildren estimated their mean IQ as 97.8 with a standard deviation of 7.3. Write a program to randomly generate the IQs of three virtual Slombovian schoolchildren (rounded to the nearest whole number)?

8.2. Generate a random float number in the range 0.0 to just less than 30.0.

8.3. Generate a random float number in the range 10.0 to just less than 30.0 without using the `random.uniform()` function.

8.4. Randomly select three names without replacement (i.e. do not allow each name to be selected more than once) from aList = ['Matthew', 'Mark', 'Luke', 'John', 'Hamish'].

8.5. Randomly select three names with replacement (i.e. allow each name to be selected more than once) from aList = ['Matthew', 'Mark', 'Luke', 'John', 'Hamish'].

8.6. Write a program to randomly select a single card from a deck of playing cards.

8.7. You are the manager of a small manufacturing enterprise with 5 employees. Put their name in a list. Due to the recession, you need to reduce your staff by one. As your employees are all valued equally, the only way to do this is to select one at random. Write a program to print the revised list of the remaining 4 employees in alphabetical order.

8.8. Write a program to randomly select the winning lottery ticket from 100 tickets numbered 1 to 100 using two different methods. Write the program to prove that the two methods produce the same result.

Chapter 9. Branches

A situation frequently arises where you may want the program to take one line of action if a particular condition pertains and a quite different line of action (or maybe no action at all) if it does not pertain. This is referred to as a **branch**. Branches are handled in Python (as in many other languages) using an **if** control structure.

An `if` control structure, as we shall see, can take different forms, but the general syntax for the simplest is:

```
if condition:
    suite
```

where `if` is a keyword, `condition` is an expression that evaluates as either `True` or `False`, and `suite` is a block of code that is processed if the condition evaluates as `True`. The line containing the condition (known as the **header**) must end with a colon. The code forming the **suite** is identified by being indented (i.e. set in from the left margin). The statements in the suite are only processed if the condition is `True`. If the condition evaluates as `False`, Python skips over the suite and resumes execution at the next line of code – i.e. the first line that is not indented.

We will look at more complex forms of the `if` control structure later, but first we will explore conditions and suites in a bit more detail.

Conditions

A condition is an expression that evaluates to either `True` or `False`. A condition frequently consists of two expressions (each of which may be simply a number or a variable) connected by a **comparison operator**. Table 9.1 lists the most common comparison operators.

Because conditions are expressions, entering them in interactive mode will cause Python to process them and return a result. Try entering the following in interactive mode:

```
>>> x = 5          # Assigns a variable
>>> y = 8          # Assigns a variable
>>> x == 3         # Tests if x is equal to 3
>>> y > 7          # Tests if y is greater than 7
>>> x >= 5         # x greater than or equal to 5
>>> y != 8         # Tests if y not equal to 8
>>> y < x          # Tests if y less than x
```

```
>>> 8 >= y              # 8 greater than or equal y
>>> y = 3               # Assignment, not a condition
>>> 4 = x               # Syntax error
>>> 4 == x    # Tests if 4 and x equal
```

Note that the first two lines (with a single equal sign) are assignment statements, whereas the third line (with a double equal sign) is a condition.

==	Equal to (N.B. two = signs)
!=	Not equal
>	Greater than
<	Less than
>=	Greater than or equal to
<=	Less than or equal to

Table 9.1. Selected Comparison (Conditional) Operators

Lines 7 to 11 possibly require comment. Line 7 illustrates that it is possible to compare two variables, whereas line 8 indicates that it does not matter whether a numeric literal is on the left or right side of the expression (provided you are careful to specify the correct operator). However, it is more common (and intuitive) in such situations to place the variable to the left of the operator and the literal on the right. Line 9 is not a condition at all – it assigns a new value to the variable y. If you wanted to test for equality, the correct operator would be a double equal sign. Line 10 is also an assignment, but it generates a syntax error because you cannot assign a new value to a number. Line 11 tests for equality (although it would be more usual to write it as x==4).

Care needs to be taken when testing floats for equality due to the fact that they are not completely accurate. For example, you might expect

```
>>> 2/3 == (1-1/3)
```

to return True, but on my machine it returns False.[39] It would therefore be safer to test whether the difference between the two expressions is less than some small amount. For example:

```
>>> 2/3-(1-1/3) < .00001
```

returns True.

Conditional comparisons are not confined to numbers and numeric variables. Strings and other sequence may also be compared. For

---

[39] It might conceivably evaluate to True on other platforms. However, the point is that it cannot be depended upon to evaluate to True in all situations

example:

```
'love' != 'hate'
```

will evaluate as True - not because the words have opposite meanings, but simply because the strings are different.

It should be noted that we met another operator in Chapter 6 that is very useful with sequences, namely the in operator. Thus, for example, if aList=[1,2,3,4,5] then:

```
3 in aList
```

will return True, but

```
[1,2] in aList
```

will return False because aList does not contain the list [1,2] as one of its items. However,

```
>>> 'end' in 'The end is nigh'
```

will return True for the reasons noted in Chapter 6.

The identity operator is also evaluates to True or False. This may be used to test if two identifiers are bound to the same object. For example:

```
>>> a=[1,2,3]
>>> b=a
>>> a=a+[4,5,6]
>>> a is b
```

will evaluate to False, indicating the objects are different.

Logical Operators

In some instances you may wish to create more complex conditions by testing two or more conditions simultaneously. This may accomplished by joining the simple conditions using a **logical operator**. These are listed in Table 9.2.

and	True if both conditions are True
or	True if at least one condition is True
not	Reverses result (i.e. True becomes False)

Table 9.2. Logical Operators

For example, you could test whether a variable x has a value between 5 and 10 using:

```
x  >   5 and x < 10
```

This will only return True if x is greater than 5 <u>and</u> x is also less than 10.

Failure of either condition will cause `False` to be returned (e.g. if x is 4 or 11, or 5 or 10 for that matter).

In some situations the `and` operator can be replaced by a **chained comparison**. Thus, for example:

```
x > 5 and x < 10
```

could be written more concisely as:

```
5 < x < 10
```

Some programmers prefer to spell it out using `and`, but chained comparisons are arguably more elegant.

The `or` operator will cause `True` to be returned if either or both conditions is/are `True`. Thus, for example:

```
x > 5 or x < 10
```

will always return `True` no matter what value x takes because if it is not larger than 5 then it must be less than 10! This would therefore be a rather meaningless test, but in other situations `or` is very useful if you only require a minimum of one condition out of two (or possibly more) conditions to be true.

It will be noted that some comparison operators contain an implicit `or`. For example:

```
x <= 10
```

is the equivalent of:

```
x < 10 or x = 10
```

The `not` operator reverses the outcome of the condition that follows it. Thus:

```
not x == 10
```

would be equivalent to:

```
x != 10
```

and:

```
not x > 10
```

would be equivalent to:

```
x <= 10
```

(Note that the last operator must be `<=` to accommodate the situation where x is equal to 10).

As can be seen, the same ends can be achieved in the above examples more simply using comparison indicators, but `not` may be useful in more complex situations. One such situation is in conjunction with the `in` operator. For example, you might have a program which invites the user to enter a userID of their choice which they will be able to use as part of their logon to gain access to a system, but you may wish to make sure the selected userID does not already belong to another user. This could be done using a condition such as:

```
newID not in existing_userID_list
```

Comparison and logical operators, like arithmetic operators, are processed by Python in a particular sequence. The precedence or processing sequence is fairly intuitive: arithmetic operators are processed before comparison operators which are processed before logical operators. However, as with arithmetic operators, you can use parentheses to override the defaults, or more simply to improve readability or avoid ambiguity.

Boolean Equivalents

Some values for other data types are treated as if they were `Boolean` values. For example, the following are regarded as equivalent to `False`:

- 0 or 0.0 for an `int` or `float` respectively.

- `None`

- An empty sequence, e.g. [] (empty `list`), () (empty `tuple`) or " (empty `string`).

- An empty mapping, e.g. {} (empty dictionary – see Chapter 12).

Non-zero numeric values and non-empty sequences and non-empty mappings are treated as `True`.

This provides a useful mechanism for testing whether a sequence `x` is empty or not using:

```
if x:
```

This might be followed by a suite indicating what action should be taken if the sequence is not empty. (An alternative would be to use `if len(x)>0:`)

Combining any of the above using logical operators in interactive mode can sometimes give surprising results. For example,

```
>>> [] or True
```

returns `True`, but

```
>>> [] and True
```

returns `[]` (and not `False` as you might expect). However, if used in an `if` statement, `[]` would be treated exactly the same as `False`.[40]

You could now attempt exercises 9.1 and 9.2.

Suites

If the condition is `True`, then Python is instructed to process a set of instructions provided as a **suite**. A suite is simply a block of one or more lines of indented code. In other words, instead of beginning at column 1, each line in a suite is indented by a fixed amount. Each line in a suite must be indented by the same amount. The amount by which they are indented is left to the discretion of the programmer, but the Python convention is four spaces. The programmer may also decide whether to indent using the <Tab> key or by pressing the <Space Bar> a set number of times. However, different text editors may convert tabs to a different number of spaces, so inconsistencies might arise if you mix tabs and spaces in the same program. You should therefore opt for either spaces or tabs and then stick to it. An even better approach is to use IDLE, as IDLE will automatically indent when it is deemed appropriate without the need to use either spaces or tabs. The only minor issue is knowing how to tell IDLE to stop indenting at the end of the suite. To do this, you simply press the <Back Delete> key to remove the indent.

If the suite contains a single line of code, this may be placed on the same line directly following the condition. For example:

```
>>> if x == 10: print('x is equal to 10')
```

However, although this works it is regarded as bad style, as an indented command is easier to read:

```
>>> if x == 10:
        print('x is equal to 10')
```

Note that when you enter the first line in interactive mode, IDLE does not display a prompt on the second line, but it automatically places the cursor at the correct position to receive the second line. If you enter the snippet directly into the Python interpreter it will display a ... on the second line

---

[40] This apparent anomaly is because Python evaluates Boolean expressions using a method known as 'short circuit logic'. However, these details need not concern us.

to indicate more code is expected, but you will need to insert the indentation yourself.

Suites normally contain multiple lines with the same indent. Python recognises the first line without an indent following the suite as the point where it should continue execution if the condition is `False`.

In many situations you may have one `if` statement inside another. If this is the case, the suite for the inner `if` statement is simply indented more than the suite for the outer `if` statement. For example, the following (**weather.py**) provides clothing advice based on randomly-generated weather conditions:

```
import random
precip = random.choice(['raining','dry'])
wind = random.choice(['windy','calm'])
print('It is '+str(precip)+' and '+str(wind)+'.')
if precip=='raining':
    print('Wear a raincoat',end='')
    if wind=='windy':
        print(', but forget the umbrella')
    print('.')
print('Enjoy your walk.')
input('Press <ENTER> to finish.')
```

The first three lines randomly generate some weather conditions using the methods described in Chapter 8. The only thing to note is that the options lists are provided directly as the arguments for the `random.choice()` methods, rather than as object references. The fourth line prints out the current weather conditions. The fifth line checks whether it is raining: if it is, the user is advised to wear a raincoat in line 6; if not, control skips ahead to the next non-indented line, which invites the user to enjoy their walk. If it is raining (and only if it is raining), line 7 uses a second `if` statement to check whether it is windy. If it is, line 8 (which is double-indented) advises the user to leave their umbrella behind, otherwise no further advice is given. Line 9 inserts a full-stop (or period) at the end of the clothing advice, but the level of indentation requires care. If no indentation was used in line 9, then a redundant full-stop would be printed even if no clothing advice had been issued (i.e. if it was not raining). A double-indentation, on the other hand would only insert a full stop if it was windy. A single level of indentation is therefore the correct option as this will insert a full-stop if clothing advice was issued (i.e. if it is raining) irrespective of whether it is windy or not (i.e. it forms part of the 'true' suite for the outer `if` statement). You will need to run the program several times to see all four possible outcomes.

Hopefully you can appreciate how indentation (which is one of Python's most characteristic features) makes the code for complex logic easy to read. You should also be able to appreciate why it was stated earlier that Python lines normally begin at the start of a line – anything else would be regarded as a suite and would most likely generate a syntax error.

The if Control structure

We are now in a position to consider other forms the `if` control structure can take. As noted, the simplest form is:

```
if condition:
    suite
```

If the condition evaluates as `True` then the suite is processed, otherwise control is passed to the next non-indented line of code.

if ... else

The simple `if` statement works fine as long as you do not want to do anything if the condition evaluates as `False`. However, there may be situations where you may wish to take some different course of action. This may be accommodated using the `else` keyword. The general syntax is:

```
if condition:
    suite1
else:
    suite2
```

If the condition is `True`, then suite1 is processed, otherwise suite2 is processed. After the appropriate suite is processed, control is passed to the next non-indented line. Note that, like the line containing the condition, the `else` keyword is followed by a colon signifying the beginning of a suite.

Let us consider an example (**coin_toss1.py**):

```
import random
options = ('heads','tails')
guess=int(input('Heads(1) or tails(2)? Enter 1 or 2 : '))
guess=options[guess-1]
toss=random.choice(options)
print('The coin has landed up',toss)
if guess == toss:
    print('You win. Lucky guess. Best of three ...')
else:
    print('I win. That\'s more money you owe me.')
```

```
input('Press <ENTER> to finish')
```

This program uses the random number generator to generate a random toss of a coin, so we need to import the random module in line 1. In line 2 we define a tuple called 'options' containing the possible results of tossing a coin. In line 3 we ask the user to guess heads or tails by entering a 1 for heads or 2 for tails. (We will look at how we can make sure the user gives a valid answer in Chapter 10, but for present we will just assume they can cope with simple instructions). The answer they give will be input as a string, so we need to convert it to an integer using the `int()` function. We will use this to assign the appropriate item in 'options' in line 4. Because tuples are indexed from 0, we need to subtract 1 from the user's input to select the correct item.[41] In line 5 we use the `random.choice()` function to simulate a coin toss by randomly selecting an item from 'options'. This is assigned to the variable `toss`. The outcome is printed in line 6. In line 7 we use an `if` statement to see if the user's guess and the random selection are the same. If they are, we print a begrudging message, otherwise we go to the `else` suite and print a triumphalist message.

Re-running the program each time we want to toss a coin is tedious, so in Chapter 10 we will look at how we can do multiple coin tosses without having to re-run the program each time.

if ... elif ... else

In some instances we may not have a simple either/or situation. Python provides an `if ... elif ... else` control structure to accommodate these situations. This takes the form:

```
if condition1:
    suite1
elif condition2:
    suite2
else:
    suite3
```

where `elif` can be read as 'else if'. If condition1 is `True` then suite1 is executed, else if condition2 is `True` then suite2 is executed, else if neither condition is `True` suite3 is executed. Only one `elif` is listed above, but you can in fact have any number. The `else` section is not essential, but its inclusion is regarded as good practice, even if it is only used to test for situations that you may have overlooked.

---

[41] We could of course have just asked the user to input a 0 or 1, but offering 1 or 2 as the choices seems more natural.

The following program (**card_select2.py**) simulates the random selection of a playing card:

```python
import random
suits=('Spades','Hearts','Diamonds','Clubs')
suit=random.choice(suits)
r=random.randint(1,13)
if r >= 2 and r <= 10:
    rank = str(r)
elif r == 11:
    rank = 'Jack'
elif r == 12:
    rank = 'Queen'
elif r == 13:
    rank = 'King'
elif r == 1:
    rank = 'Ace'
else:
    print('Logic error.')
print('The selected card is',rank,'of',suit)
input("\nPress <ENTER> to finish")
```

There are neater ways of achieving the same ends, but this way illustrates the `if` ... `elif` ... `else` control structure. The first three lines select the suit of the card. The fourth line uses the `random.randint()` function to select an integer number r in the range 1 to 13. The fifth line tests whether this is in the range 2 to 10, and if so converts the number to a string which is assigned to the variable 'rank' for output later. The next eight lines test if r corresponds to a face card and if so assigns 'rank' to the appropriate string. Finally, the `else` section prints a message if none of the previous conditions evaluate to `True`. This of course should never happen, but by now you will probably have discovered that you are not as infallible as you once thought you were, so there is no harm in building in a check for possible oversights.

Situations occasionally arise where a suite may be required following a branch but you do not actually want to do anything. The `pass` statement may be used in such situations. This tells Python to do nothing at all, yet continue as if it had processed a suite. The following (**vowel_tester.py**) does not do anything particularly useful, but it illustrates the principle:

```python
vowels=('a','e','i','o','u')
consonants=('b','c','d','f','g','h','j','k','l','m','n',\
            'p','q','r','s','t','v','w','x','y','z')
char=input('Enter a letter: ')
char=char[:1].lower()
if char in vowels:
    print('The letter entered is a vowel')
elif char in consonants:
    pass
```

```
else:
    print('*** Error: Not a letter')
input('\nPress <ENTER> to finish')
```

The program uses two tuples to define which letters should be recognised as vowels and which should be recognised as consonants. The user is then invited to enter a character. The string entered by the user is truncated to a single character (in case they enter more than one character) and converted to lower case to simplify comparisons. The `if` statement then prints a message if a vowel is detected, whereas the `elif` clause does nothing if a consonant is detected, but allows execution to proceed. If the user typed a letter as instructed, there would be no other possibilities, but you cannot rely on users doing as they are told, so the else clause traps other situations (i.e. where they type something beginning with anything other than a letter, or even nothing at all). Note that the `pass` statement allowed us to distinguish between a consonant and situations which generate an error (although an alternative would have been to simply replace `pass` with a `print()` function to indicate that we had found a consonant).

The `pass` statement is often used as placeholder during program development – i.e. you can use a `pass` statement to mark places where you need to add more code after you have finished working on other parts of the program.

Conditional Expressions

An `if ... else` control structure can often be replaced by a single line known as a **conditional expression**. Conditional expressions take the general form:

```
expression1 if condition else expression2
```

Expression1 is processed if the condition is `True` otherwise expression2 is processed. The following snippet illustrates:

```
>>> speed=56
>>> print('Slow down') if speed>30 else print('Speed okay')
```

This will print a message to slow down if a car's speed (`speed`) is above the legal limit (defined as 30) or else print a message to say the speed is okay.

The above could have been written using `if ... else` as:

```
>>> speed=56
>>> if speed>30:
```

```
    print('Slow down')
else:
    print('Speed okay')
```

This is more verbose, but some would argue it is easier to read.

You should now try the remaining exercises.

Exercises

9.1. If x=3 and y=6, what would you expect if you entered the following:

```
x >= 3
y < 6
y <= x
6 <= y
3 != 8
7 = 4
'no' == 'not yes'
[2,3] in [1,2,3,4,5]
'shot' in 'self defence'
x**2-3==y
[]==True
```

Check your answers using IDLE.

9.2. Using the same values as in 9.1, evaluate the following before checking your answers using IDLE.

```
x<=3 and y>5
x!=y and y!=x
x!=y and not y!=x
not x==3
not x==3 or y==6
not (x==3 and y==6)
'hell' in 'Hello world!'
not y**2<x**3
```

9.3. Write a program to generate a random integer in the range 1 to 9. Print the number and a message to say that it is a low number if it is in the range 1 to 3, a medium number if it is in the range 4 to 6, or a high number if it is in the range 7 to 9.

9.4. Write a conditional expression to print 'Odd' if an integer number is odd or 'Even' if it is even.

9.5. This one requires a bit of lateral thinking, but see if you can suggest a one line conditional expression to replace the 6 lines in the if ... elif ... else control structure in the suggested answer to exercise 9.3. (Do not worry about the formatting, just get it to print 'High', 'Medium' or

'Low').

9.6. The program **id_check2.py** in Chapter 7 checks whether the userID entered by a user is in a list called 'valid'. Write a program to invite a new user to enter a userId of their choice and then add it to the list of valid IDs, if it is not already in use, for future logons or else print an error message to say the userID is already in use.

9.7. Write a program inviting the user to guess a number between 1 and 10. Print a message to indicate if they guessed correctly, too low or too high.

9.8. Write a program to accept an answer to a yes / no and then print a message saying that the user answered 'yes', 'no' or 'could not be determined.' Remove any white space. Permit answers in upper or lower case (or a mixture of both).

Chapter 10. Loops

We saw in the previous chapter how **branches** may be used to determine which pieces of code should be executed and under what conditions. Not surprisingly branches are one of the most widely used control structures in every computer language. A second very common control structure is a **loop**. Loops may be used to execute a single set of commands multiple times. Python provides two main types of loop: the **for** loop and the **while** loop. Both are explored in the present chapter.

For Loops

The basic syntax of a `for` loop is:

```
for var in iterable:
    suite
```

where `for` and `in` are essential keywords, and `iterable` is any iterable data type. An iterable data type is one containing a number of items that can be returned one at a time. We have seen three types of iterable, namely lists, tuples and strings (as discussed in Chapters 6 and 7), but we will see further examples later. Each item in the iterable is assigned in turn to a variable `var` (which may be given any name). As with an `if` statement, the header line must be terminated by a colon to signify the beginning of the suite. The `suite` forms the body of the loop, and consists of one of more lines of code that are indented following the rules outlined in the previous chapter. The suite is executed once for each item in the iterable.

A simple example may help (**super_length.py**): [42]

```
text="supercalifragilisticexpialidocious"
count=0
for i in text:
    count += 1
print('The string"'+text+'"contains',counter,'characters.')
input('\nPress <ENTER> to finish')
```

The first line assigns some text to a string called `text`. The second line initialises a variable called `count` to zero, whilst the third line assigns in

---

[42] In this case, it would have been simpler to use `counter=len(text)` instead of the `for` loop in lines 2 to 4 in this example, but the example illustrates how a simple `for` loop works.

turn each item (i.e. character) in the string `text` to a variable called `i`. The body of the loop in the fourth line increments `count` by one, thereby creating a count of the number of times the loop is executed and hence the number of characters in the string. The fifth line prints the final count of the number of characters after the loop has been completed.

In this case the variable `i` is not referred to within the loop – it is simply used as an indicator of where we are within the string. When used in this way, it is quite common to use a simple name like `i`, which has no significance outside the loop, for the variable rather than a more complex name such as `variableToIndicateCurrentItem`. However, this is a matter of personal preference.

The variable may be used to process items within the iterable inside the loop. For example, the following program (**stitch_in_time.py**) defines a list called `words`, containing a number of words which are concatenated within the loop to form a string which is printed when all the words have been added:

```python
words=['A','stitch','in','time','saves','nine.']
outString=""
for word in words:
    outString = outString + word + " "
print(outString)
input('\nPress <ENTER> to finish')
```

It is possible to nest one loop inside another. The main thing to note is that the inner loop must be completely contained within the outer loop (although given Python's use of indentation to define the code blocks, it is very difficult, if not impossible, to go wrong). The following program (**nested_loop.py**) labels the squares on a chessboard using algebraic notation (i.e. the system used for chess puzzles in most newspapers):

```python
column = ['a','b','c','d','e','f','g','h']
for row in range(8):
    outString=""
    for col in column:
        outString=outString+col+str(8-row)+" "
    print(outString)
input('\nPress <ENTER> to finish')
```

The first line creates a list called `column` containing the letter names for the 8 columns. The second line creates the outer loop which prints the board row by row. The `range()` function will be explained shortly, but suffice it to say that it causes the outer loop to be repeated 8 times. At the beginning of each iteration (i.e. line 3), the output string `outString` is initialised as an empty string. The fourth line initiates the inner loop which builds up the output string one column at a time. The variable `col` is assigned to each item in `column` in turn. This, along with the current row number, is added to `outString` in line 5. When the inner loop has finished, the outer loop prints the output string for the row in line 6. This completes the outer loop, which then begins the next iteration to repeat the process for the next row.

The key thing to note in this example is that the code block in the inner loop is 'double-indented' – i.e. line 5 is indented relative to the `for` statement in line 4, whilst line 6 is 'single-indented' to indicate it does not form part of the inner loop, but is part of the outer loop (which begins at line 2).

If you use IDLE to enter your program, IDLE will automatically indent the line following a statement that should be followed by an indented code block. When you reach the end of the code for the suite, you need to manually un-indent the first line after the suite by pressing the <Back Delete> key once. Note, however, that if you insert a `for` statement in the middle of existing code, you will need to indent each line within the loop manually by inserting a tab at the beginning of each line. IDLE provides a very convenient way to do this: select all the lines that require indentation, then press the <Tab> key once (or alternatively select the Indent Region menu option on the Format menu).

Nested indentations may sound complicated, but IDLE makes things very simple for you. You will find that indented code soon becomes very easy to read.

The range() Function

If you just wish to use the items in a sequence as a loop counter, you could use something like:

```
>>> total=100
>>> for i in [1,2,3,4,5]:
        total-=1
        print(total)
```

This decrements the value of 'total' each time the loop is executed, and therefore prints out 99, 98, 97, 96, and 95. This works fine, and would be okay if you only want to implement the loop a small number of times. However, setting up the list would be very cumbersome if you wanted to count down from 1000 to zero. Fortunately the `range()` function allows us to do this more simply.

The `range()` function generates a sequence of integer numbers. In its simplest form, it takes a single argument. This specifies the number of elements that the sequence should contain. However, the numbers generated start at 0, thus if you were to specify:

```
>>> for i in range(10):
        print(i)
```

Python will print 0 through to 9. You might have expected the numbers 1 to 10, but at this stage you should be getting used to computer scientists and their funny counting.

If `range()` contains two parameters, the first is the start number and the second is the end point (i.e. one more than the last number to be included). Thus:

```
>>> for i in range(7,10):
        print(i)
```

would print 7, 8, and 9.

If `range()` contains three parameters, the third parameter is the increment to be used. [43] Thus:

```
>>> for i in range(2,10,2):
        print(i)
```

will print 2, 4, 6, and 8. Note that the end point (10) is not included in the range. The increment can of course be negative, in which case the start parameter must be larger than the end parameter. For example:

```
>>> for i in range(10,4,-2):
        print(i)
```

would print 10, 8 and 6.

If you enter:

```
>>> range(10)
```

by itself at the command prompt, Python will display `range(0,10)` – i.e. it simply gives you back the start and end values. To display the individual items you need to convert the range to either a list or a tuple. Thus:

```
>>> list(range(10))  or
>>> tuple(range(10))
```

would do the job.

---

[43] These rules, it will be noted, are the same as for slicing sequences, except that a comma is used as the separator rather than a colon.

The following program (**green_bottles1.py**) illustrates the use of a negative increment to print out ten verses of the really irritating song 'Ten Green Bottles':

```
for i in range(10,0,-1):
    print("")                      # Puts a space between verses
    print(i, "green bottles, hanging on the wall,")
    print(i, "green bottles, hanging on the wall,")
    print("And if one green bottle should accidentally "+
        "fall,")
    print("There'd be", i-1, "green bottles,")
    print("Hanging on the wall.")
print("\nThat was great! Let's do it again ... starting "+
    "at 100.")
input("\nPress ENTER to finish")
```

In this case the counter variable i is used within the loop.

Break And Continue

The break and continue commands, if included in the body of a loop, may be used to stop execution of the suite. The continue command will cause execution of the present iteration to cease and the next iteration to begin; the break command causes execution of the loop to cease completely, as if the last item in the iterable had been reached. Both commands are generally used in junction with an if statement. The following simple program illustrates (**break.py**):

```
sum=0
for i in range(20):
    if i%2 == 0:
        continue
    print(i,'is odd')
    sum += i
    if sum>25:
        break
print('The lowest sum of odd numbers >25 is',sum)
input('\nPress <ENTER> to continue')
```

This program calculates the cumulative sum of odd numbers and stops when the total exceeds 25. (Okay, maybe not something you need to do everyday, but it might come in handy sometime!). If neither of the two if statements were present, the program would print the numbers 0 through to 19 (and erroneously say that each number was odd). The first if statement tests whether the number is actually odd or even. If the number is even, then the continue statement tells Python to ignore the rest of the current iteration, with the result that only odd numbers will be processed. Lines 5 and 6 print out the odd numbers and keep a running total. The second `if` statement tests whether this total exceeds 25. If it is less than 25 then the next iteration of the loop begins. If it larger than 25, the `break` statement causes execution of the loop to cease and the first statement following the loop prints a summary message.

Try exercises 10.1 to 10.8 before moving on to the next section.

List Comprehensions

One particular combination of operations involving a `for` loop is so common that Python provides a special structure known as a **list comprehension**. In many situations one may wish to create a new list using the items from an existing sequence that satisfy certain conditions. For example, suppose you had a list called `days` containing the days of the week, and you wanted to create a new list containing only the days that include the letter 's'. To do this you might write the following (**list_select1.py**):

```
days=['Monday','Tuesday','Wednesday','Thursday','Friday',
      'Saturday','Sunday']
sDays=[]
for day in days:
    if 's' in day.lower():
        sDays.append(day)
print(sDays)
input('\nPress <ENTER> to finish.')
```

This creates a list containing the days of the week in line 1 and a new empty list `sDays` in line 2. It then it iterates through the items in days, checking whether each item contains the letter 's'. The days containing an 's' are appended to the list `sDays`. `sDays` is printed once the loop terminates.

The 'business' part of the program (i.e. lines 3 to 5) can be replaced by a list comprehension. A list comprehension allows you to do in a single line of code what might otherwise take several lines. The general syntax for a list comprehension is:

```
newList = [expression for item in iterable if condition]
```

where `newList` is a new list, `expression` is an expression, `item` is a variable name used to identify each item in an `iterable`, `condition` is a condition, and `for`, `in` and `if` are keywords. The right hand side of the equation is enclosed in square brackets. If the condition is `True` for a particular item in the iterable, then the expression (normally some expression based on the item) is added to the new list. Note that the new list does not need to be initialised (e.g. using `sDays=[]`).

The previous example can be reduced using a list comprehension to (**list_select2.py**):

```
days=['Monday','Tuesday','Wednesday','Thursday','Friday',
     'Saturday','Sunday']
sDays=[day for day in days if 's' in day.lower()]
print(sDays)
input('\nPress <ENTER> to finish.')
```

The expression in this case is simply the untransformed item, but if we wanted to abbreviate each day to its first three letters, the list comprehension could have been written as:

```
sDays=[day[0:3] for day in days if 's' in day.lower()]
```

The `if` condition is optional. If omitted, the expression defined by the comprehension is applied to every item.

You should now attempt exercises 10.9 and 10.10.

While Loops

A `while` loop combines elements of a `for` loop and an `if` statement – i.e. like a `for` loop it repeatedly loops through a series of statements defined as a suite, but it only does so provided a condition is `True`, a bit like an `if` statement.

The basic syntax of a while loop is:

```
while condition:
    suite
```

where `while` is a keyword, and the other components are the same as in an `if` statement. If the condition evaluates to `True`, the suite is executed. However, after the block has been executed, rather than continuing to the next line of code (as in an `if` control structure) Python returns to the beginning of the loop and evaluates the condition again. If it is still `True`, the code block is executed a second time. And so on. It is absolutely essential that the body of the loop contains code that will at some stage change the condition from `True` to `False` (or else contains a `break` statement), otherwise the loop will continue iterating indefinitely. (If the event of this happening, press CTRL+C to interrupt execution).

Let's toss a few coins to illustrate (**coin_toss4.py**):

```
import random
tosses = 0
heads = 0
tails = 0
while tosses<100:
    flip = random.randrange(2)
    if flip == 0:
        heads += 1
    else:
        tails += 1
    tosses += 1
print("\nNumber of heads =", heads)
print("Number of tails =", tails)
input("\nPress ENTER to finish")
```

The first four lines import the random module and initialise a few variables for counting purposes. Line 5 tests whether the variable `tosses` is less than 100. As we have just initialised `tosses` to 0, the condition is `True` so the loop is executed. This tosses a coin and increments the count of the number of heads or tails accordingly. It also increments the value of the `tosses` variable. This is critical – if `tosses` is not incremented, the condition will never be `False` and the program would loop indefinitely. Control then returns to the beginning of the loop where, although the value of `tosses` has been incremented, the condition is still `True`. The loop is therefore processed a second time. This continues until the end of the 100th iteration when `tosses` has the value 100. When we test the condition at the beginning of the 101st iteration, it evaluates to `False`, so we skip the loop and continue to the next statement which begins the output of the results.

The second example randomly generates 10 even numbers between 2 and 10 inclusive (**random_integer_loop**):

```
import random
i=10
while i:
    print(random.randrange(10, 0, -2))
    i -= 1
input("\nPress ENTER to finish")
```

A counter `i` is initialised to 10 in line 2, and then tested in line 3. Although this may not look like a condition, it will be remembered from Chapter 9 that the value 0 is regarded as `False`, and every other value is regarded as `True`. Thus line 3 is equivalent to:

```
while i>0:
```

which you might prefer for clarity. Line 4 selects and prints a random number – this could alternatively have been written as:

```
print(random.randrange(2, 12, 2))
```

Line 5 decrements the counter and control is passed back to the beginning of the loop. At the end of the 10th iteration when control is passed back, the counter has a value of 0 and is treated as `False`, terminating the loop.

Using While Loops To Check Input

An inappropriate user response to a prompt for input is one of the most common reasons for programs to fail at runtime. This is generally not a serious problem if you are only writing programs for yourself, as you will usually spot the problem fairly quickly, enabling you to re-run the program with more appropriate responses. However, if you are writing programs for other people to use, it is good practice to get the program to check whether the user's responses are likely to problematic. We will explore preferable approaches to error handling in Chapter 13, but for the present we will look how `while` loops may be used in this regard.

Problems might arise if the user accidentally pressed the <Enter> key before typing a response to a prompt. The first program (**input_check1.py**) simply checks whether the user has entered anything at all before pressing the <Enter> key:

```
reply=""
while not reply:
    reply=input("Type in something ... anything : ")
print("\nResponse received")
input("\nPress ENTER to finish")
```

The variable `reply` is initialised to an empty string in line 1. The `while` loop begins in line 2. As an empty sequence of any type is equivalent to `False`, `reply` will evaluate to `False` and `not reply` will evaluate to `True`, therefore the loop will be executed. The body of the loop in line 3 waits for input, after which control is passed back to line 2. If the user types anything before pressing <Enter>, then `reply` will now be `True` and `not reply` will be `False`, therefore the loop will not be executed a second time and control will pass to the `print()` function in line 4. However, if the user did not enter anything, `reply` will still be `False` and the loop will run again. And so on, ad infinitum, until the user eventually types something.

The second example (**input_check2.py**) does exactly the same thing but uses a slightly different approach:

```
while True:
    reply=input("Type in something ... anything : ")
    if reply:
```

```
        break
print("\nResponse received")
input("\nPress ENTER to finish")
```

Line 1 creates an indefinite loop – i.e. the program will loop indefinitely unless we trigger a `break` statement. Line 2 waits for input, and line 3 tests whether `reply` is a non-empty string. If it is, then the `break` command breaks out of the loop in line 4, otherwise you keep looping until the user types something.

The second approach is perhaps less intuitive than the first, but it can be easily extended to test for other conditions. For example, the following program tests whether the user has entered an integer between 5 and 10 inclusive (**input_check3.py**):

```
while True:
    reply = input("Enter an integer between 5 and 10 : ")
    if reply:
        intNumber = int(reply)
        if 4<intNumber<11:
            break
    print('*** Invalid response. Try again.***')
print(intNumber,"is a valid response")
input("\nPress <ENTER> to finish")
```

As before, line 1 sets up an indefinite loop, line 2 assigns the user's input to `reply` and line 3 tests whether the user actually entered anything. If not, control skips over the `if` code suite (i.e. lines 4 to 6) to line 7 which prints an error message, and passes control back to the beginning of the `while` loop line 1 to try again. If the user has entered something, it is converted to an integer in line 4 and then tested if it is in the desired range in line 5. If not, we skip the suite for the second `if` statement and jump to line 7, which prints an error message and returns control to the beginning of the `while` loop. If the data value is within the desired range, line 6 breaks out of the `while` loop established in line 1, and we proceed to the rest of the program, which in this case is simply a confirmatory message in line 9.

However, before you rush off to the pub to celebrate the triumph of logic over wanton stupidity, consider what would happen if the user entered a float number or even some text. If you test this using **input_check3.py** you will discover that their stupidity has outsmarted us. We could of course build in further error traps. However, if you are thinking that it should not be this difficult to make sure the user provides a valid response, you would be correct. As noted, we will look at a much neater solution in Chapter 13. Nevertheless, the `while True` ... `if` ... `break` combination is one you will find useful in many other circumstances, as we shall see in the following section.

Using While Loops To Re-Run Programs

In many situations you may wish to give the user the option to re-run a program when it has finished. For example, if the program was a game, you might wish to offer the user the option to try again after they have been successfully dispatched by your fire-breathing dragon. This can be achieved using a `while` loop in much the same way as above, except that almost the whole program is placed inside the loop.

The basic format is as follows (**re-run.py**):

```
while True:
    #Start doing something
    #Finish doing something
    if input('Run the program again? ').lower()=='n':
        break
input("\nPress ENTER to finish")
```

The body of the loop will be repeated until the user enters either 'N' or 'n' in response to the question asking if they want to go again.

To illustrate, the following program (**coin_toss5.py**) counts the number of heads and tails in 100 tosses of a coin and then asks whether the user wishes to run the program again:

```
import random
while True:
    tosses = 0
    heads = 0
    tails = 0
    while tosses<100:
        flip = random.randrange(2)
        if flip == 0:
            heads += 1
        else:
            tails += 1
        tosses += 1
    print("\nNumber of heads =", heads)
    print("Number of tails =", tails)
#Contine question starts here
    while True:
        ans=input("\nRun again (Y/N)? ").lower()
        if ans in ['y','n']:
            break
        else:
            print("Invalid response. Answer 'Y' or 'N'.")
    if ans=='n':
        break
```

```
input('\nPress <ENTER> to finish')
```

There are a total of three `while` loops. Most of the program is within an indefinite loop set up in line 2. The only way to escape this is using the `break` statement in the second last line. It will be noted that the `import` statement in line 1 is outside the loop, as we only need to import the **random** module once.

The first half of the program uses a second `while` loop to do 100 tosses of the coin before printing the results, although a `for` loop could have been used just as easily - i.e. `for tosses in range(100)`. The second half of the program, after the comment, uses a third `while` loop to wait until the user gives a valid response (i.e. 'Y', 'y', 'N' or 'n') to the question asking if they want to run the program again. If the answer is 'N' or 'n' for no, then the program breaks out of the main loop, otherwise control returns to the beginning of the main loop and the coin is tossed another 100 times.

Showtime

Try the remaining exercises (i.e. 10.11 onwards). These test everything you have learnt so far. You may find them more challenging than those tackled so far, so do not expect to get the correct answer straight away. Take your time and do not look up the answer unless you are completely stomped. It may be better to break each problem down into simpler steps and work towards a solution incrementally. Remember also that there is no single correct answer. If your program works, then it is 'correct' no matter how different it may be from the suggested solution (although check that it does in fact work under all circumstances).

Exercises

10.1. ASCII codes 32 to 126 represent printable characters. The character representation of an ASCII code (indeed any Unicode ordinal) can be displayed using the `chr()` function. Write a program to display ASCII codes 32 to 126 and their corresponding characters. (N.B. the answer is actually much shorter than the question).

10.2. Print each letter of the alphabet, identifying whether it is a vowel or a consonant.

10.3. Modify the program **card_select2.py** in Chapter 9 to select 10 cards. For simplicity you may allow each card to be selected more than once.

10.4. Modify the program **coin_toss1.py** in Chapter 9 to play the coin toss game 10 times, and then print a message summarising the user's success rate.

10.5. Randomly select one name from the list ['Matthew', 'Mark', 'Luke', 'John', 'Hamish'] 100 times, allowing replacement (i.e. multiple selection). Provide a summary of the number of times each name was selected.

10.6. Write a program to count how many times there are more than 7 heads in 100 repetitions of 10 simulated tosses of a coin.

10.7. If you look closely at the output from the program **green_bottles.py** you will note that the last two verses use the word 'bottles' where 'bottle' would be more correct. Adjust the program to be grammatically correct.

10.8. The sentence 'The quick brown fox jumps over the lazy dog.' is a pangram – i.e. it includes each letter of the alphabet at least once. Write a program to test whether the sentence is or is not a pangram. (Hint: when testing, change 'jumps' to 'jumped' to see if you get the same result).

10.9. Use a list comprehension to create a list of months containing the letter 'r' from a list of all months.

10.10. Write a program to create a list of words with more than three letters in the quote 'Now is the winter of our discontent'. See if you can reduce the 'business' part to a single line.

10.11. Write a program to accept some text from the user and then print it out in reverse order.

10.12. As noted in the text, the program **input_check3.py** accepts integer numbers within a permitted range. Rewrite the program to accept any positive or negative integer, but reject all other inputs (e.g. text, floats, etc.).

10.13. Write a program inviting the user to guess a random integer number between 1 and 100. If they guess wrong, tell them whether their guess is too high or too low and invite them to try again. If they fail to guess correctly in 6 guesses, tell them they have lost, and ask them if they wish to play another game. At the end of each game, display a running total of their successes and failures.

10.14. Rewrite the suggested answer to exercise 6.14 (**encrypt1.py**), so that it can encrypt multiple sentences one at a time, ending each sentence with a full stop (i.e. encrypt the first sentence, terminate it with a full stop, encrypt the second sentence, terminate it with a full stop, and so on). Test it on the message: 'What do you mean: The eagle has flown the coup. This means nothing to me. Please resend your message in plain Slombovian.' (N.B. Use fullstops in the message rather than the grammatically more correct exclamation marks or question marks.)

10.15. Write a program to decrypt messages encrypted using the solution to exercise 10.14. Test it on: 'O ci se mosusuth ecpmereryabnorid. Tt**Pneagentdvyeusrsh **rg so do eo reea** ilh na lerno ct.' – a copy of which can be found in the file **message.txt**.

10.16. Write a program to select the winning numbers for next week's National Lottery.

Chapter 11. Functions And Modules

In the previous chapters we looked at examples of how one might test whether a number entered by the user fell within a specified range, or whether the user had correctly answered a yes/no question. Each operation requires several lines of code, so it would obviously be tedious to have to rewrite the same lines of code every time we required a user to enter a number or answer a simple question. Fortunately there is a very simple solution: we can write the code once and save it as a **function**; the function can then be called anytime it is required using a simple call statement. In this way the business of checking the user's response can in effect be 'subcontracted' to the function each time it is required.

We have already seen several examples of functions. Some, like the len() function (used to count the number of items in a sequence), are an integral part of the Python language and are referred to as **built-in functions** (or **BIF**s). Others, such as the random.random() function (used to generate a pseudorandom number), are optional extras that can be imported as part of a **module** supplied with Python as part of the **standard library**. We can also import modules containing functions provided by a third party source in much the same way. We will look at built-in, standard library and third party functions later, but the main focus of this chapter is on user-defined functions (i.e. functions you write yourself).

In addition to preventing unnecessary duplication of the same code, functions are also useful for simplifying the structure of a large program. Even if each function is only used once, each step in a complex program can be 'subcontracted' to a function, thereby reducing the main program to a small number of function calls. By transferring the nitty-gritty details to functions, the structure of the main program may become much easier to follow.

A third advantage of using functions is that they can be 'recycled' – i.e. once you have written a function for a particular purpose in one program, it can often be re-used for the same purpose in other programs. This obviously saves you the trouble of having to 'reinvent the wheel' each time you need to do something similar. Over the course of time you will probably build up a collection of functions for the tasks you perform most frequently. These functions could be cut and paste into programs as they are required, but a better approach is to save them in a **module**. This module can then be imported into programs requiring one of your functions in much the same way as you import the `random` module to access a number of random number functions. The final sections in this chapter look at how you can create your own modules and access third party modules.

Functions

A function is a piece of code that performs a particular task outside of the main program. Each time you require a particular operation to be carried out, you call the function. When the program is executed, the call statement passes control to the function, the instructions in the function are executed, and control is then passed back to the call statement. Each function is defined only once, but may be called as many times as you like.

Before you can use a function, you must define it (unless it is a built-in function or a function imported as part of a module, in which case it is already defined). The function definitions are separate from the main program. Some languages use a keyword (such as 'main') to identify the main program, but in Python anything not identified as a function definition is assumed to be part of the main program. Some languages allow you to place the function definitions after the main program but, because Python interprets the lines in a program sequentially, Python requires the functions to be defined before they are called. The function definitions are therefore normally grouped together near the beginning of the program. To understand the overall structure of the program, you may need to scroll down past a number of function definitions to find the main program near the bottom.

Defining A Function

In its simplest form, a function definition takes the general form:

```
def functionName():
    suite
```

where `def` is a keyword (short for define), `functionName` is whatever name you decide to give to your function (subject to the same rules as variable names), and `suite` is one or more lines of code defining what the function should do. Note that the first line (known as the **function header**) always terminates with a colon and the suite (known as the **function body**) must be indented. Note also that the function name is always followed by a set of parentheses.

Calling A Function

The function is called in the main program using its name (including the parentheses). The following trivial example (**hello_world4.py**) illustrates:

```
def greetings():
    print('Hello world!')
    return

#Main program starts here
greetings()
input('\nPress <ENTER> to finish')
```

This is not actually a very good use of a function as it manages to expand a one line program (cf. **hello_world1.py** in Chapter 3) to several lines (plus comments and blank lines). However, it illustrates the basic features. The first line is the function header for a function called greetings(). The second and third lines form the function body. The end of the function body is indicated by the end of the indentation. The return statement returns control to the call statement in the main program.[44] However, control is automatically passed back to the main program when Python reaches the end of the suite, so the return statement in this case is redundant and could have been omitted without making any difference. However, as we shall see, a return statement at the end of the code block is often essential in other contexts (see 'Returning Results' below). Some Python programmers regard the inclusion of a redundant return statement as bad style, whereas others believe it makes the program more readable. Its inclusion does not do any harm.

The function in this example is followed by a blank line. This is not essential. Like all white space it is ignored by the interpreter, but the use of blank lines to separate different sections of a program may make it easier to read. If there are a lot of functions, placing them in alphabetical order may also make them easier to find in a large program, but you can place them in any order provided they precede any statements that call them. The comment line indicating the beginning of the main program could also be omitted, but I will include one in the examples in the present chapter for clarity.

---

[44] Functions do not necessarily need to be called from the main program: they may also be called from within another function. However, in the interests of clarity, the call statement will be assumed, for the purposes of this chapter, to always come from the main program it (unless otherwise stated).

The main program in this example contains little other than a call to the function. When called, the function extends the usual salutations to the global community and then returns control to the main program, which then immediately proceeds to the next line, which in this example prompts the user to terminate the program.

On some occasions a function may have more than one `return` statement. For example, an `if` statement may create two separate branches, each of which may need to be terminated by its own `return`. The following program (**multiple_returns.py**) illustrates:

```
def do_stuff():
    while True:
        ans=input('Would you like to do something(Y/N)? ')\
            .lower()
        if ans in ['y','n']:
            break
    if ans[0]=='n':
        return
    while True:
        print('\nWhat would you like to do?\n'+
            ' 1 Say hello\n 2 Say goodbye')
        opt=(input('Enter 1 or 2: '))
        if opt=='1' or opt=='2':
            break
    if opt=='1':
        print('\nHello world!')
    else:
        print('\nGoodbye cruel world!')
    return

#Main program starts here
do_stuff()
input('\nPress <ENTER> to finish')
```

Most of this program forms part of the function `doStuff()`. The main program at the bottom simply calls the function then shuts down once control has been returned. The function when called asks the user if they would like to do something. If they answer 'n', the first `return` is invoked, control is returned to the main program and nothing else happens. However, if they answer 'y', the function asks a second question. Depending on their answer to the second question, a short message is printed and the second `return` is implemented. In this case the second `return` could have been omitted, as the end of indention signifies the end of the function so control would be passed back to the main program anyway.

The `do_stuff()` function includes a few simple (but by no means foolproof) tests of the validity of the responses provided by the user. Given that you are likely to require similar tests elsewhere either in the same program or in other programs, these tests could be 'subcontracted' to other functions (which could be reused as required). Thus, the `do_stuff()` function might include calls to functions with names like `yn()` and `get_integer()`.

There are two loops in **multiple_returns.py**, neither of which contains a `return`. However, it should be noted that a `return` statement can be used to break out of a loop in much the same way as a `break` statement. For example (**get_input.py**):

```
def get_input():
    while True:
        x=input('Type something: ')
        if x:
            return

#Main program starts here
get_input()
print('Something was typed')
input('Press <ENTER> to finish.')
```

This uses a `while` loop to loop indefinitely until something is typed before pressing the <ENTER> key. However, when something is typed, instead of using `break` to break out of the loop, the `return` statement returns control to the main program.

Passing Values To Parameters

The above examples do not require any input from the main program. However, in many instances functions are designed to perform some operation using data values supplied by the main program. The data values supplied by the main program are referred to as **arguments**, and they are represented inside the function by **parameters**. The arguments and parameters may have the same names or different names, but even if they have the same names they refer to different objects (i.e. the function creates its own local data objects). The function header identifies the parameters required. The general form is:

```
def functionName(parameter1, parameter2):
    suite

#Main program starts here
functionName(argument1, argument2)
```

where `parameter1` and `parameter2` are two parameters required by the function. Although two parameters are shown here, you can have as many or as few parameters as you want (including, as we have seen, none at all). Each of these references an object (e.g. a variable or sequence) required by the code in the function body. The objects referred to by parameters are initialised when the function is called using the values passed as the arguments in the calling statement (i.e. `argument1` and `argument2`). The arguments in the call statement may be literals, object references (e.g. variable names), or even expressions. The following program (**hello_you2.py**) illustrates:

```
def greet (name):
    print('Hello',name)
    return

#Main program starts here
greet('world')
userName=input('What is your name: ')
greet(userName)
friendName=input('What is your friend\'s name: ')
greet(userName+"'s friend "+friendName)
input('\nPress <ENTER> to finish')
```

The first 3 lines defines a function called `greet()` which takes a parameter called `name`, and then prints a hello message using `name`. The function is called in the first line of the main program using the string literal 'world' as the argument. This is assigned to `name` within the function, which uses it to print out our now-familiar greeting. The next line asks the user to enter their name and assigns the input string to the variable `username`, which is passed as the argument in the second call to `greet()`. Finally, the program asks the user to input the name of a friend which is assigned to `friendName`. The third call to greet passes an expression using the variables `username` and `friendName`.

Python uses a technique known as **pass by reference**. In other words, it is the object references of the arguments that are copied rather than their values. For example, if the variable `userName` is passed as an argument with the value 'Daphne', the corresponding parameter `name` would be assigned the object reference (or 'pointer') to the string object with the value 'Daphne'. The function call sets the object references of the argument and parameter to point initially to the same object, rather than creating a new object with the same value. However, if any change is made to the value of the object within the function, the local variable in the function is rebound to point to a new object with the new value, whilst the variable in the main program remains unchanged. The variables in the main program are therefore isolated from any changes made in the function. These subtleties need not concern you too much in the normal course of events, but they are occasionally important to understanding exactly what is happening in some situations.

If there is more than one parameter, how does Python know which argument in the call statement to assign to which parameter? The answer is quite simple: by default the parameters are assigned by their position – i.e. the first argument in the call statement is assigned to the first parameter listed in the function definition, the second argument in the call statement is assigned to the second parameter in the definition, and so on. When making a call to a function, it is obviously important to place the arguments in the correct sequence. Consider, for example, the following:

```
def func(name, age, sex)
    ...
    return
```

```
func(myAge, myName, mySex)
```

This would assign `myAge` in the main program to `name` in the function `func`, and `myName` in the main program to `age` in the function. This is probably not what is intended. In this case the call might generate a type error (e.g. if `name` was a string and `age` was an integer), but in other situations the error could pass unnoticed.

Keyword Arguments

An alternative to **positional arguments** is to use **keyword arguments**. If you know the parameter name used within the function, you can explicitly use the parameter names in the call statement. In this case, the sequence does not matter. Any of the following calls would work correctly in the above example:

```
func(myName, myAge, mySex) or
func(name=myName, age=myAge, sex=mySex) or
func(age=myAge, sex=mySex, name=myName)
```

You can even mix positional and keyword arguments in a call statement but, if you do, the positional arguments must all come in the correct sequence before the first keyword argument. Once you include a keyword argument, all subsequent arguments must also be keyword arguments. Thus:

```
func(myName, sex=mySex, age=myAge)
```

would be valid, but

```
func(age=myAge, myName, mySex)
```

would not.

Default Values

If the number of arguments in the call statement does not match the number or parameters in the function definition, Python will normally issue an error message. However, parameters may be assigned a default value in the function definition statement. These are referred to as **optional parameters**. Optional parameters do not require an argument in the call statement unless you wish to override the default. Optional parameters are particularly useful when using keyword arguments, but they may also be used with positional arguments provided you do not disrupt the sequence (i.e. if you omit an argument to indicate that you wish to accept the default value, then any further arguments need to be passed using keywords). The following (**hello_world5.py**) illustrates several possibilities:

```
def greetings(name='world', salutation='Hello'):
    print(salutation+' '+name+'!')

#Main program starts here
greetings()
greetings('Marmaduke')
greetings(salutation='Salutations')
greetings('cruel world', salutation='Goodbye')
greetings(salutation='Well hello there,', name='beautiful')
input('\nPress <ENTER> to finish')
```

The function `greetings()` is defined with two parameters `name` and `salutation` which are assigned the default values 'world' and 'Hello' respectively. It will be noted that the function definition has no `return` statement. In this case it does not matter as Python knows to return to the call statement at the end of the function, but a `return` statement could have been added after line 2 if you wanted to be explicit. The main program contains 5 function calls. The first specifies no parameters, so both defaults are used. The second overrides the first parameter (`name`) with 'Marmaduke'. The third overrides the second parameter (`salutation`) but leaves `name` set to its default ('world'). Because the first parameter is left at its default, the second parameter must be referred to using its keyword. The fourth call uses a positional parameter followed by a keyword one. If there had been any additional optional parameters, they would need to have been specified using keywords if you wished to override the defaults. The fifth call uses two keyword parameters, but they are out of sequence.

Once you have run the program, you could test other calls in interactive mode using IDLE. For example:

```
>>> greetings(name='Sheila', salutation="G'day")
```

Arbitrary Argument Lists

Python supplies a useful facility for situations where you may not be sure how many arguments need to be passed. This can be accomplished be prefacing a parameter name by an asterisk. The following example (**add_numbers.py**) illustrates:

```
def add(*numbers):
    total=0
    for number in numbers:
        total+=number
    print('The numbers add up to:',total)
    return

#Main program starts here
add(1,2,3,4,5)
add()
aList=[6,7,8,9]
add(*aList)                          # N.B. Asterisk in call
input('\nPress <ENTER> to finish')
```

The function has a single parameter, but the asterisk at the beginning of its name indicates it can take an unspecified number of arguments. These arguments are actually passed as a tuple which is referred to in the function as `numbers`. The `for` loop in the function instructs Python to cycle through the items in the tuple, adding each one to the running total in turn. Once the `for` loop completes, the total is printed and control is returned to the main program.

The main program contains three calls to the function. The first passes five arguments, which the function sums before printing out the total. The second passes no arguments. This does not cause the function a problem because the `for` loop simply passes control onto the next statement, which displays the total as zero. A list `aList` with four items is established before the third call to the function. However, note that the argument `aList` is preceded by an asterisk in the function call. In the absence of an asterisk, the object reference for `aList` would be passed, and the `aList` would become the first and only item in the tuple `numbers`. The asterisk tells Python to copy the items in `aList` as separate items in the tuple. The same would apply if the `aList` had been a tuple.

In this example the only arguments passed are the numbers which are to be added together. However, in other situations you may wish to pass other arguments. This causes no problems provided the 'asterisk' parameter is listed last in the parameter list, and an argument is provided for each positional parameter in the parameter (i.e. no arguments can be omitted to indicate acceptance of their default values).[45]

Function Names As Arguments

Whilst the arguments passed to a function are normally literals, object references (i.e. variable names) for numbers or sequences, or expressions, it is also possible to pass function names. The following short program **(flexi_func.py)** illustrates:

```
def math(x,y,z):
    z(x,y)
def add(x,y):
    print('The sum of the numbers is:',x+y)
def subtract(x,y):
    print('The difference between the numbers is:',x-y)

#Main program
math(5,3,add)
math(5,3,subtract)
input('\nPress <ENTER> to finish')
```

The main program contains two function calls to the function `math`, each with three arguments (the integer literals 5 and 3, and a function name, `add` or `subtract`). Function `math()` in turn makes a call to function `z()`, where `z` is determined by the third argument passed to it (i.e. if the third argument passed to `math()` is `add`, then `math()` calls `add()` and the two values are added together; if the third argument is `subtract`, `math()` calls the function `subtract()`).

Returning Results

In the examples so far, the functions do what they need to do (e.g. print something) without having to return a result of some sort to the main program. However, in many situations we require a two way flow of information between the function and the main program – i.e. the main program sends some arguments for the function to work with, and in return receives some results. This is the real purpose of the `return` command. The results that are to be returned are simply listed in the `return` command in comma separated list. Thus, the basic form of a function definition takes the general form:

```
def functionName(parameter1, parameter2):
    suite
```

---

[45] It is also possible to pass a variable number of keyword arguments by prefixing the parameter name with **. This parameter must come after the * parameter in the parameter. The keyword arguments are passed using a dictionary (see Chapter 12).

```
        return result1, result2
```

where `result1` and `result2` are results to be returned to the main program. Although two results are shown here, you may return as many as you wish (or none at all).[46]

The results that are returned are usually assigned to variables in the main program using a statement taking the form:

```
name1, name2 = functionName(variable1, variable2)
```

where `name1` and `name2` are the names of the variables that are to receive the values of `variable1` and `variable2` respectively.

To illustrate, the following example calculates the area and circumference of a circle (**circle2.py**):

```
def circle(radius):
    PI=3.14159
    area=PI*radius**2
    circumference=2*PI*radius
    return area, circumference

#Main program starts here
a,c = circle(10)
print('Area = ',a, ', Circumference = ',c, sep="")
t = circle(5)
print('Area = ',t[0], ', Circumference = ',t[1], sep="")
input('\nPress <ENTER> to finish')
```

In this example the main program makes two calls to the function `circle()` which calculates the area and circumference of a circle using the parameter `radius`. The first call sets radius to 10 and the function calculates the area and circumference which are returned and assigned to the variables `a` and `c` respectively in the main program.

The second call sets radius to 5 but it only has one variable (`t`) to receive two answers. So, how does this work? The results can be thought of as being returned as a comma separated values. We saw previously that values separated by commas can be assigned to a tuple, so in this case `t` would be a tuple with two values. The `print()` function uses subscripts to print the values.

---

[46] Strictly speaking functions always return a result. If you do not specify a result to be returned, or do not even include a `return` statement, the function will return the value None.

Scope: Local And Global Variables

The availability of a variable in different parts of a program is referred to as its **scope**. Variables initialised in the main program are said to be **global**; whereas variables initialised within a function, including parameters (which are initialised with the values passed as arguments) are said to be **local**. Local variables are only available within the function in which they are initialised, whereas global variables can be accessed, although not modified, within any function (even if they have not been explicitly passed as an argument). The following example (**scope.py**) illustrates:

```
def func(u):
    u+=1
    w=v+1
    x=w
    print('u in function =',u)
    print('v in function =',v)
    print('w in function =',w)
    print('x in function =',x)
    return w

# Main program
u=1
v=1
print('u in main program before call =',u)
print('v in main program before call =',v)
w=func(u)
print('u in main program after call =',u)
print('v in main program after call =',v)
print('w in main program after call =',w)
print('x in main program after call =',x)
input('\nPress <ENTER> to finish.')
```

(N.B. This program will generate an error when run, for reasons explained below). The main program begins by initialising variables u and v to 1. The values of u and v are printed for confirmation. Function func() is then called using only u as an argument. The function func() initialises a local variable u with the value supplied by argument u. The u in func(), initially references the same object as the u in the main program. However, when it is incremented in the first line of the function, a new object is created for the incremented value. Thus, when we print u in the function, it has a value of 2. The u in func() is a local variable, whereas the u in the main program is a global variable. Although v was not passed as an argument, the function is able to 'see' it and display its value because it is a global variable. However, although the function can read a global variable it cannot change it – any attempt to do so (e.g. by inserting a line beginning v+=1) would generate an error – try it to confirm. Nevertheless, the value of the global variable v can be used to initialise a local variable w, which in this example is set equal to v+1. This value (2) is displayed for confirmation before we create another local variable x, which is initialised with the same value as w (i.e. 2). This is displayed before we return the value of w to the main program, where it is assigned to a new global variable also called w.

The main program prints the values of u and v. Both are equal to 1. The value of v should not cause any surprise as we were unable to change it in the function, but u was incremented to 2 in the function. However, it was the local variable u that was incremented; the global variable in the main program remains unchanged (unless it is specifically assigned to a value returned by the function). The next line prints the value of the global variable w, which was assigned a value by the local variable w.

Finally, the attempt to print the value of x in the main program causes the program to crash because x is local to the function and is therefore not visible to the main program. (In fact the local variables are made available for garbage collection as soon as the function terminates).

The names of the local variables u, v and w were deliberately given the same names as the global variables u, v and w in the main program in the above example to emphasize that the same names can refer to different objects. This is sometimes referred to as **shadowing**. However, it is regarded by many programmers as bad practice as it can become confusing trying to keep track of which variables have what values (as you may have discovered as you tried to follow the example above!). It is therefore preferable to use different names within functions.

The Global Statement

If we had wanted the function to change the value of either u or v in the main program in the example above, we could have assigned u or v to a variable explicitly returned by the function. For example, using the call statement u = func(u) would change the value of u to the value of the local variable returned by the function.

An alternative approach is to define a variable in a function as global using a global statement. Thus, in the above example, we could define the variable x as global by inserting the line

```
global x
```

at the beginning of the function. This would make it available to the main program, thereby avoiding the error message when the program is re-run.

There are situations where this may be useful, but in general the use of `global` statements should be avoided. Good program design should adhere, as far as possible, to the principles of **encapsulation**. Encapsulation can be thought of as meaning 'self-contained'. If you intend to write functions that can be re-used in other programs, then it is inadvisable to give those programs read/write access to variables within the function by making them global as the main program could accidentally change the value of the variable in an unforeseen manner. Likewise, it is inadvisable to directly access global variables within functions as the function will only work if the main program contains appropriately named variables. To avoid these problems you should write your function to be as self-contained as possible. All the values it requires from the main program should be passed as arguments, and any results that need to be sent back to the main program should be passed back using `return` statements.

If you have managed to follow everything in this section, then Einstein's general theory of relativity should be a stroll in the park. If not, hang in there, it will all become clear eventually.

Using A main() Function

There is no necessity for the lines in the main program to be grouped at a single location; although it would be very messy, the main program could be interspersed between definitions for various functions as illustrated below (**messy.py**):

```
print('This is an example of poor structure.')
def function1():
    print('This line is printed by a function.')
function1()
print('And now we are back to the main program.')
def function2():
    print('This is a line from another function.')
function2()
print('Even with comments, this would be hard to follow.')
input('\nPress <ENTER> to finish')
```

Even in a very short program, this is very messy and makes it very difficult to distinguish between functions and main program. Imagine if the program was much larger and made frequent calls back to functions defined previously!

It is clearly preferable to group the lines forming the main program together. However, because functions need to be defined before they are called, this means that the main program is generally located at the end of the program. It can be irritating to have to scroll up and down a large program to find where it begins, so a simple expedient preferred by some programmers is to place the main program inside a function that can be placed at the beginning of the program. Unlike other languages, Python does not reserve a particular name for the main function, but a sensible choice would be `main()`. You still require a main program at the end of the program, otherwise nothing will happen when you run the program, but this might consist of little more than a `main()` statement to call the `main()` function. The overall structure of a program might therefore look something like this:

```
def  main():
    #Statements forming the main program
    return
def func():
    #Statements defining a function called by main()
    return

main()
print('\nPress <ENTER> to finish')
```

One minor benefit of designing your program like this is that any variables initialised by the `main()` function will be local variables. This will help flag situations where your other functions are not fully encapsulated - if they depend upon being able to read global variables from a main program they will generate an error. If your functions work with a `main()` function, then you can have more confidence that they will work in any situation.

Another Trap For The Unwary

If attempting to adhere to the rules of encapsulation, it is important to be aware of a potential pitfall if working with a mutable sequence (e.g. a list). For example, consider the following program (**pitfall1.py**):

```
def update():
    print('List within the function:',aList)
    aList[0]='Twice'
    return

#Main program starts here
aList=['Once','upon','a','time']
print('Initial list:',aList)
update()
print('List after function call:', aList)
input('\nPress <ENTER> to finish')
```

The main program defines a list `aList` and then calls the `update()`

function, which changes the first item in aList within the function. The contents of aList is not changed in the main program, nor was it passed as a argument to the function. One might therefore expect its value to remain unchanged in the main program, but if you run the program you will see that its value in the main program is in fact changed by the function. This would seem to contradict what I said about it not being possible to change the values of a variable in the main program unless it is either defined as global in the function or reassigned using a return statement.

Strictly speaking the value of aList in the above example has not changed. The variable aList is an object reference which points to a list object containing other pointers to where the string objects are stored in memory. The location of the list object is not changed; what has changed is the value of one of the pointers it contains - a subtle but crucial distinction.

Using a different parameter name for the list within the function (**pitfall2.py**) does not resolve the problem:

```
def update(listName):
    listName[0]='Twice'
    print('List within the function:',listName)
    return

#Main program starts here
aList=['Once','upon','a','time']
print('Initial list:',aList)
update(aList)
print('List after function call:', aList)
input('\nPress <ENTER> to finish')
```

The function explicitly defines its own list (listName). However, the list in the main program (aList) is still changed because the argument passed by the function call (aList) is only a pointer to a list object in memory. The parameter in the function (listName) is also a pointer. All that happens is the pointer in the function is set to point to the same list object as the pointer in the main program. Any changes to the pointers within the list object in the function will therefore be reflected by the list in the main program.

It may be useful in some situations to be able to modify a mutable list using a function (e.g. you could write functions to append additional items or change existing ones), but it also creates dangers. If using a function to modify the contents of a list (or, indeed any other mutable collection, such as a dictionary – see Chapter 12), you need to be aware that it may also affect the contents of the object in the main program, irrespective of whether it is passed as an argument or not.

If you want to safeguard against the possibility of a list in the main program being changed by accident, there is a solution, as illustrated by the following (**pitfall3.py**):

```
def update(listName):
    listName[0]='Twice'
    print('List within the function:',listName)
    return

#Main program starts here
aList=['Once','upon','a','time']
print('Initial list:',aList)
update(aList[:])
print('List after function call:', aList)
input('\nPress <ENTER> to finish')
```

This program is almost identical to **pitfall2.py**, but the argument in the call statement is slightly different. Instead of passing a name pointing to the location of the list, the call statement `update(aList[:])` passes all the items in the list. The function creates a new list for these items and uses `listName` to point to them. The next line changes the value of the first item, but only does so in the list pointed to in the function by `listName`. The contents of `aList` in the main program remain unchanged.

You should now attempt exercises 11.1 to 11.8.

Modules

One of the main advantages of writing a function is that it can be re-used in other programs. One way to do this would be to cut and paste the function into your programs as required. However, a less labour-intensive approach is to create a **module** (or possibly several modules) containing your favourite functions. This module can be imported into any program, making the functions it contains available without any need to cut or paste.

Creating A Module

Creating a module is very straightforward. All you need to do is create a Python file containing all the functions you want to save in your module. Thus, for example, the following contains the source for a module with two functions (**testlib1.py**):

```
def hello(name='world'):
    print('Hello '+name)
    return

def goodbye(name='cruel world'):
    print('Goodbye '+name)
    return
```

The name you give the file determines the name of the module. In this instance the file is called **testlib1.py**, so the module will be recognised in your programs as 'testlib1' (without the extension). [47]

The other decision you need to make is where to save the file. One option is to save the module file in the same folder as the programs that need to access it. The main drawback with this approach is that the module is more difficult to access from programs saved in other folders. You could of course make a duplicate copy of the module file in each of the other folders, but this would be a bad idea: if you ever need to update the module file, then you would need to remember to make changes to all the duplicate copies. This could get messy, so it is preferable to save a single copy of the module file at a location which is accessible to all Python programs. Any folder in the Python path would work.

To identify which files are in the path, you can enter the following in interactive mode:

```
>>> import sys, pprint
>>> pprint.pprint(sys.path)
```

The first line imports two built-in modules (`sys` and `pprint`) supplied as part of the Standard Library (see below), whilst the second uses these to print the current Python path.[48] Although you could save your module in any of the folders listed in the path, the one called 'site-packages' is specifically intended for third party modules and is therefore the recommended choice.

Copy the module file **testlib1.py** to the 'site-packages' folder. After copying, you should probably either delete the original file or change its name. This will ensure that there is only one copy of **testlib1.py** – i.e. the

---

[47] You can use any combination of lower and upper case characters for a module name, but the official recommendation is to use lower case letters throughout, with an underscore where necessary to improve readability.

[48] The `pprint()` function in the `pprint` module, which stands for 'pretty print', simply prints each folder name on a separate line for readability.

---

one in the 'site-packages' folder – thereby removing any possible confusion as to which copy you are accessing.

Accessing A Module

Once you have saved your module, you can access its functions in any program using the `import` command (in much the same way as described for the `random` module in Chapter 8). The convention is to place all the `import` statements at the beginning of the program, before any function definitions.

Each module has its own **namespace**. This means is that the functions inside a module cannot be seen from outside unless they are prefaced by the name of the module using a dot notation. This avoids confusion with other functions with the same name in other modules (whether they were written by you, provided by Python, or provided by a third party). The following (**library_test1.py**) illustrates a few calls to the functions in our new module:

```
import testlib1
testlib1.hello()
testlib1.goodbye()
testlib1.hello('Marmaduke')
testlib1.goodbye('Marmaduke')
input('\nPress <ENTER> to finish')
```

If you examine the folder where you saved your module file, you may discover that a new file with a .pyc extension (possibly in a subfolder) was added when **testlib1.py** was imported. The 'pyc' extension indicates that it is a compiled Python file. This file is used by any future calls to the module (thereby eliminating the need to re-compile), so you could in theory delete the source (**testlib1.py**) and programs importing the module would still work. However, it is advisable to retain the source file in case you ever need to make changes. If you do make changes to the module (e.g. add additional functions), Python will recognise this and automatically create a new compiled file.

Remembering to prefix the function name with the module name can prove irksome, so it should be noted that there is an alternative method to import a module which does not require the module name to be specified each time a function is called. Using this approach, the above example would become:

```
from testlib1 import *
hello()
goodbye()
```

```
hello('Marmaduke')
goodbye('Marmaduke')
input('\nPress <ENTER> to finish')
```

The problem with this approach is that it in effect copies all the names in the module into the current namespace. Thus, if you already have any functions (including built-in functions or functions in modules imported previously) with the same name as those being imported (in this example, `hello()` and `goodbye()`), importing a module by this method would cause the pre-existing functions to be overwritten.[49] It is therefore safer to use the first method even if it involves a little extra typing.

Identifying Executable Files

A module is much the same as any other Python source file, except that a module is not intended to be directly executable. Any program file can be treated as a module – i.e. you can import it and use its functions in much the same as a purpose-built module. However, each module is executed when it is first imported, so there is a danger when importing a program file as a module that the whole program could be inadvertently executed with unforeseen consequences. A common safeguard, therefore, is to place most of the main program in an executable file within a `main()` function which is only called if the file has not been imported as a module. To do this, the main program generally contains a line similar to:

```
if __name__ == '__main__':
    main()
```

Each object (including program files and modules) has a built-in attribute called __name__ (spelt with double underscores before and after). When a module is imported, __name__ is set to the name of the module; but when a program is executed directly __name__ is set by default to the string '__main__'. The above code therefore tests if a file has been imported, and if not the `main()` function is called. If the file has been imported, the test will return `False` and the `main()` function will not be executed.

To illustrate, we could re-write **library_test1.py** as follows (**library_test2.py**):

```
import testlib1

def main():
    testlib1.hello()
```

---

[49] If necessary you can revert back to the originals by restarting the shell (e.g. by pressing CTRL+F6 in IDLE).

```
    testlib1.goodbye()
    testlib1.hello('Marmaduke')
    testlib1.goodbye('Marmaduke')

if __name__ == '__main__':
    main()
input('\nPress <ENTER> to finish')
```

If you try to execute a module, nothing much happens. This could cause some confusion for a user who did not realise the file was a module, but similar code may be included in a module to display a message if the user attempts to execute it. For example, you could include something like:

```
if __name__ == '__main__':
    print('This is a module file and should be imported.')
    input('\nPress <ENTER> to finish')
```

This is included in the module file **testlib2.py**.

Docstrings And Help

As you build up a library of functions saved in one or more modules, you may forget what some functions do, what parameters they take, or what data they return. Fortunately Python provides a simple solution, known as a **docstring** (documentation string). Each function may (many would say 'should') contain a docstring to provide information about what it does and any other relevant details. To create a single line docstring, you simply enclose the desired text between either single or double quotes in the line immediately following the def header. You can also create a multi-line docstring by inserting a triple quoted string. The file **testlibdoc.py** illustrates both approaches:

```
def hello(name='world'):
    "Displays 'Hello' + name"
    print('Hello '+name)
    return

def goodbye(name='cruel world'):
    """
    Displays 'Goodbye' + name

    Only one argument: name
    If none specified, default name is 'cruel world'.
    No results are returned.
    """
    print('Goodbye '+name)
    return
```

The above should be copied to the 'site-modules' folder.

To test out our docstrings, using IDLE in interactive mode enter:

```
>>> import testlibdoc
>>> testlibdoc.hello()
```

As you enter the left parenthesis after 'hello', a prompt will pop up indicating the parameter list, including any default values. IDLE does this whether there is a docstring or not. However, IDLE also displays the first line of your docstring.

If you now enter:

```
>>> testlibdoc.goodbye()
```

a prompt will again pop up as you enter the open parenthesis to display the parameter list and the first line of the docstring. However, it does not display the rest of the triple quoted comment. So, what was the point of including it?

The extended docstring comes into its own when it is accessed using the `help` function. If you enter:

```
>>> help()
```

in interactive mode, Python will display a `help>` prompt. If you enter:

```
help> modules
```

at this prompt, you will get a list of all the available modules (including your own). Entering any of these names at the following prompt will cause its docstring information to be displayed. Thus, for example, if you enter:

```
help> testlibdoc
```

your docstring will be displayed in full. If you fully document your functions, this can prove invaluable.

You can also get the docstring on a particular function by entering its name, e.g.

```
help> testlibdoc.goodbye
```

(Note that the function name does not include the parentheses). If you cannot remember the name of the function, a list should appear after you enter the fullstop.

You may also view 'keywords' and 'topics' in a similar manner. To leave help, just press the <Enter> key without typing anything.

Some authors suggest a few conventions for docstrings:

1. The first line should begin with a capital, and provide a brief

description of what the function does without specifically including its name.

2. If multi-line, the first line should be followed by a blank line.

3. The remaining text should be organised into paragraphs, each separated by a blank line.

However, these are conventions, not rules, so you are at liberty to adopt your own styles.

Built-In Functions And Modules

Python provides over 60 **built-in functions** (or **BIFs**) that can be accessed without the need to import a module. We have already met several of these (e.g. `len()`, `float()`, `input()`, `tuple()`, `list()`, `print()`, etc.), but there are many others. If you wish to explore what is available, a full list appears in the documentation on the Python Standard Library on the Python website. The documentation is version specific, and the web addresses are subject to change, but the documentation on the built-in functions in version 3.3.0 can currently be viewed at:

http://docs.python.org/py3k/library/functions.html.

If this does not impress you, then you should check out the available modules in the Standard Library. There are well over 200 modules provided, each of which contains several functions and/or methods. To check out what is available, go to the index page for the Standard Library currently at:

http://docs.python.org/release/3.3.0/library/index.html.

And if that does not leave you feeling overwhelmed and awestruck, then you should check out the index of packages supplied by third party sources at:

http://pypi.python.org/pypi.

At the time of writing, this contains almost 26,000 packages.

You should now attempt exercises 11.9 to 11.13.

Exercises

11.1. Write a function to transpose two words (passed as arguments) in a sentence (as in exercise 7.9). Return the sentence unchanged if either word is not present.

11.2. Write a function to test whether a sentence passed as an argument is a pangram (see exercise 10.8). Return `True` if it is and `False` otherwise.

11.3. Write a function to calculate the factorial of an integer number n.

11.4. If I offered to give you 20 million dollars provided you give me 1 cent on first day of January, 2 cents on second day, 4 cents on the third day, and so on until the end of the month, should you accept my offer? Write a program using a function to calculate the total amount you would give me.

11.5. Write a function to randomly select a card. Use the function in a program to randomly select 5 cards (i.e. a poker hand), ensuring that no card is selected twice.

11.6. Write a function to accept the answer to a yes/no question, returning either `True` for 'yes' or `False` for 'no'. Allow the question to be passed as an argument, but assign a default prompt if no argument is passed. Get the function to keep repeating the question until it receives 'yes', 'no', 'y' or 'n', but allow any combination of upper and lower case. Write a short program to test the function.

11.7. Write a function to test whether the user has entered an integer in specified range. Provide default values for the range of permitted values. Write a program to test the function.

11.8. Write a function to test whether the user has entered a floating point number in specified range. Provide default values for the range of suitable values.

11.9. Create a module called **mylib** containing the functions in exercises 11.6, 11.7 and 11.8. Include docstrings. Test your module using IDLE in interactive mode.

11.10. Modify **number_guess2.py** (see Answers, Chapter 10) using the module created in the previous question.

11.11. Rewrite **lottery_numbers1.py** (see Answers, Chapter 10) using functions, including a `main()` function. Use **mylib** for the input of integer values.

11.12. Write a program to enter a series of non-zero integers between -10.0 and +10.0 and calculate the mean (i.e. average) of these numbers. Use **mylib** where appropriate. Write the program using a `main()` function and use other functions to simplify the program structure.

11.13. Create a module containing functions to encrypt and decrypt a sentence using the Slombovian method (see exercises 10.14 and 10.15). Write a program to encrypt user entered text, and then decrypt the encrypted form to see if you can recover the original.

Chapter 12. Sets And Dictionaries

Python provides a number of **collection** types (i.e. structures that allow multiple data items to be grouped and referred to by a single name). We saw three examples in Chapters 6 and 7 (i.e. lists, tuples and strings). In this chapter we will look at two other collection types, namely **sets** and **dictionaries**. The items in both these types are unordered (i.e. in no particular sequence), in contrast to lists, tuples and strings where the individual data items are organised in a particular sequence and can therefore be addressed using an index which identifies their position within the sequence.

Sets

A set is a mutable unordered collection of zero or more hashable objects, where 'hashable' in the present context basically means immutable. A set can therefore include ints, floats, strings or tuples, but not lists or other sets. However, there is also an immutable form of set, known as a **frozen set** (see below). Because they are immutable, frozen sets can be included as items within both sets and other frozen sets.

A set can be defined using the general syntax:

```
name = { itemA, itemB, itemC, itemD }
```

This, it will be noted, is basically the same as for a list or a tuple, except that the set definition uses curly braces (rather than square brackets or parentheses). However, unlike a list or a tuple, the sequence in which the items are entered is irrelevant as the items are stored in unpredictable manner. Because the items in a set are unordered, sets cannot be sliced or strided, nor can an index be used to identify specific items.

As an example, you could define a set using:

```
>>> fruit = { 'apples', 'oranges', 'pears', 'bananas' }
```

The contents of the set `fruit` can be displayed by entering:

```
>>> fruit
```

in interactive mode, or

```
print(fruit)
```

within a program. The likelihood is that the items will be displayed in a different sequence to the one in which they were entered.

A set can also be created using the `set()` function. If the argument is a list, tuple or string, the `set()` function will create a set containing the same items. Thus, an alternative to the above would have been:

```
>>> fruit = 'apples', 'oranges', 'bananas', 'pears'
>>> fruit = set(fruit)
```

or alternatively:

```
>>> fruit = set(('apples','oranges','pears','bananas')) or
>>> fruit = set(['apples','oranges','pears','bananas'])
```

The first line defines a tuple with four items, whilst the second converts it to a set. The alternative forms combines these operations in a single line using a tuple and a list respectively.

The `set()` function may also be used to copy an existing set. Thus,

```
>>> new_fruit = set(fruit)
```

would create a new set called `new_fruit` with the same items as `fruit`. Note, however, that:

```
>>> new_fruit = fruit
```

would simply create a new identifier pointing to the same set object as `fruit`. In this cases, any changes to `fruit` would also affect `new_fruit` and *vice versa*.

If no argument is provided the `set()` function will create an empty set. This, in fact, is the only way to create an empty set. One might assume that:

```
>>> zilch = {}
```

would work, but this in fact creates an empty dictionary (for reasons which will become more obvious shortly).

The `in` and `not in` operators may be used to test for membership. Thus,

```
>>> 'bananas' in fruit
```

will return `True`.

Sets are iterable, so `in` can also be used in a `for` loop. For example:

```
>>> for each_item in fruit:
        print(each_item)
```

will print each of the items, although not in any particular order. If you wanted to print the items in alphabetical order you could pass `fruit` through a `sorted()` function:

```
>>> for each_item in sorted(fruit):
        print(each_item)
```

The `len()` function may be used to count the number of items in a set. Thus,

```
>>> len(fruit)
```

will return 4.

One very useful feature of a set is that each item can only occur once. Thus, if you were to enter:

```
>>> fruit={'apples','oranges','pears','bananas','pears'}
```

'pears' would only be stored once, and `len(fruit)` would still return 4.

This property is often used to eliminate duplicate items in other collection data types. For example, if you had an unsorted collection of names containing duplicates in a list called `names`, you could use the `set()` function to produce a new list without duplicates. For example:

```
>>> names = ['Jim','Joe','Angus','Fred','Joe','Jim']
>>> names = sorted((set(names))
>>> print(names)
```

The `set()` function in the second line converts the list to a set, removing the duplicates as it does so, whilst the `sorted()` function puts the items into alphabetical order function. The `sorted()` function also converts the set back into a list.

Modifying Sets

Method	Use	Sample Syntax
add()	Adds item x to set s (if it does not already exist)	s.add(x)
discard()	Removes item x if it is present in s	s.discard(x)
remove()	Removes item x if present in s, or else raises an exception	s.remove(x)
pop()	Returns and removes a random item from s, or raises an exception if s is empty	x=s.pop()
clear()	Removes all items in set s	s.clear()
copy()	Copies s to new set n	n=s.copy()

Table 12.1. Methods For Modifying A Set

Although the items within a set are immutable, sets themselves are mutable (i.e. items may be added to or deleted from the set). Python provides a number of methods for modifying the contents of a set (Table 12.1).

Add()

The `add()` method may be used to add an item to a set. Thus, we could add 'pineapples' to our `fruit` set using:

```
>>> fruit.add('pineapples')
```

The set is modified *in situ*, so we do not need to allocate an identifier for the modified version.

discard() and remove()

There are two methods for removing a specified item. The difference between them is that `discard()` does nothing if the item does not exist, whereas `remove()` will raise an exception (i.e. crash the program with an error message). Thus, using `fruit` as defined above:

```
>>> fruit.discard('tomatoes')
```

will do nothing, but would have removed 'tomatoes' if it had existed, whereas:

```
>>> fruit.remove('tomato')
```

will cause python to display an error message and traceback information.

One might be inclined to opt for `discard()` to avoid having your programs crash, but there may be situations where it is important to know if you are attempting to remove a non-existent item. In such cases it would therefore be preferable to use `remove()`, but catch the exception using techniques to be described in Chapter 13. This would allow you to display a warning message whilst allowing the program to continue.

pop()

The `pop()` method removes an item from the set, but because the items in a set are unordered there is no way of knowing in advance which item will be removed. The removed item may be assigned to a variable for further processing. To give a trivial example:

```
>>> x=fruit.pop()
>>> print('The item removed was',x)
```

clear()

The `clear()` method removes all items, leaving an empty set.

copy()

The `copy()` method copies the contents of a set to a new set. Thus:

```
>>> new = fruit.copy()
```

would be equivalent to:

```
>>> new = set(fruit)
```

Set Operations

As noted, one can test for membership (i.e. whether a particular item is a member of a given set) using the `in` operator. However, sets really come into their own when they are used to compare the membership of two or more sets. **Venn diagrams** (which you may remember from you school days) provide a useful way of representing the various relationships.

The diagram below shows two sets, which we will call A and B. Each set contains two items: A contains items a and c, and B contains items b and c.

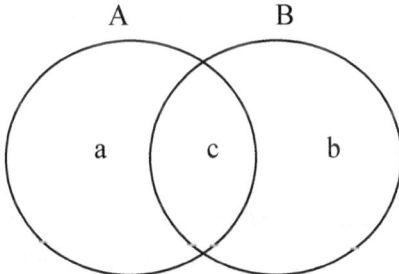

The **union** of the two sets (written A ∪ B) is the two sets added together (in this case a, b and c). The **intersection** of the two sets (written A ∩ B) is the overlap (i.e. the items common to both – in this case c). The **difference** between two sets (e.g. written A \ B) is items in the first not also included in the other – in this case a. However, the difference is asymmetric – i.e. A \ B is not the same as B \ A, which in this case would be b. The **symmetric difference** (written A Δ B) is defined as all members of either set not included in both sets (in this case a and b). Obviously A Δ B = (A ∪ B) \ (A ∩ B).[50]

The union of two sets is equivalent to logical **or**. In other words, if an item is a member of set A or a member of set B, then it is a member of the union of the two sets. Likewise the intersection is equivalent to a logical **and**. The difference is equivalent to the items in one set **minus** the items in the other set. The symmetric difference is equivalent to the logical **exclusive or**.

Union, intersection, difference and symmetric difference can be applied in Python using the operators |, &, - and ^ respectively. To illustrate, let us consider the program **wedding_guests1.py**:

```
def sprint(text,s):
    print('\n'+text+' ('+str(len(s))+'):')
    for i in sorted(list(s)):
        print('   '+i)

#Main program starts here
bride = {'Mary','Anne','Liz','Gloria','Jane','Helen',
         'Fred','Patsie','Mags','Glenda','George','Harry'}
groom = {'Jim','Joe','Anne','Gloria','John','William',
         'Arthur','Claire','Jane','Jerry','Mark','Joan'}
s=(bride|groom)                  #Union
sprint('All guests',s)
s=(bride&groom)                  #Intersetc
sprint('Common friends',s)
s=(bride-groom)                  #Difference
sprint('Bride only friends',s)
s=(groom-bride)                  #Difference
sprint('Groom only friends',s)
s=(bride^groom)                  #Symmetric difference
sprint('Revised guest list',s)
input('\nPress <ENTER> to finish.')
```

This program sorts lists of the friends of either the bride or groom before a wedding. The first few lines do not require much comment: they simply define a function which prints out a heading and the contents of a set passed as arguments. The main program begins by defining two sets: one is a list of friends of the bride and the other the list of friends of the groom. The next line creates a new set s using the or operator (|) to union the two sets. The function prints out a list of the 21 people who are a friend or either the bride or the groom or both.

The next line calculates the intersection of the two sets using the and operator (&) – i.e. the 3 people who are a friend of both the bride and the groom. Following this the minus operator (-) is used twice to calculate

---

[50] Okay, maybe not 'obviously'. However, if you check it using the Venn diagram you will see that it is correct.

people who are friends of the bride only and friends of the groom only.

At this point the bride notices that the three friends that they have in common are all female, and decides that she does not really wants them at her wedding. So husband-to-be is persuaded to drop them from the guest list.[51] The revised guest list is calculated in the final part of the program using the ^ operator to calculate the symmetric difference using exclusively or logic.

Python also provides methods for these operations (Table 12.2). The `union()`, `intersection()`, `difference()` and `symmetric_ difference()` methods each take the name of a second set as an argument and create a third set for the output. The program **wedding_guests2.py** is the same as **wedding_guests1.py** but uses methods instead of operators. The relevant section is:

```
n=bride.union(groom)
sprint('All guests',n)
n=bride.intersection(groom)
sprint('Common friends',n)
n=bride.difference(groom)
sprint('Bride only friends',n)
n=groom.difference(bride)
sprint('Groom only friends',n)
n=bride.symmetric_difference(groom)
sprint('Revised guest list',n)
```

Table 12.2 also includes a number of methods that include 'update' in their name. These do much the same as the first four methods in the table, but the results are saved to the set making the call (i.e. the calling set is changed *in situ*). It will be noted that three of the methods simply append '_update' to the name of the non-update version, but there is no 'union_update() method – it is simply called `update()`.

The final three methods in Table 12.2 test for conditions and return `True` or `False`. The first, `isdisjoint()` tests if two sets have no items at all in common; the second, `issubset()` tests whether the calling set `s` is a subset of the set `t` passed as the argument (i.e. if all the items in `s` are also in `t`); the third, `issuperset()` tests the converse (i.e. if all the items in `t` are also in `s`).

---

[51] Okay, I know the bride's logic is a little suspect: it is probably the groom's female friends that she does not know that she needs to be more concerned about! However, it is not easy trying to think up plausible examples.

Method	Use	Sample Syntax
union()	Creates new set n containing all items in s plus those in t	n=s.union(t)
intersection()	Returns a new set n containing only items in both s and t	n=s.intersection(t)
difference()	Returns items in s not in t as new set n	n=s.difference(t)
symmetric_ difference()	Creates a new set n containing every item in s and t not in both sets	n=s.symmetric_ difference(t)
update()	Adds every item in t to s (if not already present)	s.update(t)
intersection_ update()	As intersection() but result is saved to s	s.intersection_update(t)
difference_ update()	Removes items in t from s	s.difference_update(t)
symmetric_ difference_ update()	Items in s plus items in t, but not items in both, are saved to s	s.symmetric_ difference_update(t)
isdisjoint()	Returns `True` if s and t have no items in common	if s.isdisjoint(t): ...
issubset()	Returns `True` if s is a subset or equal to t	if s.issubset(t): ...
issuperset()	Returns `True` if s is a superset or equal to t	if s.issuperset(t): ...

Table 12.2. Methods For Set Operations[52]

The comparison operators `==` (equal) and `!=` (not equal) can be used to test if two sets contain or do not contain the same items.

---

[52] The names of some methods are too long to fit on one line in Table 2.12. Names is broken following an underscore should be printed on a single line, and should include the underscores as part of the name, e.g. `symmetric_ difference_ update()`.

Set Comprehensions

In addition to the methods already mentioned, sets can also be created using a set comprehension. This is analogous to a list comprehension (as discussed in Chapter 10). For example, if we needed to create a set of people with surnames beginning 'P' using a list of surnames, we could use a statement such as:

```
>>> p_set = { name for name in surnames if name[0]=='P' }
```

The syntax is exactly the same as for a list comprehension except curly braces are used instead of square brackets.

Frozen Sets

Sets are mutable, but there may be situations where you want the items in the set to remain fixed. In such situations we can define a **frozen set** using a `frozenset()` function, which behaves much the same as a `set()` function. For example, we could define a frozen set called `weekend` to contain weekend days using:

```
>>> weekend = frozenset(['Saturday','Sunday'])
```

Because a frozen set is immutable, the methods used to modify a set (as listed in Table 12.1, with the exception of `copy()`), are inapplicable. Attempts to modify a frozen set will raise an exception. Likewise, the 'update' methods listed in Table 12.2, which attempt to modify a set *in situ*, are inapplicable with frozen sets, but the other methods work perfectly.

You should now attempt exercises 12.1 to 12.7.

Dictionaries

A dictionary can be used to store a collection of data values in a way that allows them to be individually referenced. However, rather than using an index to identify a data value, each item in a dictionary is stored as a key-value pair. The **key** can be looked up in much the same way that we can look up a word in a paper-based dictionary to access its definition – i.e. the word is the 'key' and the definition is its corresponding 'value'. However, unlike a paper-based dictionary, the items in a Python dictionary are unsorted (similar to a set). Slicing and striding cannot be used with a dictionary.

The key for each item must be unique, in the same way that each word in a paper-based dictionary occurs only once. Any attempt to assign the same key to a second item will cause an error. The keys must be hashable – in effect any immutable type (e.g. strings, ints, floats or even tuples) - but the corresponding values can be any type. Given that each item has a unique key, the order in which the items are entered and stored does not matter. Dictionaries are mutable, so items may be added or deleted as required.

Creating A Dictionary

A dictionary may be created using a statement with the general form:

```
dictName = {key1:value1, key2:value2, key3:value3}
```

where `dictName` is the name of the dictionary (which in this case contains 3 items), `key1, key2` and `key3` are the keys for the three items, and `value1, value2` and `value3` are the values of the items. As noted, the keys may be any immutable type, although strings are often used, whilst the values may be any valid data type, including ints, floats, strings, lists, tuples, sets or even other dictionaries. The items (i.e. key-value pairs) are separated by commas. A colon is used within each item to separate the key (which is always to the left) from its corresponding value (to the right). Like a set, the entire definition is enclosed within curly braces. When entering the data, either in a program or interactive mode, the data items may be entered for clarity on separate lines by inserting a line feed (i.e. by pressing the <ENTER> key) after each comma.

Dictionaries may also be created using the `dict()` function. The argument may take several different forms. For example, it could take the form of a list containing a number of comma-separated tuples, each of which has two items. The first item in each tuple is taken as the key and the second as the corresponding value. For example:

```
items = [(key1, value1),(key2, value2),(key3, value3)]
dictName = dict(items)
```

or, more concisely:

```
dictName=dict([(key1,value1),(key2,value2),(key3,value3)])
```

An alternative, and arguably more intuitive syntax, is to use equal signs to link keywords with values:

```
dictName = dict(keyword1=value1, keyword2=value2)
```

The keywords should conform to the same rules as other identifiers (e.g. variable names). The keywords should not be enclosed in quotes when defining a dictionary, but they do need to be placed in quotes when retrieving data (see below).

To illustrate, the program **epl2001.py** creates a dictionary called `places2001`. This records the final positions of football clubs in the English Premier League at the end of season 2000-1.[53] The key section is:

```
places2001 = {
'Champions':'Manchester United',
'Runners Up':'Liverpool',
'Relegated':('Manchester City','Coventry','Bradford'),
}
print("Dictionary 'places2001' has been created.")
input('\nPress <ENTER> to finish')
```

The three data items in this example are entered on separate lines. The key for each of the items is a string. The values for the first two items are strings indicating the team finishing in the top two positions, whilst the value for the third item is a tuple containing strings for each of the three relegated clubs.

Having run the program, if you now enter `places2001` in interactive mode Python will display the contents of the dictionary. Note that the sequence of the data items may well be different to the order in which they were entered.

A dictionary for the following year could be created using the `dict()` function with tuples (**epl2002.py**):

```
places2002 = dict([
('Champions','Arsenal'),
('Runners Up','Liverpool'),
('Relegated',('Ipswich','Derby','Leicester'))
])
print("Dictionary 'places2002' has been created.")
input('\nPress <ENTER> to finish')
```

Note that the keys and values are separated by commas (as is the norm in tuples) rather than colons. The tuples that form the list are also separated by commas.

Likewise, using the keyword approach, the positions for the 2011 season could be defined using (**epl2003.py**):

```
places2003 = dict(
Champions='Manchester United',
Runners_Up='Arsenal',
Relegated=('West Ham','West Brom','Sunderland')
```

---

[53] Aw, c'mon ladies – don't give up on me now! The only reason that I am using a football example is that men are not as bright as you, and therefore need something that they can relate to.

```
)
print("Dictionary 'places2003' has been created.")
input('\nPress <ENTER> to finish')
```

Note that an underscore was inserted in 'Runners_Up' key name to conform with the usual rules for identifiers – 'RunnersUp' could also have been used.

There are other variants, but the above should provide you with a reasonable choice of methods. Irrespective of the entry method used, entering the dictionary name at an interactive prompt will cause the dictionary to be displayed using the 'colon' format (i.e. the first format). I will therefore confine myself to this approach when defining dictionaries in the remainder of the chapter.

Retrieving Data From A Dictionary

As mentioned, the entire contents of a dictionary can be displayed by entering the name of the dictionary at an interactive command prompt (or by including `print(dictName)` within a program). However, individual items may be displayed by specifying a key within square brackets. Thus, for example, entering:

```
>>> places2001['Champions']
```

should cause 'Manchester United' to be displayed. Note that if the key is a string, as in this example, it must be enclosed in quotes. Also, as already noted, if the dictionary was defined using the 'keyword' approach, the keyword should be enclosed in quotes (even though it was not in quotes when creating the dictionary).

It is important to note that if the specified key does not exist, Python will stop execution and raise an exception (i.e. crash with an error message). It is therefore advisable, when writing scripts, to check if the key exists before attempting to access an item. This can be done using the `in` operator to create a condition taking the form:

```
key in dictName
```

where `key` is the key to be tested and `dictName` is the dictionary. This evaluates to `True` or `False`, and can therefore be used in an `if` statement. For example, the following snippet (from **epl2001_read.py**) tests if the key 'Runners Up' exists in `places2001`:

```
if 'Runners Up' in places2001:
    print('The Runners Up were:',places2001['Runners Up'])
else:
    print('Error: Key does not exist')
```

In this case it does, so the 'Runners Up' item in `places2001` is printed. However, if the key had been erroneously specified as 'RunnersUp' (with no space), the condition would be `False` and the error message would be printed, but the program would continue to run rather than crashing with a `KeyError` message.

It should perhaps be noted that `in` tests whether a key is present. It cannot be used to test whether a specific value is present. This (in some senses) is the opposite of its use with a list, where it can be used to test if a value is present (but not whether an index is present). For example, you could not use the `in` operator to test whether 'Manchester United' is one of the data values.

The `get()` method may also be used to retrieve values in a safe manner. This takes the form:

```
dictName.get(key, default)
```

where `dictName` and `key` are as above, and `default` is a default value. If the key exists, the `get()` method returns the item value, but if it does not exist then it returns the default value. The default value could, for example, be a string containing an error message. If no default is specified, the method returns the value `None` (which can be treated as `False` in an `if` statement).

The following program illustrates (**champions1.py**):

```
import mylib
#Create dictionary
champions = {
    '2000':'Manchester United',
    '2001':'Manchester United',
    '2002':'Arsenal',
    '2003':'Manchester United',
    '2004':'Arsenal',
    '2005':'Chelsea',
    '2006':'Chelsea',
    '2007':'Manchester United',
    '2008':'Manchester United',
    '2009':'Manchester United',
    '2010':'Chelsea',
    '2011':'Manchester United',
    '2012':'Manchester City'
    }
#Query dictionary
print('English Premier League Champions')
while True:
    while True:
        key=input('Specify a year (2000-2012): ')
        if key:
```

```
            text=champions.get(key)
            if text:
                print(text+' were champions in '+key+'\n')
                break
        print("Error: Not a valid year")
    if not mylib.yn('Another year (y/n)? '):
        break
input('\nPress <ENTER> to finish')
```

The first part of the program sets up a dictionary called `champions` containing Premiership league champions for each year between 2000 and 2012. The data values are saved as strings (as might be expected). The keys are also saved as strings, although in this case integers could have been used (provided the response to the question asking for a year is converted using `int()`).

This is followed by an indefinite `while` loop that will continuously re-run the interrogation part of the program until the user indicates that they do not want 'Another year', thereby triggering the `break` statement to terminate the loop. It will be noted that the question uses the `yn()` function that we saved in Chapter 11 as part of the `mylib` module.

A second indefinite loop inside the outer loop requests the user to enter a date between 2000 and 2012. The `if key:` statement tests whether the user has typed in anything. If not an error message is printed. If the user has typed in something, the `champions.get()` method either assigns `None` or the retrieved data value to `text`. The `if text:` statement tests whether this is `None`, in which case control passes to the line printing out the error message and the loop is repeated, otherwise the value is printed and the `break` statement exits the loop.

Editing A Dictionary

As mentioned, dictionaries are mutable so it is possible to delete items, add additional items, and change existing ones.

To change an existing value, the format is simply:

`dictName[key] = value`

where `dictName` and `key` are as above, and `value` is the new value to be assigned.

The exact same format is used to add a new item, except that `key` must be a previously unused key. If the dictionary already has a key with that name, then the value to which it refers will simply be overwritten with the new value. To make sure you do not inadvertently overwrite an existing value, you could include a simple test along the lines:

```
if key in dictName:
    print('Key already exists')
else:
    dictName[key]=value
```

To delete a dictionary item (i.e. a key-value pair), you can use the `del` keyword. The format is simply:

```
del dictName[key]
```

If the key does not exist, Python will issue an error message and execution will cease. To prevent this happening, you could again include a simple test:

```
if not key in dictName:
    print('Key does not exist')
else:
    del dictName[key]
```

or more simply:

```
if key in dictName:
    del dictName[key]
```

Copying Dictionaries

If you need to make a copy of a dictionary, the simplest way is to use the `dict()` function:

```
newDict = dict(oldDict)
```

where `oldDict` is the dictionary to be copied and `newDict` is the name to be given to the copy. As in other situations,

```
newDict = oldDict
```

would just create a second identifier for the same object.

Dictionary Methods

Python provides a number of methods that may be used with dictionaries. The main ones are summarised in Table 12.3.

get()

We have already seen the `get()` method. This may be used to get the current value for a key. It therefore works in much the same as a simple `dict[key]` command except that it prevents the program crashing if the key does not exist. If the key does not exist, then the optional default value is returned. If no default value is specified, then `None` is returned.

Method	Use	Sample Syntax
get()	Returns a value / tests for presence of key	v=dict.get(key, def)
setdefault()	Returns an existing value or else creates a new item	v=dict.setdefault(key, def)
pop()	Returns a value and deletes the item	v=dict.pop(key)
popitem()	Returns value and deletes the last item in the dictionary	v=dict.popitem()
clear()	Deletes all items	dict.clear()
copy()	Copies a dictionary	new=dict.copy()
update()	Updates a dictionary with the values of another dictionary	dict.update(dict2)
fromkeys()	Creates a new dictionary using keys provided in a sequence	dict={}.fromkeys(seq,val)
items()	Create an iterable view object with all key:value pairs	iter=dict.items()
keys()	Create an iterable view object containing just the keys	iter=dict.keys()
values()	Create an iterable view object containing just the values	iter=dict.values()

Table 12.3. Selected Dictionary Methods

The following snippet uses a default value to provide feedback. Assuming a dictionary called `dict` already existed, the following snippet asks the user to enter a key and then either displays its value or a message saying that the key does not exist:

```
k=input('Enter a key:')
value=dict.get(k, 'missing')
```

```
print('The value for "'+k+'" is '+value)
```

N.B. The snippet assumes that all the keys are strings – if not they would need to be converted.

setdefault()

The `setdefault()` method is similar to the `get()` method – i.e. it returns the value for the specified key if the item exists, or else returns the default value if one is specified or `None` if no default is specified. The difference is that if the item does not already exist, `setdefault()` creates a new item with either the specified default value or `None`. The following program illustrates (**setdefault.py**):

```
dict={1:'one',3:'three'}
print('Initial dict =',dict)
a=dict.setdefault(2,'two')              #Call 1
print('Value returned by call 1:',a)
print('Dictionary =',dict)
a=dict.setdefault(2,'four')             #Call 2
print('Value returned by call 2:',a)
print('Dictionary =',dict)
a=dict.setdefault(4)                    #Call 3
print('Value returned by call 3:',a)
print('Dictionary =',dict)
a=dict.setdefault(4,'four')             #Call 4
print('Value returned by call 4:',a)
print('Dictionary =',dict)
dict[4]='four'
print('Final Dictionary =',dict)
input('\nPress <ENTER> to finish')
```

The first `setdefault()` call in line 3 does not find the requested key so it creates a new item with the default value 'two'. The second call in line 6 finds the key, so it simply returns the existing value without assigning the default 'four'. The third call does not find the requested key, so it creates a new item. However, as no default value was defined, it assigns the value `None`. The fourth call finds a key so it does not make any changes, even though the current value is `None`. To change the value we use `dict[4]='four'`.

pop()

The `pop()` method may be used to return a value for a key, but the key-value pair is then removed from the dictionary. If the key does not exist, the program will crash with an error message, so it is advisable to test if the key exists before 'popping'. For example:

```
if k in dict:
    value=dict.pop(k)
```

```
    print('Value removed is',value)
value=dict.pop(k)
```

The first `pop()` in this snippet follows a test for the key's existence. If the key exists, then the value is printed and removed; but if it does not exist then nothing happens. Either way, the second `pop()`, which does not follow a test, will generate an error because the item no longer exists.

popitem()

The `popitem()` method is similar to `pop()` except it returns and deletes the last item in the dictionary. It does not take any arguments. Given that the items in a dictionary are not stored in any particular sequence, it is unpredictable which item will be returned. The method is useful if you wish to process the items in a dictionary but do not know their keys and are indifferent to the sequence in which they are processed.

clear()

The `clear()` method deletes all items in the dictionary. It does not require any arguments. After running, the dictionary still exists, but it has no contents.

Using the `clear()` method is not quite the same as assigning an empty dictionary. To illustrate, enter the following in interactive mode:

```
>>> d1={'key': 'value'}
>>> d2=d1
>>> d3=d1
>>> print(d1,d2,d3)
>>> d1={}
>>> print(d1,d2,d3)
>>> d2.clear()
>>> print(d1,d2,d3)
>>> d1.setdefault('key','one')
>>> print(d1,d2,d3)
>>> d3.setdefault('key','three')
>>> print(d1,d2,d3)
```

The first three lines set up a single dictionary with three object references: d1, d2, and d3 – i.e. they all reference the same object rather than pointing at three different objects with the same values. The fifth line 'empties' d1, but it does this by binding d1 to a new object. However, as the following `print()` statement illustrates, d2 and d3 are unaffected and continue to point to the original location. However, when the `clear()` method is used on d2 in the next line, it actually changes the value of the object that d2 is bound to, and as d3 is bound to the same object its value is also changed. The final four lines confirm that d2 and d3 still refer to the same object, but d1 refers to a different object.

copy()

The copy() method makes a copy of the dictionary. It does not require any arguments, but an identifier for a new dictionary must be provided to receive the results, i.e.

```
newDict = oldDict.copy()
```

The copy() method makes a new copy of the values rather than just copying the pointer. To illustrate, enter the following in interactive mode.

```
>>> d1={'key':'value'}
>>> d2=d1
>>> d3=d1.copy()
>>> d1['key']='new'
>>> print(d1,d2,d3)
```

Line 2 'copies' the dictionary d1 by binding d2 to the same object as d1. The copy() method in line 3 binds d3 to a new object with the same values as d1. When d1 is changed in line 4, d2 is also changed (as it points at the same location), but d3 remains unchanged.

update()

This method updates the items in one dictionary with the items in another. If the second dictionary contains keys not in the first, then these items are added. The following simple program illustrates (**dict_update1.py**):

```
dict1={1:'one',2:'too',4:'for',6:'sex'}
dict2={2:'two',3:'three',4:'four',5:'five',6:'six'}
dict1.update(dict2)
print('New dictionary =',dict1)
input('\nPress <ENTER> to finish')
```

It will be noted that the value for key 2 is changed by update(), whilst a new item is added for key 3.

fromkeys()

The fromkeys() method creates a new dictionary using keys passed as a sequence. All items are assigned the value None or a value which may be passed as a second argument. The general syntax may appear strange:

```
new = old.fromkeys(seq, value)
```

where *new* is the dictionary you wish to create, *old* is an existing dictionary, `seq` is a string, list or tuple and `value` is an optional default value.

The `old` dictionary is unaltered by the method, and seems to serve no other purpose than to act as somewhere to call the method from. An empty dictionary {} suffices. The method creates a key for each item in the sequence. For example:

```
>>> new = {}.fromkeys('Hello world! ')
```

would produce a dictionary called `new` with 9 keys (one for each character in the string 'Hello world!' including spaces and punctuation, but ignoring duplicate 'o's and 'l's). Each item would have a default value of `None`.

items(), keys() and values()

The final three methods in Table 12.3 return a **view object**. A view object is an iterable read-only object that allows us to view the contents of a dictionary. However, given that we can view a dictionary directly, why should we bother creating a view?

One reason is that views are sometimes easier to work with, although in many instances the advantages (if any) are marginal. If we run **champions1.py** to create the `champions` dictionary, we could print it using:

```
>>> print(champions)
```

but the output is not very user friendly. Using the `sorted()` function:

```
>>> print(sorted(champions))
```

displays the keys in order but does not display the values. To see the keys and their corresponding values we need to iterate through the sorted dictionary:

```
>>> for item in sorted(champions):
        print(item, champions[item])
```

As can be seen, when we iterate through the dictionary `item` refers only to the keys. To display the values we must print `champions[item]`.

The equivalent using the `items()` method to create a view object is:

```
>>> for item in sorted(champions.items()):
        print(item[0], item[1])
```

In this case `item` refers to a key-value pair, which we can separate using indices.

A neater approach is to unpack the tuple into two variables. For example, using k for the keys and v for the values:

```
>>> for k,v in sorted(champions.items()):
        print(k,v)
```

The keys() and values() methods allow us to select out only the keys or the values in a similar manner. Thus if we wanted to print the champions in alphabetical order, we could use:

```
>>> for v in sorted(champions.values()):
        print(v)
```

This would be more complicated to do working directly with the dictionary.

One useful property of a view is that if the dictionary on which it is based is changed, the view is automatically updated. For example, if we create a view, then pop an arbitrary item, the view will be automatically updated to reflect the changed dictionary:

```
>>> c = champions.items()
>>> champions.popitem()
>>> for c,v in sorted(c):
        print(c,v)
```

Note that we cannot pop the item from a view – the view simply reflects the contents of the dictionary.

Another useful property of item and key views is that they may be used for set operations, either with other views or with sets, using the operators | (union), & (intersection), - (difference) and ^ (symmetrical difference). For example, if we had a dictionary called leaders listing countries (as keys) and the heads of state as values) and a set called female which contained countries with a female head of state, we could print a list of female heads of state using:

```
>>> for k in (leaders.keys() & female):
        print(leaders[k])
```

Likewise, to list the male (or, to be more precise, non-female) heads of state we could use:

```
>>> for k in (leaders.keys() - female):
        print(leaders[k])
```

Dictionary Comprehensions

Like lists and sets, dictionaries can be created using a comprehension. The general syntax is:

```
newD = [kexp:vexp for item in iterable if condition]
```

where `newD` is a new dictionary, `kexp` and `vexp` are expressions defining the key and the value, `item` is an item in an iterable (e.g. a key-value pair in a dictionary), `condition` is an optional condition, and `for`, `in` and `if` are keywords.

For example, if **champions1.py** had been run to create the `champions` dictionary, the following would create two new dictionaries selecting only the key-value pairs for the years Chelsea won and Arsenal won:

```
>>> chelsea = {i:champions[i] for i in champions
               if champions[i]=='Chelsea'}
>>> arsenal = {k:v for k,v in champions.items()
               if v=='Arsenal'}
```

The Chelsea dictionary is created by iterating through `champions` directly, whereas the Arsenal dictionary is created using an item view.

You could now attempt exercises 12.8 to 12.13.

Nested Dictionaries

The values in a dictionary may be strings, numbers, sequences or even other dictionaries. The latter provides a useful mechanism for setting up a simple database. The following illustrates (**contacts.py**):

```
contacts = {
    'John':{'phone':123456, 'email':'john@gmail.com'},
    'Paul':{'phone':234567, 'email':'paul@hotmail.com'},
    'George':{'phone':345678, 'email':'george@yahoo.com'},
    'Ringo':{'phone':456890, 'email':'ringo@live.com'}
    }
while True:
    name=input('Name : ')
    key=input('Phone (p) or Email (e) : ')
    if key=='p':
        print(contacts[name]['phone'])
    elif key=='e':
        print(contacts[name]['email'])
    else:
        break
input('\nPress <ENTER> to finish')
```

This program would require a bit more 'idiot-proofing' before being released for general use – as it stands, if any of the questions are answered with anything other than a valid response, the program just terminates without necessarily providing a message to indicate what the problem was.

The first part of the program sets up a dictionary called 'contacts' with four items, each corresponding to a different person. Each of these items is itself a dictionary with two items called 'phone' (containing a phone number, and 'email' (containing an email address). As far as Python is concerned there is no necessity for these dictionaries to have keys with the same names, or even the same number of keys. However, it makes it easier to recall the information if each 'record' has the same 'fields'. It will be noted that the phone numbers are saved as strings. They could have been saved as integers, but strings are preferable because integers discard any leading zeros, which would cause problems if an area code began with a zero.

The suite within the `while` loop is used to recall the information. The first question asks the user which person they want information on, and second asks the user to indicate whether that information should be a phone number or email address by entering the letter 'p' or 'e'. If a valid response is given to both questions, the program will return the requested information, otherwise it will exit the `while` loop and the program will terminate. The `while` loop will continue prompting for further names until an invalid response is given (e.g. by simply pressing <ENTER> before typing a name).

You should now attempt the remaining exercises. The final 4 exercises form a progression so, before attempting the first one, you may wish to read the others to avoid providing an over-elaborate answer.

Exercises

12.1. Using IDLE, enter the following lines in interactive mode. Try to predict what IDLE will display (if anything) before you press <ENTER> at the end of each line.

```
>>> a={1,2,3,4,5,6}
>>> b={2,4,6}
>>> a|b==a
>>> a&b==b
>>> a.difference(b).isdisjoint(b)
>>> c=a-b
>>> c&b==a
>>> c|b==a
>>> d=a
>>> a.difference_update(b)
>>> d==c
>>> c.union_update(b)
>>> c.update(b)
>>> c==a|b
```

12.2. The file **Nato.txt** contains a list of countries that are members of the North Atlantic Treaty Organization (NATO). It also contains a list of countries that are members of the European Union (EU). Write program to count and list the countries that are in the EU but are not members of NATO.

12.3. The election for leadership of the Munificent Party is hotly contested between two candidates: Gannon and Johnson. Gannon has received promises of support from representatives Hunter, Green, Driscoll, Barlow, Manning, Davies, Stevenson, Thomas, Glover, Hearn, Adams, Robinson, Craddock, Miller, Connell, McPhee, and McAllister. Johnson has received promises of support from Shaw, Dean, Glover, Smith, Hunter, English, Weir, Barlow, Wright, Newton, Knox, Jennings, Wilson, Green, Stevenson, Arnold, Adams, Brown, Hearn. Given that the number of promised votes is roughly similar, the election will be determined by those who have currently pledged support to both candidates deciding who to support. Compile an alphabetised list of the undecided voters that the candidates need to lobby.

12.4. Using the data from the previous question, compile an alphabetised mailing list of all the voters.

12.5. Write a program using sets to test whether a sentence is a pangram. If it is not a pangram, print a list of the letters missing.

12.6. The file **Supporters.txt** contains a list of football supporters, their nationality and the team they support. Write a program using sets to test (a) whether all Irish men in the sample support either United or Liverpool and (b) whether all supporters of either United or Liverpool are Irish.

12.7. Write a program to create an empty set, then allow the user to enter items one at a time until they press <ENTER> by itself. If the user enters a valid integer or a valid float, convert to an int or float, otherwise leave the item as a string. Display the final set at the end.

12.8 Rewrite the **champions1.py** example using integers for the keys (i.e. the years).

12.9. If you entered the following into IDLE, what value would be printed by the final line?

```
>>> d={5:'five',4:'four',3:'three',2:'two',1:'one'}
>>> dview=sorted(d.items())
>>> for k,v in dview:
        print(k,v)
```

```
>>> d.pop(4)
>>> d.pop(2)
>>> print(len(dview))
```

12.10. One of the problems with the solution to exercise 12.6 is that the sets are created manually. It would be very easy to accidentally omit a name from a set. Repeat exercise 12.6, but create a dictionary to contain all the information in the source file and then use this to create the sets.

12.11. The `update()` method updates the values in one dictionary with the values in a second dictionary. If items in the second dictionary are not present in the first, `update()` adds them to the first as new items. Write a program to update the items in a dictionary using those in a second dictionary, but do <u>not</u> add any new items if they do not already exist.

12.12. Write a program to accept text from the user. Use a dictionary to count how many times each letter occurs with the text.

12.13. The file **eurovision1.py** creates a dictionary showing the winning country in the Eurovision Song Contest. (N.B. Four countries tied for first place in 1969). Write a program to create a table showing the winning countries in alphabetical order and the number of times each won. Produce a second table listing countries by the number of times they won, highest to lowest.

12.14. Write a program to define a dictionary containing five names and phone numbers. (You do not need to include email addresses or any other information at this stage). Request the user to enter a name. Display the phone number if the user enters a valid name, otherwise prompt the user to try again. Provide a mechanism to allow the user to look up another phone number or terminate the program.

12.15. Modify the phonebook program in 12.14 so that instead of typing a name the user selects from a numbered list of the available names alphabetically ordered. Allow the user to enter '0' to terminate the program. Block all invalid responses. (Hint: You could use functions in your `mylib` module to do the checks).

12.16. Extend the phonebook program to provide a count of the number of names in the phonebook, list them, add additional names and phone numbers, edit existing items, and delete items. Trap all invalid responses. (You could run the suggested answer (**phonebook3.py**), without looking at the source, to get an idea of how the program might appear to the user).

12.17. Extend the phonebook program in 12.16 to include information on the person's address (as a single field) and email.

Chapter 13. Exception Handling

The python interpreter is very good at identifying syntax errors before it executes a program, but syntactically-correct programs sometimes crash due to run-time errors. This may not be too serious a problem if you are simply writing a short program for your own use, as Python will issue an error message to indicate the nature of the problem, plus some traceback information to identify where the error occurred, therefore it is usually a simple matter to fix the problem and run the program again. However, if the program is large, or is intended for use by other people, it is good practice to try to anticipate potential problems in advance and, where possible, take evasive active.

The run-time errors identified by the interpreter are referred to as **exceptions**, although an exception does not necessarily indicate an error – an exception can also arise for other reasons. Also, as will be explained later, it is also possible to trigger (or **raise**) an exception deliberately to help control program flow.

If an exception arises it will cause the program to crash unless steps are taken to **handle** the exception. This involves writing code to instruct Python what to do should an exception arise. This could take the form of providing more detailed diagnostic information about the precise nature of the exception or (better) provide a mechanism for circumventing the problem, thereby permitting program execution to continue without a crash.

If a program calls a function, which might in turn call another function, and so forth, an exception at the lowest level could be handled at the lowest level or passed up to the next level above (i.e. the calling routine). If it not handled by the calling routine, control will pass to next level up (if any) in the call stack, and so on. Only if the exception is not handled at any level will execution cease with the by now familiar error and traceback information.

This chapter looks at how these exceptions can be handled. This is often treated as an advanced topic, but some authorities suggest that it should in fact be one of the first things than new programmers should learn. It is certainly one of the first things that a programmer should consider when writing a new program, but discussion was deferred until now because an understanding of both the nature of the problems and how they should be addressed requires some knowledge of the topics covered in earlier chapters.

Exceptions

The following snippet (**exception1.py**) provides an example of a program crash:

```
numerator=5
denominator=0
quotient=numerator/denominator
```

Although it contains no syntax errors, the program crashes when you attempt to run it because any number divided by zero gives an infinite quotient, which computers simply cannot handle. Python produces an error message similar to:

```
Traceback (most recent call last):
  File "G:\Python Book\Examples\Chapter 14\exception1.py",
line 4, in <module>
    quotient=numerator/denominator
ZeroDivisionError: division by zero
```

The final two lines indicate the nature of the exception, whilst the previous line indicates where the problem arose.

In this instance the outcome could have been easily anticipated given that the value of the denominator is assigned in the code. However, a similar outcome might have arisen if the value of `denominator` was assigned by an expression or input by the user. Given that any value other than zero would work perfectly, problems of this type could easily go undetected during testing, so the onus is on the programmer to anticipate where problems might conceivably arise and take pre-emptive steps to block them.

We previously looked at other attempts to pre-empt potential problems (e.g. the **InputCheck*** programs in Chapter 10), but the exception handing facilities in Python provide a neater and more comprehensive mechanism.

Catching Exceptions

Exceptions can be caught using a **try ... except** construct. In its simplest form this consists of two keywords (`try` and `except`), each followed by a block of code:

```
try:
    try_suite
except:
    except_suite
```

where *try_suite* is the code in which a potential problem might arise, and *except_suite* is the code used to define an appropriate response. If the code in *try_suite* does not raise an exception, control jumps to the first line following the *except_suite*. If an exception is raised, the *except_suite* is processed and control passes to following line without returning to the *try_suite*.

A simple example may help (**exception2.py**):

```
try:
    numerator=100
    print('Numerator is '+str(numerator))
    denom=float(input("Enter a denominator: "))
    print('\n100 divided by',denom,'gives',numerator/denom)
except:
    print('\n*** There is a problem of some sort ***')
print('\nThe remainder of the program follows here')
input('\nPress <ENTER> to finish')
```

This assigns a value of 100 to numerator, requests a value for denom from the user, and then attempts to divide numerator by denom. The outcome depends upon what the user enters for denom. If the user enters a valid number, the program prints the result of the division and proceeds to the end of the program, ignoring the *except_suite*. However, if the user enters a zero, this triggers a zero division exception, which causes the *except_suite* to display a message saying there is a problem. After the message is displayed, control continues to the first line after the *except_suite*, which in this case is the end of the program. A similar outcome will occur if the user enters some text or any other invalid response. To confirm, run the program again and instead of entering a zero enter a letter or even just press <ENTER> without typing anything. However, although the exception handler stops the program from crashing, it does so at the expense of not processing the *try_suite* (i.e. not doing the division). This could be problematic if the code that followed depended upon the division being completed, but we will look at ways to ensure that the *try_suite* is executed shortly.

In this case the program will trap any type of exception. In other words, any input other than a valid number will be handled in the same way and produce the same warning message. Having all exceptions handled in exactly the same way may not be particularly useful. The feedback from the program above, for example, provides no indication of the nature of the problem. However, the *except_suite* can be tailored to respond in different ways to different types of exception by replacing the simple except statement with:

```
except exception_type:
```

where `exception_type` is an exception type. Table 13.1 lists some of the more common exception types, but there are many others.

Exception Type	Example
IOError	Attempt to open a non-existent file
IndexError	An index in a sequence is out of range
KeyError	A dictionary key does not exist
NameError	The name of a variable or function does not exist
SyntaxError	Syntax error in program
TypeError	Inappropriate type for a particular operation
ValueError	An argument has an inappropriate value
ZeroDivisionError	Denominator in a division is zero

Table 13.1. Some Common Exception Types

If a type is specified, the suite following it will only be processed if the exception is the correct type; if the exception is not the correct type, control will skip over the except suite. One can include several except suites, each defining a different action for a different type of exception.

If you are unsure about the name for a particular type of exception, one simple expedient is to use IDLE's interactive facilities to generate an error of the required type to see what message is displayed by the interpreter.

The except statements are checked in sequence and only the suite for the first one with a matching type is processed. The general format is:

```
try:
    try_suite
except type1:
    except_suite1
except type2:
    except_suite2
else:
    else_suite
finally:
    finally_suite
```

This checks for two different types of exception (*type1* and *type2*). You must include at least one except statement, but you can have as many as you want. The else and finally keywords and their associated suites are optional. The *else_suite* is only processed if there are no exceptions, whilst the *finally_suite* is processed in all situations. This might be used, for example, to close any open files (see Chapter 15) irrespective of whether an exception was raised or not. The program **exception3.py** illustrates some of these features:

```
try:
    numerator=100
    print('Numerator is '+str(numerator))
    denom=float(input("Enter a denominator: "))
    print('100 divided by',denom,'gives',numerator/denom)
except ZeroDivisionError:
    print('*** Error: Zero divide ***')
except ValueError:
    print('*** Error: Not a valid number ***')
except Exception:
    print('*** Error: Unanticipated problem ***')
else:
    print('Division completed without problems')
finally:
    print('\nNow proceeding to the rest of program')
print('The remainder of the program follows here')
input('\nPress <ENTER> to finish')
```

This does much the same as the previous example except that a zero division exception is specifically flagged by the first `except` statement, non-numeric input is flagged by the second `except` statement, whilst the third `except` statement catches all other types of exception. If there are no exceptions, the `else` block displays a message that the division was completed without any problems, and the `finally` block confirms that we will be proceeding to the remaining part of the program irrespective of whether there was an exception or not.

If appropriate, the same suite may be used for more than one type of exception. In such cases the `except` statement takes the form:

```
except(type1,type2):
```

Note that the exception types must be enclosed within parentheses.

If including a catch-all `except` statement, it should be placed after the suites for the specified exception types, otherwise the type-specific exceptions will not get processed.

A plain `except:` statement with no type specified could have been used as the catch-all (as we saw in **exception2.py**), but it is preferable to use:

```
except Exception:
    except_suite
```

as in this example, where `Exception` begins with a capital. Although using a plain `except:` statement is not actually illegal, it is regarded by many programmers as bad practice as it also catches some exceptions that we might not want to have handled. For example, programs can normally be interrupted using a CTRL+C, but instead of terminating execution, a plain `except:` passes this to the *except_suite* and execution would continue – which is probably not what the user wants. (You can confirm that CTRL+C is not handled by `except Exception:` by entering CTRL+C instead of a denominator in either **exception2.py** and **exception3.py**).

Using `Exception` also permits more information about the nature of the problem to be displayed. An exception, like everything else in Python, is an object. It can therefore be assigned to a variable. This may be done using the `as` keyword in the `except` statement:

```
except type as errorName:
      print('Exception raised -',errorName)
```

where *errorName* is whatever name we wish to use (although common conventions are to use the single letter `e` or `err`). This may be used to display more detailed information about the exception.

To illustrate, the following program (**exception4.py**) requests a float number to be used as a numerator and an integer to be used as the denominator in a division. Run the program and enter a letter in response to each question to deliberately raise exceptions.

```
while True:
    try:
        num1 = float(input("\nEnter a float numerator: "))
        num2 = int(input("Enter an integer denominator: "))
        num = num1 / num2
    except ValueError as e:
        print("*** Value Error -",e)
    except Exception as e:
        print("*** Error -",e)
    else:
        print("\nValid input. The quotient is", num)
        break
print('The remainder of the program follows here')
input("\nPress <ENTER> To Finish")
```

Although entering a letter in each case generates a `ValueError` exception, the error messages that are displayed are quite different and therefore more informative. Also, try entering a zero in response to the denominator question. This triggers a zero division error. This is not specifically caught in this program, but the 'catch-all' suite handles it fairly seamlessly. Indeed, if you just need to display error messages when something goes wrong, rather than take some sort of corrective action (as described in the next section), an `except Exception as e` suite may be all you need.

The **exception4.py** program uses an indefinite loop to cycle until the user enters two suitable answers. The use of `Exception`, rather than a bare `except:`, ensures that a keyboard interrupt exception will not be caught, which means that in the event of an emergency it would be possible to stop the program by pressing CTRL+C. Note the use of the `break` statement in the *else_suite* to break out of the loop when valid input has been received.

Handling Exceptions

Just flagging an exception and then continuing as if nothing had happened is not necessarily much of an improvement over a program simply crashing – in fact, in many situations it could make things worse. It would obviously be much better to fix the problem before proceeding. The strategy that needs to be adopted depends upon the nature of the exception.

For instance, unless you are dabbling in some arcane field of pure mathematics, the denominator in a division should never in normal circumstances be zero. What you need to do is envisage the exceptional circumstances under which a zero might arise and then take corrective action. For example, if you were calculating the percentage of people in each of a number of areas having a particular attribute (e.g. percentage aged over 65), a zero division might arise if an area was uninhabited. In such circumstances both the numerator and the denominator would be zero, so although recording the percentage of 0.0 is arguably reasonable, it might be preferable to assign a special code to indicate that the area is uninhabited. The Python value `None` is a suitable choice. This is what the following code (**zero_divide_fix1.py**) does:

```
try:
    numerator=int(input('Numerator value (integer) : '))
    denom=int(input('Denominator value (integer) : '))
    percent=float(numerator/denom*100)
except ZeroDivisionError as e:
    if numerator==0:
        percent=None
        print('*** Warning - Percentage set to None.')
    else:
        print('Denominator error -',e)
```

```
except Exception as e:
    print('Exception raised -',e)
else:
    print('Percentage calculated:',percent)
input('\nPress ENTER To Finish')
```

If the denominator is zero, the program checks whether the numerator is also zero and if so it assigns a value of None. There are also other things that could go wrong (e.g. entering a float number instead of an integer), but in these cases the program simply flags the error without making a correction. The *else_suite* ensures the answer is only printed if there are no exceptions.

So how can we ensure that the program will only proceed if it has a valid percentage? The solution is to place the entire try ... except construct within a while loop, and only break out of the loop when we have a valid percentage. Before looking at how our program might be adjusted, let us look at a simpler example using a similar approach (**integer_test1.py**):

```
while True:
    try:
        a=int(input('Enter an integer: '))
        break
    except ValueError:
        print('*** Not a valid integer ***')
    except Exception as e:
        print('Unanticipated error -',e)
print("\nValue input = "+str(a))
input("\nPress ENTER To Finish")
```

This requests the input of an integer value within a while loop which will run indefinitely until a valid integer is entered. If a valid integer is entered, the break statement is executed, and execution proceeds to the first statement after the *except* suites, which prints the entered value. If an exception of any type is detected, the exception is processed and control is passed back to the beginning of the loop where the user is invited to enter another integer.

This, it will be noted, is a much more elegant approach than that adopted in **input_check*** programs in Chapter 10. It also handles a wider range of situations (e.g. negative values). However, as it stands, it does not restrict the acceptable values to a specific range, but this could be easily added by using an if statement to make the break statement conditional on the value entered being within the acceptable range.

Returning now to our **zero_divide_fix1.py** program, how would we use a while loop to prevent the program from progressing until the numerator and denominator values were valid? Try this for yourself before checking the suggested solution (**zero_divide_fix2.py**):

```
while True:
    try:
        numerator=int(input('\nNumerator (integer) : '))
        denom=int(input('Denominator value (integer) : '))
        percent=float(numerator/denom*100)
    except ZeroDivisionError as e:
        if numerator==0:
            percent=None
            print('*** Warning - Percentage set to None.')
            break
        else:
            print('Denominator error -',e)
    except Exception as e:
        print('Error -',e)
    else:
        print('Percentage calculated:',percent)
        break
input('\nPress ENTER To Finish')
```

The changes required are fairly minimal. A 'while True:' line was added at the beginning and most of the remainder of the program is indented. Two break statements were added to break out of the loop when there are no exceptions or when the zero divide was fixed.

Idiot-Proof Functions

Although handling exceptions is simple, there is little point on reinventing the wheel every time you wish to do something simple like input an integer value. The obvious solution is to write the code as a function and save it, along with other commonly used functions, in a module.

The **integer_test1.py** program above, for example, might be written in a more generalised form using a function. This, along with some code to test, is shown in **integer_test2.py**:

```
def get_int(prompt='Enter an integer: ',min=0,max=1e100):
    while True:
        try:
            x=int(input(prompt).strip())
            if min<=x<=max:
                return x
            else:
                print('*** Error: Value outside range ***')
        except ValueError:
            print('*** Error : Not an integer ***')
        except Exception as e:
```

```
            print('*** Error :',e)

#Main program starts here
a=get_int()
b=get_int('Enter another integer (+/-100): ',-100,100)
print("\nValues entered: "+str(a)+', '+str(b))
input("\nPress <ENTER> to finish")
```

The function provides a default prompt string plus default minimum and maximum permitted values. These can be over-ruled as illustrated by the second call statement.

Raising Exceptions

An exception usually indicates an error, but it does not necessarily need to do so. Although beyond the scope of the present volume, it is possible to define your own exceptions. It is also possible to 'commandeer' one of the built-in exception types for your own purposes using the syntax:

```
raise exception_type('text')
```

where `raise` is the command used to raise an exception, `exception_type` is the type of exception you wish to raise, and `text` is the text you want to have displayed to explain the nature of the exception.

An example may help. The following program (**number_sum1.py**) calculates the sum of all integer numbers less than 10 that are not divisible by either 2 or 3. (It would probably be quicker to do it in your head, but the program is intended to illustrate the use of the `raise` command).

```
sum=0
for i in range(10):
    try:
        if (i%2 and i%3):
            sum += i
        else:
            raise ValueError(str(i)+' multiple of 2 or 3')
    except ValueError as e:
        print(e)
print('The sum of qualifying numbers is: '+str(sum))
input('\nPress <ENTER> to finish')
```

The key section is the *try_suite*. The `if` statement tests whether `i` is exactly divisible by 2 or 3. Only if `i` modulo 2 and `i` modulo 3 are both non-zero (equivalent to `True`) will the number be added to `sum`. If not, the `else` clause raises an exception using the syntax outlined above. When you run the program, the text for the `ValueError` exception is printed out

7 times (i.e. once for each number other than 1, 5 or 7) before the answer (13 = 1+5+7) is printed.

If you wished to sum a longer series of numbers satisfying the same criteria, the voluminous output messages before the answer could get a bit irritating. It should therefore be noted that there is no necessity to print anything. The following (**number_sum2.py**) achieves this for numbers less than 100 by omitting the *text* argument in the `raise` command, and also by using `pass` to do nothing if an exception is raised.

```
sum=0
for i in range(100):
    try:
        if (i%2 and i%3):
            sum += i
        else:
            raise ValueError()
    except:
        pass
print('The sum of the qualifying numbers is: '+str(sum))
input('\nPress <ENTER> to finish')
```

Of course, in this example the same end result could have been achieved even more concisely by omitting the whole `try ... except` construct and the `else` clause:

```
sum=0
for i in range(100):
        if (i%2 and i%3):
            sum += i
print('The sum of the qualifying numbers is: '+str(sum))
input('\nPress <ENTER> to finish')
```

but the objective was simply to illustrate the syntax.

Exercises

13.1. The **zero_divide_fix2.py** covers most contingencies, but it would not block percentages larger than 100 or less than zero. Modify the program to ensure that the calculated percentage must be within the range 0 to 100.

13.2. The program **day_of_week2.py** (Answers, Chapter 6) invites the user to indicate the current day by entering a number between 1 and 7, but there is nothing to stop the user entering a higher or lower value. Rewrite **day of the week2.py** to remove this loophole.

13.3. Write a function to accept only a valid float number (similar to the `get_int()` function in **integer_test2.py** above).

13.4. Write a function to accept an answer to a yes/no question passed as an argument. Return `True` if the answer is 'y' or 'yes' (case insensitive) or `False` if 'n' or 'no' (upper or lower case).

13.5. Write a function to accept only a valid text string in response to a prompt provided as an argument. Check for unanticipated errors. Provide an option to accept or reject an empty string.

13.6. Create a module called **mylib** to contain the `get_int()` function in **integer_test2.py**, plus the functions created in exercises 13.3 to 13.5. Include docstrings. Replace the old **mylib** module in the 'site-packages' folder.

13.7. When working with sets, the `pop()` method raises an exception if the set is empty. Devise a way to `pop()` all the items in a set without crashing the program.

13.8. Rewrite the **enter_set_items1.py** program in Answers, Chapter 12 using `try … except` constructs.

13.9. If a dictionary item does not exist, attempts to display it, delete it or pop it may raise an exception (depending on the method used). Attempts to change an item's value will create a new item if the item does not exist; whilst attempts to add a new item could inadvertently overwrite an existing one. Write functions to read, delete or pop values without crashing the program if the item does not exist, add an item only if it does not already exist, and edit an item only if it does exist. (Hint: Exception handling may help, but not in all situations).

Chapter 14. Advanced Formatting

The `print()` function, as we have seen, may be used to output a mix of strings, numeric variables and other objects passed as arguments. The default formatting provided by `print()` is perfectly adequate for most purposes, but on some occasions more control over the output format may be desirable. For example, if printing a floating-point number you may wish to display only two digits after the decimal point; or, if printing a table, you may wish to right adjust the items in a column. This can be achieved using the `str.format()` method, introduced in Python 3. This provides a very flexible mechanism for controlling the format of a string to be passed as an argument to `print()`. This chapter explores the `str.format()` method in some detail.

Replacement Fields

The syntax used by the `str.format()` method is quite complex but extremely versatile.[54] We will begin by looking at how the method may be used to create strings containing values from variables, before looking at how these values can be formatted.

If we had a string called 'name' containing a person's name and an int called 'age' containing their age, we could print this information using a simple `print()` function. For example:

```
>>> name = 'Horatio'
>>> age = 7
>>> print(name,'is aged',age)
```

Using the `str.format()` method, the third line might could be replaced by:

```
>>> s='{0} is aged {1}'.format(name,age)
>>> print(s)
```

The `print(s)` simply prints the string `s` created by the previous line using the `str.format()` method. The two lines would normally be combined as a single line:

```
>>> print('{0} is aged {1}'.format(name,age))
```

However, separating into two lines may help clarify the role of the

---

[54] It is actually described on the Python website as a 'mini language'.

method.

So what is happening in the first line? The bit enclosed in the quotes is the string to be created. Like all objects, strings have methods. The bit after the dot is the string's `format()` method. In this example, the string contains some literal text plus two replacement fields (i.e. the items in braces), whilst the method has two arguments, namely the variables 'name' and 'age'. The first of these is assigned to replacement field 0 and the second to replacement field 1. Needless to say, we are back to counting from zero. The replacement fields must be numbered from 0, but they may be in any sequence within the string. However, the arguments must be listed in the correct sequence. Thus:

```
>>> print('{1} is aged {0}'.format(age, name))
```

would do exactly the same as the previous example. (Note that the arguments `age` and `name` are in reverse sequence).

The method may also use keyword arguments. For example:

```
>>> s='{pers} is aged {yrs}'.format(yrs=age, pers=name)
```

does exactly the same as the previous example except it refers to the replacement fields as `pers` and `yrs`. The sequence of the arguments does not matter if using keywords.

As with functions, it is possible to mix sequential and keyword arguments, but if doing so the sequential arguments must be listed before the keyword ones. For example:

```
>>> s='{0} is aged {yrs}'.format(name, yrs=age)
```

If an argument is a sequence, then an index can be supplied either in the replacement field or as part of an argument. For example, if `months` is a 12-item list containing the names of the months of the year, we could print 'March' using either:

```
>>> print('{0[2]}'.format(months))
```

or

```
>>> print({0}).format(months[2])
```

Note that the index in the first example is enclosed within the curly braces for the replacement field.

Using the `str.format()` method to substitute data values in replacement fields may seem unnecessarily complicated compared with using a simple `print()` function, but its main advantage is that it provides a mechanism to control the formatting using specifiers.

Format Specification

Each replacement field can be formatted using specifiers. The specifiers for strings, ints and floats are somewhat similar, but they differ in detail so we will consider each type separately. In each case the format specification begins with a colon immediately after the number or keyword in the replacement field, followed by one or more specifiers. Each specifier is optional and may be omitted (unless it is required by another specifier), but if included the specifiers must be in a specific sequence. The entire specification is enclosed within the replacement field braces.

Table 14.1 provides a summary of the specifiers and if used the sequence in which they must included (reading from top to bottom).

	String	Int	Float
specifier	:	:	:
fill character	anything but }	anything but }	anything but }
alignment	< ^ >	< ^ > =	< ^ > =
sign		- + space	- + space
base prefix		#	#
zero pad		0	0
width	int	int	int
precision	.int		.int
type		b o x X d n c	e E f g G % n

Table 14.1. Format Specifiers

String Specifications

A string specification may specify a fill character, how the string should be aligned within a field, and the minimum and maximum field widths.

If required, the first specifier is a **fill character**. This specifies what character to use to fill out the string if the string passed by the argument is shorter than the specified width. You can use any character except a right brace, as this would be interpreted as the end of the format specification. If included, the fill character must be followed by an alignment specifier (and, if the fill character and alignment are to have any meaning, by a width specifier). If no fill character is specified, the field will be padded out (where required) with blank spaces.

The **alignment** specifier specifies how the argument is to be aligned within the field. There are three possible alignments for strings: left align <, right align > and centre ^. If a fill character is specified, an alignment indicator must be included.

The **width** specifier is an integer specifying the width of the field (in characters). If the width is larger than the length of the argument then the string will be padded out with the fill character or spaces. If the specified width is less than the length of the argument then it is simply ignored.

To illustrate:

```
>>> s='{0:*^20}'.format(' Urgent ')
```

would set s equal to '****** Urgent ******' (i.e. the argument ' Urgent ' is centre aligned in a field of width 20, which is padded out with asterisks. Note that in this example the string calling the method is simply a replacement field containing a format specification – i.e. there is no other text.

Although not included in this example, there is also an option to include **precision** specifier. This takes the form of an integer preceded by a dot. This specifies number of characters to be displayed. If it is larger than the length of argument then it is ignored, but if it is smaller then the argument string is truncated at the number of characters specified. Thus:

```
>>> print('{0:.2} tresspass'.format('Do not'))
```

would print 'Do Tresspass'. Although we omitted the fill, align and width options, these could have been included if required.

Suppose we wanted to pad out the string with dots. How does Python distinguish between a dot used to specify precision and a dot used as a fill character? The answer is that a fill character must always followed by an alignment specifier, so if a dot is not followed by an alignment specifier then it must be part of a precision specifier. To illustrate, if you enter the following:

```
>>> print('{0:.<25}'.format('And so on '))
>>> print('{0:.25}'.format('And so on '))
```

you will see that the dot is treated as a fill character in the first line, but as part of the precision specifier (which is ignored because it exceeds the length of the argument) in the second line.

You could now try exercises 14.1 and 14.2.

Integer Specifications

The format specification for integers includes the same options as a string (except for the precision specifier), plus a few additional options.

As before the first specifier after the colon is treated as a **fill** character if it is followed by an alignment indicator. The possible **alignments** for integers are the same as for strings (i.e. left align <, right align > and centre ^), plus an additional one =. An equal sign indicates that the fill should only be applied between the sign (if present) and the number. In most instances you will probably want to use blanks as the fill character (irrespective of the alignment), in which case the fill specifier may be omitted. For example:

```
>>> print('{0:=10}'.format(-12345))
```

will print '-   12345'. If you wanted to print '-12345   ' you could enter:

```
>>> print('{0:<10}'.format(-12345))
```

If you wanted '   -12345' you could enter:

```
>>> print('{0:>10}'.format(-12345))
```

(although the right align specifier > is actually unnecessary, as integers are right aligned by default).

The alignment specifier may be followed by a **sign** specifier. This has three possible values: a minus sign -, a plus sign + or a blank space. A minus sign (the default in the absence of a sign specifier) indicates that only minus signs should be shown, a plus sign indicates that both plus and minus signs should be shown, whilst a space indicates that only minus signs should be shown but positive numbers should be prefaced by a blank space. Enter the following to observe the effects:

```
>>> print('{0:-}'.format(12345))
>>> print('{0:+}'.format(12345))
>>> print('{0: }'.format(12345))
```

The next optional specifier is a **base prefix** specifier. If you wish the number to be output as anything other than a base-10 number, you need to include a type specifier (as discussed below). If a base prefix specifier # is also included, it causes the string representation of a non-decimal number to be prefixed by '0b' (binary), '0o' (octal), '0x' (lower case hexadecimal) or '0X' (upper case hexadecimal) as appropriate. Examples are included in the discussion of the type specifier. If no type specifier is included the base prefix specifier is ignored.

The nest possible specifier is a **zero pad** specifier. This is simply a zero

0. If included it results in any number shorter than the field width being padded out with preceding zeros. A field width, which is the next specifier, must of course be included. For example:

```
>>> print('{0:010}'.format(12345))
```

specifies a field width of 10, padded with zeros. The same effect could also be achieved using a fill plus a right align specifier:

```
>>> print('{0:0>10}'.format(12345))
```

but the zero pad specifier is more concise.

The zero pad specifier tends to make any alignment specifiers redundant. For example, the left align specifier in the following is simply ignored:

```
>>> print('{0:<010}'.format(12345))
```

The next specifier is the **width specifier**. As for strings, this simply specifies the width of the field. However, there is no equivalent of the precision identifier. Attempts to include one will generate an error.

The final specifier for integers is a **type specifier**. Numbers by default are displayed as base-10 (decimal) numbers, but they may also be expressed as base-2 (binary), base-8 (octal) or base-16 (hexadecimal), by setting the type specifier character to b (binary), o (octal), x (hexadecimal using lower case letters) or X (hexadecimal using upper case letters). You can also specify d for decimal, although this is unnecessary as it is the default. The following two lines print the number 1023 in a variety of ways. The second line includes the base prefix (as described above).

```
>>> print('{0} {0:b} {0:o} {0:x} {0:X}'.format(1023))
>>> print('{0:#} {0:#b} {0:#o} {0:#x} {0:#X}'.format(1023))
```

It will be noted in passing that these lines use a single argument but with multiple placeholders. Also although we included a type prefix for the decimal output in the second line (first item), it did not do anything as decimal numbers do not have a prefix.

There are two other options for the type specifier for integers. The letter n is the same as d (i.e. decimal or base-10) except that it uses the locale-specific separators when outputting the number. By default large numbers are output without commas (or other separators) to indicate thousands. However, you can instruct Python to import the locale-specific settings specified for your machine by entering:

```
>>> import locale
>>> locale.setlocale(locale.LC_ALL, "")
```

If you now enter:

```
>>> print('{0:n}'.format(-1234567))
```

Python will display '-1,234,567' (assuming that commas are the normal separator in your locale – if not, Python will display the appropriate separator for your particular locale). Note that each comma counts as a character when calculating the field width.

To remove the locale-specific settings and return to the default without separators (referred to as the C locale), you could enter:

```
>>> locale.setlocale(locale.LC_ALL, "C")
```

although there is not much need to do this as all you need to do is omit the n specifier (or replace it by d) if separators are not required.

A c specifier causes the Unicode character corresponding to the number to be output.[55] For example:

```
>>> print('{0:c}'.format(169))
```

displays the ASCII character having code value 169 (i.e. ©).

You could now attempt exercises 14.3 and 14.4.

Float Specifications

The specifiers for float numbers are similar to integers with two exceptions. The first is that you can use a precision specifier to control the number of digits to be displayed – we will return to this shortly. The second is that there are different options for the type specifier.

The main **type specifiers** are f, e and E. The f specifier causes the number to be output as a standard floating point number, whereas e and E cause it to be output in exponential form. Enter the following to observe the effect:

```
>>> print('{0:}'.format(1234.5678))
>>> print('{0:f}'.format(1234.5678))
>>> print('{0:e}'.format(1234.5678))
>>> print('{0:E}'.format(1234.5678))
```

The first two produce similar outputs, although the f specifier results in

---

[55] Unicode is an international standard that provides numeric codes for over 100,000 characters from over 90 different scripts. It is implemented by different character encodings. The most common is UTF-8, which uses 1 byte for ASCII characters and up to 4 bytes for all other characters. You can use the ord() function to identify the code for a character on your keyboard. For example, >>> ord('€') will identify the code for the euro sign as 8364.

---

the number being padded with a couple of trailing zeros. The e and E options result in a number (the 'coefficient') with a single digit to the left of the decimal point followed by the letter 'e' or 'E' and a second number (the 'exponent') with a positive or negative sign - the only difference between e and E is whether a lower or upper case 'e' is used in the output. The exponent indicates the power to which you should raise the coefficient – i.e. if the sign is positive, the exponent is the number of places you should move the decimal place in the coefficient to the right; if negative, it is the number of places it should be moved to the left. The exponential form is very useful for expressing extremely large or extremely small numbers compactly, although it may result in a loss of precision.[56]

The g and G 'general' options basically leave the decision whether to use the f or e/E format to Python. Again the only difference between g and G is the case of the letter 'e' in the output. Thus:

```
>>> print('{0:g}'.format(1234.5678))
```

expresses the number in standard floating point format, whereas:

```
>>> print('{0:g}'.format(12345678))
```

expresses the larger number in exponential form. In both cases there is a slight loss in precision.

The % specifier multiplies the argument by 100, expresses the answer in f format and adds a percentage sign. It is particularly useful when the argument is a quotient. For example:

```
>>> print('Pro government voters: {0:.2%}'.format(27/87))
```

As with integers, the n specifier may be used to output locale-specific separators. (N.B. All the other type specifiers used with integers will generate an error if used with floating-point numbers).

The **precision** specifier (which, if used, must come before the type specifier) specifies the number of digits to display after the decimal point when used with the f type, or the number of digits after the decimal point in the coefficient when used with the e or E types. It is often used in conjunction with a width specifier, but if the width specifier is not large enough it is ignored. Note that if you use the g or G type specifier, or no specifier at all, the precision value may be over-ruled. These points are

---

[56] The exponent is much more significant than the coefficient. It is amazing how many students accurately remember the coefficient to several decimal places but have no recollection of the exponent!

illustrated by the following examples:

```
>>> print('{0:10.2f}'.format(1234.5678))
>>> print('{0:10.2e}'.format(1234.5678))
>>> print('{0:5.2e}'.format(1234.5678))
>>> print('{0:10.2G}'.format(1234.5678))
>>> print('{0:10.2}'.format(1234.5678))
```

Note that if the precision specifier value is less than the number of digits to the right of the decimal point in the argument, there will be a loss of precision. Numbers are rounded up or down to the nearest number that complies with the format specification.

You could now attempt exercises 14.5 and 14.6.

Flexible Formatting

Although the arguments passed to the replacement fields are normally variables or literals that you wish to print, replacement fields may also be included in the format specifiers. This allows the format to be determined at run-time.

For example, suppose you wished to print a table with two columns of numbers and wanted each column to be the same width, but did not know in advance the maximum width required to accommodate the largest number until the program was run. The print() function for each row in the body of the table might take the form:

```
>>> print('{0:{2}.3f}{1:{2}.3f}'.format(col1,col2,width))
```

where col1 and col2 are the numbers to be printed in that row, and width is the width estimated at run-time that is required to accommodate the largest number. The format specification assumes the numbers are to be printed as standard decimal numbers (f) with 3 decimal places (.3). The value of width replaces {2} in each format specification to define the field width.

Summary

The str.format() method is normally used to provide precise formatting control over a string to be output using the print() function. However, it should be noted that the string does not necessarily need to be printed – the formatted string could be formatted for other purposes.

Also, whilst the str.format() is particularly useful for formatting the arguments that are substituted into the replacement fields, many programmers find the replacement field approach useful even when it is not used for formatting. For example, it avoids the need to remember to explicitly convert numeric values into strings using the `str()` function. Thus, many would find:

```
>>> print('My age is {}'.format(age))
```

more convenient than:

```
>>> print('My age is', str(age))
```

once they get their head around the arguably less-intuitive syntax.

It is basically a matter of personal preference, but given the additional control provided by the `str.format()` method, it is probably worth persevering with.

You should now attempt the remaining exercises.

Exercises

14.1. Predict the effect of each of the following before checking your answers using IDLE:

```
>>> print('{0:*^10}'.format(' Urgent '))
>>> print('{0:*<20}'.format(' Urgent '))
>>> print('{0:*>20}'.format(' Urgent '))
>>> print('{0:^20}'.format(' Urgent '))
>>> print('{0:*^1}'.format(' Urgent '))
>>> print('{0:>>20.7}'.format(' Urgent '))
>>> print('{0:s<6.5}'.format(' Urgent '))
>>> print('{0:!^14.8}'.format(' Not Urgent '))
```

14.2. Enter lines using `str.format()` to print each of the following:

a) ^^^ Up ^^^
b) >>>>>>>>>> Exit
c) Left adjusted   (In field, width 25)
d)   Right adjusted   (In field, width 25)
e) Left   Right   (Both within a field 25 wide)
f) ooo 000 ooo
g) >>>>>>> This way >>>
h) ~~~~Don't Make Waves~~~~~

14.3. Predict the output from line 3 onwards as you enter it into IDLE in interactive mode:

```
>>> import locale
>>> locale.setlocale(locale.LC_ALL, "")
>>> print('<{0:.>05}>'.format(345))
```

```
>>> print('<{0:>05}>'.format(345))
>>> print('{0:010}'.format(-3265))
>>> print('{0:^10}'.format(-3265))
>>> print('{0:10n}'.format(-3265))
>>> print('{0:010n}'.format(-3265))
>>> print('{0:< 10n}'.format(3265))
>>> print('{0:-> 10n}'.format(3265))
>>> print('{0:+10n}'.format(3265))
>>> print('{0:=+10}'.format(3265))
```

14.4. Enter lines using `str.format()` to print each of the following (using a field width of 12 in (a)-(f)):

a) **12345678**
b) - 12345678
c) -12345678
d) + 12345678
e) +12345678
f) 345 in hexadecimal is 0x159
g) 345 in octal is 0o531
h) 345 in binary is 0b101011001

14.5. Predict the output from the following before entering them into IDLE in interactive mode:

```
>>> print('{0:10.2f}'.format(12345.6789))
>>> print('{0:10.2f}'.format(-12345.6789))
>>> print('{0:+10.2f}'.format(-12345.6789))
>>> print('{0:+10.2f}'.format(12345.6789))
>>> print('{0: 10.2f}'.format(12345.6789))
>>> print('{0: 6.2f}'.format(12345.6789))
>>> print('{0:>6.2f}'.format(12345.6789))
>>> print('{0:.= 16.2f}'.format(12345.6789))
>>> print('{0:.=+16.2f}'.format(12345.6789))
>>> print('{0:.^+16.2f}'.format(12345.6789))
>>> print('{0:+6.2%}'.format(3/4))
>>> print('{0:>+10.2%}'.format(3/4))
```

14.6. Assuming a field width of 14, enter lines using `str.format()` to print each of the following:

a) ....66.67%....
b)   66.67%
c)   66.67%
d)   +66.67%
e) +   66.67%
f) 66.67%
g)   0.67
h) 0.6667

i)   6.67e-01
j)   6.67E-01
k) 6.67E-01
l) >>>>> 6.67e-01

14.7. Write a program to display Unicode characters within a range specified by the user as a column in a table. Display the numeric codes in decimal, octal and hexadecimal formats in the preceding columns. Place headings at the top of each column.

14.8. Write a program to accept dictionary keys and their corresponding definitions input by the user until the user presses the <ENTER> key. When the user has finished entering keys and definitions, print a table with two columns separated by a colon with a space on either side. Place the keys in alphabetical order right adjusted in the left column with the corresponding definitions left adjusted in the right column. Place headers at the top of each column. The output should look something like this:

```
              Key : Definition
------------------------------
          Albania : A country in Europe
Manchester United : An English football team
           Python : A programming language
```

Chapter 15. File Input And Output

You now have almost all the tools you require to write useful programs. However, a major limitation in what you have learned so far is that all the data required for a program must either be written into the program or else entered at run-time from a keyboard. Likewise, all the output from a program is transient and disappears as soon as the program is finished. This is okay provided you are working with only small amounts of data, but with larger amounts it makes more sense to save the data to a storage device. This chapter explains how to read and write to files.

The first section discuss how to read and write data from and to text files; whilst the second section looks at how to use binary files, with particular emphasis on Python's 'pickling' and 'shelving' options. Following this, the third section looks at how one can access information about the file system and individual files from within a program; whilst the final section deals in general terms with how to work with proprietary file formats.

Text Files

If you need to process large amounts of data, in either interactive or batch mode, the obvious approach is to read from or write to a file on a storage device. There are two main types of file: text and binary. **Text files** can be thought of collections of strings – i.e. they contain text, numbers etc. encoded using Unicode characters (normally ASCII). They can be opened and read using a text editor (such as Notepad). **Binary files** are encoded using binary digits (i.e. 0s and 1s). However, if you open them in a text editor they will appear as unintelligible 'hieroglyphics' because the editor treats each group of 8 as an ASCII character (or possibly each group of 32 as a Unicode character). Binary files are generally more compact, and can be processed much quicker, but they can only be read by an application that knows how to interpret the format used by the program that created them.

This section explains how to open text files for reading from and/or writing to within Python. The following section looks at binary files.

Opening Text Files

Before a file can be written to or read from, it must be opened using the open() function. When we run the open() function, it returns a file object which we can assign to a variable. We do not work directly with files, but indirectly through the file object. In its simplest form the open() function takes two parameters:[57]

```
fh = open(filename,'m')
```

where *fh* is the name (or file handle) that we are assigning to the file object, *filename* is a string variable or a string literal containing the name of the file (including its path if it is not in the current directory) and '*m*' is the file mode. The mode is specified by one or mode characters enclosed in quotes (Table 15.1).

Access Mode	Effect
r	Read from an existing file (default).
w	Write to a new file.
a	Append to a new or existing file.
r+	Read from or write to an existing file.
w+	Write to or read from a new file.
a+	Append to or read from a new or existing file.
t	Text file (default)
b	Binary file
U	Universal newline

Table 15.1. File Access Modes

The first three modes permit you to read or write to a file, but not both. Read-only files are represented by 'r', and write-only files by either 'w' (write) or 'a' (append). The difference between 'w' and 'a' is that if a file with the specified name already exists, 'w' will cause it to be overwritten (thereby losing its previous contents), whereas 'a' will append any new material to the end of an existing file. If the file does not already exist, both options will create a new file.

Files can be opened for both reading and writing by appending a '+' to 'r', 'w' or 'a'. Like 'r', 'r+' will raise an exception if the file does not already exist, whilst 'w+' (like 'w') will overwrite the current contents if

---

[57] There are actually five other parameters that could be specified, but they control fairly advanced features and can be ignored for the present.

the file does already exist. 'w+' and 'a+' both create new files if the file does not already exist.

The 't' and 'b' options can be appended to specify whether the file is a text file or a binary file. Thus 'wb' would open a binary file for writing. Given that if neither letter is specified the file is assumed to be a text file, the 't' option is essentially redundant and is rarely used.

The U option, when used with text files, translates the different newline encodings used by different platforms - i.e. ASCII 10 (LF) on Unix, Linux, Mac OS X; ASCII 13 (CR) on Mac pre OS X; or ASCII 13 ASCII 10 on Windows - into a standard ASCII 10 (i.e. \n). This can be useful if you need to process files created on different platforms.

The mode parameters may be omitted completely, in which case the file is assumed to be 'rt' (i.e. a read-only text file).

As mentioned, the 'r' and 'r+' modes throw an exception if the file does not already exist. This can be easily trapped using a `try` ... `except` construct (e.g. **open_read_file.py**):

```
try:
    fname=input('\nEnter file name: ')
    f=open(fname,'r')
    print('File "'+fname+'" is now open')
except Exception as err:
    print('*** Error - File "'+fname+'" not found')
input('\nPress <ENTER> to finish')
```

Opening a file that already exists using 'w' or 'w+' is potentially more hazardous as if you were really unfortunate you could accidentally delete the final version of your *magnum opus*. However, you can write a test using a method provided by the os module to test if the file already exists (**open_write_file.py**):

```
import os
fname=input('\nEnter file name: ')
if os.path.isfile(fname):
    print('*** Warning - "'+fname+'" exists. Not opened.')
else:
    f=open(fname, 'w')
    print('File "'+fname+'" is now open')
input('\nPress <ENTER> to finish')
```

The key line is the third one: the file is not opened if the method returns `True` (indicating the file already exists), but is opened if the method returns `False`. (N.B. The os module is described in more detail later).

Reading And Writing To Text Files

Once the file is opened, one can use the methods of the file object to read and write to the file. Some of the more commonly used methods are listed in Table 15.2.

Method	Use	Sample Syntax
read()	Reads n bytes / whole file	all=f.read()
readline()	Reads n bytes / whole line	line=f.readline(n)
readlines()	Reads lines into a list	aList=f.readlines(n)
write()	Writes string to a file	f.write(s)
writelines()	Writes a list of strings to a file	f.writelines(aList)
tell()	Returns the current position	p=f.tell()
seek()	Sets a new position	f.seek(p)
close()	Closes an open file	f.close()

Table 15.2. Selected File Object Methods

read()

The `read()` method, used without an argument, returns the entire file as a single string. If an integer argument n is provided, it returns the first n bytes (i.e. characters). The following would therefore print an entire file containing the first chapter of *A Tale Of Two Cities* by Charles Dickens:[58]

```
>>> f=open('Dickens1.txt','r')
>>> print(f.read())
```

N.B. If the file does not open then the most likely reason is that it is not in your current working directory. One solution is to preface the filename with the path to the folder where it is located (e.g. `'D:\\My Documents\\Python\\Dickens1.txt'`).

The above two lines could be rewritten as a single line:

```
>>> print(open('Dickens1.txt','r').read())
```

If reading a large file, the `read()` method could cause your machine to

---

[58] If you want to find out what happens next, the entire book can be downloaded from http://www.gutenberg.org/.

crash because the entire file is returned as a single string. It is therefore worth noting that the file object is iterable and can be used to print the lines one at a time without using a `read()` method. For example:

```
>>> f=open('Dickens1.txt','r')
>>> for line in f:
        print(line,end='')
```

Note that the `end` parameter is set to quotes with nothing in between. Each line in the file **Dickens1.txt** is terminated by a \n, so if we were to print it without setting the `end` parameter the `print()` function would add another \n by default, resulting in each line being printed with a blank line immediately following (producing a double spacing effect).

readline()

The `readline()` method, without an argument, returns a single line from the file. A line in this context is a string of characters terminated by \n. This is not necessarily a line as it would appear in a text editor with wraparound enabled - it could be a whole paragraph. For example, the file **Dickens2.txt** contains the same text as **Dickens1.txt**, but it contains less formatting due to the removal of the \n at the end of each line. If you open **Dickens2.txt** in a text editor and disable wraparound, you will see that each paragraph in the file is in effect a single line. The spaces between the paragraph, containing a \n and nothing else, also count as a line.

If an integer n is supplied as an argument to `readline()`, the method returns the first n characters in the line. However, the remainder of the line is not discarded - subsequent calls will each return the next n characters until the end of the line. The \n at the end of the line is returned, but no additional \n encodings are added. To demonstrate, run the following (**readline.py**):

```
f=open('Dickens2.txt')
while True:
    line=f.readline(20)
    print(line)
    if not line:
        break
input('\nPress <ENTER> to finish')
```

This chops each paragraph into strings 20 characters long. These strings contain no \n codes, so the text is printed in single spacing using only the \n codes provided by default by the `print()` function. However, the string at the end of each paragraph contains a \n, so it is printed with extra spacing between the paragraphs. Indeed, there are a total of four \n codes between the paragraphs – one provided by the paragraph with text, one by the blank line between the paragraphs in the source file and two added by default by the `print()` function.

The `readline()` method returns an empty string when it reaches the end of a file. This can be used, as in the above example, to test when to break out of a loop.

readlines()

The `readlines()` method reads the entire file in one call, but returns the contents as a list of strings. For example, the file **readlines.py** returns the contents of **Dickens2.txt** to a list called `text`:

```
f=open('Dickens2.txt')
text=f.readlines()
print(len(text))
input('\nPress <ENTER> to finish')
```

The third line prints the number of items (i.e. strings) in the list `text`. It will be noted that `text` contains 13 items – 7 contain the text in the paragraphs (including the title), and the other 6 the blank lines between them. If you run **readlines.py** on **Dickens1.txt**, you will find that there are 94 items because each line was terminated by a \n.

The `newlines()` method can take an optional argument which specifies the approximate number of characters to process. However, the specification can be very approximate, depending upon the buffer size used by the system. For example, entering 20 into **readlines.py** on my machine returns 629 characters – 20 characters brings you into the first paragraph, so **readlines.py** processes to the end of the first paragraph.

write() and writelines()

The `write()` method can be used to write a string to a file; whilst the `writelines()` method can be used to write a list of strings to a file. The string or the list are passed as arguments. Neither method adds newline characters, so if you require line feeds you need to make sure to include \n codes in the strings.

The following (**write_file1.py**) illustrates both methods:

```
fin=open('Dickens2.txt')
text=fin.readlines()
fout=open('Dickens3.txt','w')
fout.writelines(text)
fout.write('\nThe end\n')
```

```
fout.close()
print('File "Dickens3.txt" has been created')
input('\nPress <ENTER> to finish')
```

This opens **Dickens2.txt** for input, reads the entire file into the list `text`, opens **Dickens3.txt** for output (destroying any previous file with this name), uses `writelines()` to write the contents of `text` to the new file, and then uses `write()` to append 'The end' at the end of the output file. After running the program, open **Dickens3.txt** in a text editor to confirm it is as expected.

tell() and seek()

One question that might have occurred to you in the previous example is: how did Python know <u>where</u> to write the string within the output file? When the output file is write-only, each new item that is written is simply appended to the end of the items written previously. However, if a file is opened for read and write access (e.g. using `'r+'`), it may be necessary to jump backwards and forwards within a file. To facilitate this, each file object contains a pointer to the current location (measured in bytes from the beginning of the file). In the case of a write-only file, the pointer is simply incremented by the length of each string as it is added (likewise for a read-only file), but in the case of a read/write file it becomes necessary to be able to adjust the pointer.

The `seek()` method can be used to set the pointer to a new value, whilst the `tell()` method may be used to identify its current location. Thus, for example, `seek(0)` will set the pointer to the beginning of the file.

The following example (**write_file2.py**) illustrates:

```
f=open('Dickens3.txt','r+')
text=f.read()
f.seek(0)
f.write('File begins here:\n')
print('File "Dickens3.txt" has been modified')
f.close()
input('\nPress <ENTER> to finish')
```

The file **Dickens3.txt** is opened in read/write mode in line 1. The `readlines()` method in line 2 leaves the pointer at the end of the file, but the `seek()` method in line 3 returns it to the beginning. The `write()` method in line 4 writes some text at the beginning and the file is closed. Simple. What could go wrong?

If you open **Dickens3.txt** in a text editor, you will find that the original text at the beginning of the file has been overwritten by the new text. To insert the new text, you could have used (**write_file3.py**):[59]

```
f=open('Dickens3.txt','r+')
text=f.read()
print('Original length =',f.tell())
f.seek(0)
f.write('File begins here:\n'+text)
print('File "Dickens3.txt" has been modified')
print('Final length =',f.tell())
f.close()
input('\nPress <ENTER> to finish')
```

The write statement in line 5 rewrites the original text immediately after the new text. However, the length of the file, as indicated by the two calls to `tell()`, has changed and so has the location of everything in the file. Great care is obviously required when using pointers if inserting or deleting text.

close()

As illustrated in the previous examples, the `close()` method is used to close a file. It takes no arguments. Closing files is discussed in more depth in the following sub-section.

Closing Text Files

A file should always be closed when you are finished using it. This prevents the file from being corrupted by any further accidental write accesses; it also frees it for access by other programs. Python automatically closes files when they go out of scope (e.g. when a program terminates). If a file is opened in a function, the file can be kept open by returning its file handle to the main program, otherwise the file will be closed automatically when the function terminates. Nevertheless, although Python provides a high degree of security, it is probably better to close files explicitly when they are no longer required.

One common approach is to open read and close the file within a `try` block. The following snippet illustrates (**file_close1.py**):

```
try:
    f=open('Dickens1.txt','r')
    for line in f:
        print(line,end='')
```

---

[59] Note that if you are running **write_file3.py** after **write_file2.py**, you will need to re-run **write_file1.py** to set **Dickens3.txt** back to its original state.

```
    f.close()
    print('\n*** File closed ***')
except Exception as err:
    print('Error - ',err)
input('\nPress <ENTER> to finish')
```

Context Managers

Using a `try` block is effective, but cumbersome. Fortunately there is a neater approach which takes advantage of the fact that the file object is one of a special group of objects known as **context managers**. What this means is that it has a built-in method that is automatically run when the object is created with a `with` statement and likewise a second method that is run when the object goes out of scope. In the case of a file object, the second method automatically closes the file.

The above snippet could be rewritten as follows (**file_close2.py**):

```
try:
    with open('Dickens.txt','r') as f:
        for line in f:
            print(line,end='')
except Exception as err:
    print('Error - ',err)
input('\nPress <ENTER> to finish')
```

The syntax of the `with` statement may take a little getting used to, but the code is clearly cleaner and more compact.

You could now attempt exercises 15.1 to 15.4.

Binary Files

Binary files can be handled in much the same sort of way as text files, except that the file access mode specifier should include 'b' for binary – e.g. 'rb' or 'wb'. Also if reading from or writing to a string, the string should be a **binary string**. Unlike an 'ordinary' string (which contains Unicode characters – by default ASCII characters), a binary string contains bytes. A binary string can be initialised like an ordinary string, except that the first quote is preceded by a letter 'b'. For example,

```
x = b'This is a binary string'
```

Many proprietary applications use binary file formats which begin with a specific series of bytes to identify the file type. For example, the first four bytes in a GIF file are always 0x47, 0x49, 0x46, and 0x38 ('GIF8'). The following function illustrates how a file passed as `fname` could be tested to see if it was a GIF file (**gif_test.py**):

```
def is_gif(fname):
    f = open(fname,'br')
    first4 = tuple(f.read(4))
    return first4 == (0x47,0x49,0x46,0x38)
```

or alternatively:

```
def is_gif(fname):
    f = open(fname,'br')
    first4 = f.read(4)              #Binary string
    return first4 == b'GIF8'
```

The function returns `True` if the first four bytes in the file match 'GIF8', but returns `False` otherwise.

Pickling

Although it is possible to work directly with binary files, Python provides a much easier approach using the **pickle** module.[60] This allows you to save any object as a single entity, whether it is a simple object, like an `int` or `float`, or a more complex data structure, such as a `list`, `tuple` or `dictionary`. Indeed, virtually any data structure can be 'pickled' (i.e. preserved) as a single entity and recalled subsequently.[61]

Before pickling an object, you must import the `pickle` module and open a binary file.

In its simplest form the syntax for saving an object is:

```
pickle.dump(object_name, file_handle)
```

where `pickle.dump()` is the name of the function used for saving an object, `object_name` is the name of the object, and `file_handle` is the handle for the binary file. There is an optional third argument referred to as the `protocol`, which in most instances can be ignored. The protocol refers to the internal format used by Python. Although unique to Python, different versions of Python use different formats. There are currently four protocols (0, 1, 2 and 3). The newest and most compact is protocol 3, which is assumed by default, but if your file needs to be read by older programs, you may need to add the digit 0, 1 or 2 as a third argument.

---

[60] Older versions of Python also had a module called **cPickle,** which did much the same as **pickle** but faster. It is no longer necessary to specify **cPickle** in Python 3 as **pickle** will automatically use the faster routine where appropriate.

[61] Pickling is sometimes referred to as 'serialization' in other languages.

You can pickle more than one object in the same file using a separate `pickle.dump()` function for each.

To retrieve a pickled object, the syntax is:

`object_name = pickle.load(file_handle)`

The object does not need to be assigned the same name as when it was saved. If the names differ, the restored object will be bound to the new name. If you saved more than one object to the same file, these can be restored using a separate `pickle.load()` function for each. Note, however, that the objects must be restored in exactly the same sequence as they were saved. If reading a file created by an older version of Python, it is not necessary to specify the protocol as this will be detected automatically.

The following (**pickle_test.py**) illustrates some of the points above:

```python
import pickle

def main():
    save_pickle()
    read_pickle()

def save_pickle():
    outfile = open("Pickle", "wb")
    teams = {1:'Manchester City', 2:'Manchester United',
             3:'Arsenal',4:'Tottenham Hotspurs'}
    weekdays = ('Monday','Tuesday','Wednesday','Thursday',
                'Friday','Saturday','Sunday')
    pickle.dump (teams, outfile)
    pickle.dump (weekdays, outfile)
    outfile.close()

def read_pickle():
    infile = open("Pickle", "rb")
    clubs = pickle.load(infile)
    days = pickle.load(infile)
    print("\nEPL Champions 2012 =", clubs[1])
    print("The last day of the week is", days[6])
    infile.close()

if __name__ == '__main__':
    main()
input("\nPress ENTER to finish")
```

The `main()` function contains calls to two other functions: `save_pickle()` creates a pickle file called **Pickle** containing a dictionary (`teams`) and a tuple (`weekdays`). The file is closed. The `read_pickle()` function opens this file as 'rb' (read binary) but uses a different file handle. The dictionary is mapped to `clubs` and the tuple is mapped to days (i.e. both have different names than those used to create them). The two print() functions indicate that the data has been restored correctly. Note that clubs is a dictionary, therefore clubs[1] refers to the item with the key 1, rather than to the second item in a list.

It should perhaps be noted that there is a potential security issue associated with opening pickle files received from a third party. Because any type of object can be pickled, it would be possible to pickle a function that does nasty things. However, if you simply use pickle to dump and load your own data, then you are perfectly safe – unless, of course, you are up to no good and accidentally shoot yourself in the foot, in which case it serves you right!

Shelving

The **shelve** module may be thought of as a more advanced variant of pickle. Although a pickle file can contain several objects, they must be unpacked in sequence. The shelve module in contrast permits objects to be directly accessed using a dictionary-like syntax. It is probably easiest to demonstrate using an example. The following program (**shelve_test.py**) does much the same as **pickle_test.py**.

```
import shelve

def main():
    save_shelf()
    read_shelf()

def save_shelf():
    sh = shelve.open('Shelf')
    teams = {1:'Manchester City', 2:'Manchester United',
             3:'Arsenal',4:'Tottenham Hotspurs'}
    weekdays = ('Monday','Tuesday','Wednesday','Thursday',
                'Friday','Saturday','Sunday')
    sh['days']=weekdays
    sh['teams']=teams
    sh.close()

def read_shelf():
    sh = shelve.open('Shelf','r')
    clubs = sh['teams']
    days = sh['days']
    print("\nEPL Champions 2012 =", clubs[1])
    print("The last day of the week is", days[6])
    sh.close()

if __name__ == '__main__':
    main()
input("\nPress ENTER to finish")
```

As before, the first line imports the required module, in this case `shelve`, and then the `main()` function calls the `save_shelf()` function to save the data to a file and the `read_shelf()` function to read it back.

The first substantive difference is in the way in which the archive is opened. Rather than using the normal `open()` function to open a file, the `shelve` module provides its own `shelve.open()` function. This provides an interface to whatever Database Manager (DBM) happens to be on the machine. As a database may consist of several files, it is best not to provide a filename extension as the DBM will normally provide its own extensions to whatever name you provide. In this example we have named our database 'Shelf', but you could call it whatever you like. After running the program, you will probably find several files called 'Shelf' with different extensions. The shelve handle in this example has been called 'sh', but again you could use any name you wish.

Access Mode	Effect
r	Open existing database for read only.
w	Open existing database for reading or writing.
n	Create a new database for reading or writing.
c	Open a new or existing database for reading or writing (default).

Table 15.3. Shelve Access Modes

We have not used any access modes in this example as the default 'c' suits our purposes, but there are four access modes which may be added as a second argument to `shelve.open()` function (Table 15.3).

The first two options will raise an exception if the file does not already exist. The third option will result in the file being overwritten if it does already exist - note that it does not produce a warning message. The fourth option covers most eventualities and is treated as the default if no access code is specified. Note that there is no need to specify the file as binary as all shelves are binary.[62]

Returning to **pickle_test.py**, the tuple 'weekdays' is saved to the shelve using a dictionary-like syntax:

---

[62] It should be noted that the shelve access modes do not directly correspond to the file access modes.

```
sh['days']=weekdays
```

i.e. the object is saved using the key 'days'. The dictionary 'teams' is saved in a similar manner:

```
sh['teams']=teams
```

Note that the key can be, but does not need to be, the same as the object name. Unlike a dictionary, the keys must always be strings – i.e. you cannot use integers or other objects as keys.

The database is closed before exiting the `save_shelf()` function, and then reopened at the beginning of the `read_shelf()` function. Although the default access mode would have sufficed, the 'r' mode provides a little more security. The dictionary and the tuple are then restored and bound to 'clubs' and 'days' respectively. It will be noted that they are restored in a different sequence than they were stored; also the variable names are different to the originals. However, the keys remain constant. After displaying some data, the database is closed before returning to the `main()` function.

It is obviously important to know the keys when retrieving information from a shelve. This can be easily determined using the `keys()` function. For example, to get a list of the keys in 'Shelf' you could enter:

```
>>> import shelve
>>> sh=shelve.open('Shelf')
>>> for key in sh.keys():
        print(key)
```

in interactive mode.

An item in a shelve can be deleted using:

```
del sh[key]
```

where `sh` is the database handle and `key` is the key for the item to be deleted.

You could now attempt exercises 15.5 to 15.8.

Accessing File And System Information

Situations often arise where you need to need to get information about either the file system or an open file. We have already seen that the `tell()` method can be used to identify the current position within a file. Each file object has a number of attributes that may be accessed, whilst the `os` module provides a number of useful methods for working with the operating system.

Table 15.4 lists some of the more useful methods provided by the os module (which must of course be imported before accessing the methods).

Method	Use	Sample Syntax
getcwd()	Get current working directory	d=os.getcwd()
listdir()	List files in directory	aList=os.listdir(d)
chdir()	Set working directory	os.chdir(d)
path.isdir()	Test if a directory exists	t=os.path.isdir(d)
path.isfile()	Test if a file exists	t=os.path.isfile(fname)
stat()	Get information about a file	stat(fname)

Table 15.4. Some Useful os Methods

os.getcwd()

The getcwd() method returns the name of the current working directory (i.e. folder) as a string.

os.listdir()

The listdir() method returns a list of files in a directory whose name is passed as a string. If no argument is provided, the method returns a list of the files in the current working directory.

os.chdir()

This sets the current working directory to a directory passed as a string.

os.path.isdir()

This takes a string argument containing the name of a directory that you wish to test. If the directory exists, the method returns True, otherwise it returns False.

os.path.isfile()

This returns True or False depending on whether a file whose name is passed as a string argument exists.

os.stat()

The `stat()` method returns information about a file whose name is passed in a string as a special object. If you run the method on a file in interactive mode, you will see names of the attributes. You can get the value of any particular attribute by appending its name to the method. For example, to get the size of the file **Dickens.txt** in bytes, you could enter:

```
>>> os.stat('Dickens.txt').st_size
```

To view the full list of `os` methods, enter:

```
>>> help(os)
```

in interactive mode (making sure that `os` has been imported first). Some of the methods discussed above are actually in a different module called `os.path`. This is imported automatically by `os`, but to view the help on its methods you need to enter:

```
>>> help(os.path)
```

The `os` methods work directly with the file system rather than with a file object. However, file objects also have a number of useful attributes (Table 15.5):

Attribute	Type	Description
closed	Boolean	Indicates whether a file is closed (`True`)
mode	String	File mode (as specified in `open()`)
name	String	Name of the file
newlines	String	If U set, indicates the newline codes used
encoding	String	File encoding

Table 15.5. File Object Attributes

These require very little explanation, but a simple example may help. Assuming that a file has been opened with the handle 'fh', the following could be used to close it without the risk of raising an exception if it did not exist:

```
>>> if not fh.closed:
>>>     fh.close()
```

The other attributes are exactly what they appear to be. The `newlines` attribute is set to `None` unless the U option was enabled in the mode settings, in which case it indicates the newline codes used in the file.

Proprietary File Formats

Using Python to read and write data files organised using your own formats is all very well, but sooner or later you will probably need to read files created by a some external application or write data to a file in a format that can be read by proprietary programs. Like Python files, proprietary files may be either text files or binary files. Also proprietary file formats can either be 'open' (meaning details about the format have been placed in the public domain) or 'closed' (meaning the format is secret and may even be protected by patents).

There is no point in reinventing the wheel, so if you find you need to work with a proprietary format, the first thing you should do is check the web to see if anyone has made available for download any software you could use. The PyPI repository (pypi.python.org) is a useful place to begin. Should you find that your particular 'wheel' has not already been invented, you should do a second web search to see if you can find any information regarding the format that you could be use if you need to write your own programs.

Even if the formatting specifications have not been placed in the public domain, the fact that text files can be easily read in a text editor may enable you to deduce enough details about the format to extract the data you require. Binary file formats are obviously more complicated. However, a further web search may unearth a utility program to convert from the binary format you wish to read into a more accessible text format. Programs that convert from binary to HTML or XML may be more useful in this regard than those that convert to plain text, due to the fact that HTML and XML files contain formatting information in addition to the actual text (or data). The formatting details may be used to parse the file but, if necessary, can also be easily filtered out.

Proprietary application programs should also be considered as options for converting between file formats. Most of the major application programs have facilities for importing data from and exporting data to a number of common formats. Thus, for example, Microsoft Word may be used to import files created by several other word processors and also to export from its own binary format to HTML. Once the data are in a suitable text format, you can write your own Python program to extract the information you require. For example, if you wanted to process data that is currently saved as a PDF file (a binary format), one option (although not necessarily the most direct) would be to convert the PDF file into a MS Word format, read it into MS Word, save it as an HTML file and then parse it with a purpose-specific Python script.[63]

When working with numeric data, one of the most flexible formats is CSV (Comma Separated Values). Most proprietary spreadsheet, database and statistical packages provide options for both the import and export of CSV data (sometimes referred to as 'comma delimited'). CSV files are particularly suited for the transfer of tabular data organised into rows and columns (referred to in Chapter 6 as a 'data matrix'). Each row of the data matrix is represented in a CSV file by a line of text containing each the values in the row separated by comma delimiters. The line is terminated by an appropriate newline character. In addition, CSV files often begin with a header row containing the labels for each column as strings separated by commas. As in Python, strings are enclosed in quotes. Thus, a simple CSV file containing the information on the age, sex and marital status of 3 individuals might look something like this:

```
'Age','Sex','Marital Status'
34,'Male','Single'
68,'Female','Widowed'
21,'Female','Single'
```

CSV files can be readily read line by line into lists or tuples in a Python program. Likewise, it is a simple matter to export data from a Python program in a format that can be directly read into proprietary spreadsheets like Microsoft Excel or OpenOffice / LibreOffice.

You should now attempt the remaining exercises.

Exercises

15.1. Write a function to ask for a name of a read-only file, test if the file exists and then open it for reading. Read the file in the main program. Provide an error message if the file does not exist, and invite the user to either enter another name or else exit by pressing <ENTER> without entering a filename. (N.B. do not use a `with` statement).

15.2. Attempt exercise 15.1 using a `with` statement. What problems do you experience trying to read the file in the main program?

---

[63] In this particular case a simpler solution would be to use an online utility. The website www.pdftoword.com, for example, provides free PDF to Word conversions.

15.3. The program **id_add1.py** (Answers, Chapter 9) tests whether a user-entered id already exists, and if not adds it to a list of valid ids. Write a program to read and write the ids from/to a file. (The file **Valid.txt** may be used for testing purposes).

15.4. The file **Dickens2.txt** has only a newline character at the end of each paragraph. Hence, if it is viewed in a text editor without wraparound enabled you only see the beginning of each paragraph. Write a program to split each paragraph into lines having a maximum length to be specified by the user, without splitting words between lines, and insert \n at the end of each line. Output to a file called **Dickens4.txt**.

15.5. Write a program to open a file and read each byte within a user-specified range, for each byte printing the offset (i.e. position in bytes from the beginning of the file), the integer value of the byte, and (if the value is in the range 32 to 126) its ASCII character.

15.6. Adjust the program **phonebook4.py** (Answers, Chapter 12) to save the phonebook as a pickle so that any changes will be made available each time the program is run. (N.B. The file **Notebook.dat** contains some sample data that you can use for testing).

15.7. The programs **epl2001.py**, **epl2002.py** and **epl2003.py** (Chapter 12) contain dictionaries indicating the placings in the English Premier League for the seasons ending 2001, 202 and 2003. Using the data within these programs, write a program to shelve a dictionary for each year using the year as a key. Write a second program to allow the user interrogate this information.

15.8. Write a program to create a file containing userids and passwords. Make sure each userid is unique. Write a second program to invite the user to enter a userid and password and, using the information in the file, check whether the user has entered a valid combination.

15.9. Extend **open_read_file3.py** (see exercise 15.2) using the os module to display a list of files in the current folder. Distinguish between files and folders. Provide an option to change to a different directory.

15.10. For a directory of the user's choice, print the names of the files and their sizes in descending order of size.

15.11. Write a program that allows the user to enter information on the age, sex and marital status of a number of individuals. Save this information in a comma separated values (.csv) format. Check that you can open the file in a proprietary spreadsheet (such as Excel).

15.12. Write a program to read the file created in exercise 15.11.

Chapter 16. Command Line Options

In all likelihood you will have been running programs so far either from IDLE or by double clicking the program's file name in Windows Explorer (or similar). However, a third option, as identified in Chapter 3, is to run your Python programs from a command prompt. A command window can be opened in Windows by entering 'cmd' in the Run box on the Start button, whilst most Linux distros provide several options for opening a Console or Terminal window.

There are situations where running a program from a command prompt may be preferable to the alternative methods, especially if you want to run the program in **batch** mode (i.e. with no intervention from the user). This may be useful if you wish to run the same program, especially one that takes a long time to execute, on multiple sets of data. Running the program from a command prompt allows you to specify additional parameters which may be used to provide any additional information required by the program at run-time. Thus, once started, the user may leave the program to run its course without further intervention.

Two approaches are considered in this chapter. The first section explains how to use redirection operators to run programs in batch mode using a file to supply the information normally typed in at a keyboard and also how to redirect the output from a program normally sent to a monitor screen to a file for future exploration. The second section looks at how data can be provide as arguments on a command line.

Redirecting Input And Output

The simplest way to save output from a program is to run the program from a command prompt using a redirection operator to redirect output that would normally go to a monitor screen to a file.

Instructions for running a program from a command prompt are provided in Chapter 3 (for Windows) and Appendix A (for other operating systems), but they take the general form:

```
> python program.py
```

where `program.py` is the Python program that you wish to run. Depending on the setup, the `python` command can sometimes be omitted, whilst the program name will need to be prefaced by its path if it is not in the current folder.[64]

To redirect the output to a file simply add > to the command line followed by the name of the file (including its path if necessary). For example:

```
> python program.py > outfile.txt
```

If `outfile.txt` already exists, its contents will be overwritten, but if required you could retain its contents and use >> to append the new output:

```
> python program.py >> outfile.txt
```

If the file does not already exist, >> behaves exactly the same as >.

One drawback with redirecting to an output file is that if the program prompts the user for input during execution, the prompts will also be redirected to the output file and will no longer appear on the screen. The program will therefore appear to 'hang' while it waits for input. If you happen to know what input is required, you can enter it from the keyboard without the benefit of prompts, but running a program 'blind' can be disconcerting and error-prone.

One solution is to pre-save the answers to the prompts in the correct sequence, one answer per line, in a plain text file. A word processor could be used to create the file if you are careful not to save any formatting information, but it is much simpler (and safer) to use a simple text editor (e.g. Notepad).

The general syntax to run a program using an input file containing the answers to the prompts, without redirecting the output to a output file, is:

```
> python program.py < infile.txt
```

Note that the redirection operator for the input 'points' in the opposite direction to that for an output file.[65]

To read the input from one file whilst sending the output to a second file, you simply use two redirection operators:

---

[64] If running the program in Linux you need to specify `./program.py` even if the program is in the current directory.

[65] If the command file does not work as anticipated, check that it was not imported from a different operating system. Windows terminates each line in a text file with <CR><LF> (ASCII 13 + ASCII 10, or \r\n), whereas Linux and MacOS X use <LF> by itself. MacOS before version 10 used <CR> by itself.

```
> python program.py < infile.txt > outfile.txt
```

As with the program file, if either the input or output files are not in the current directory, you need to preface their name with their path.

For example, consider the following trivial example (**gossip.py**):

```
from mylib import *
pers1=get_string('Name of first person: ',empty=False)
pers2=get_string('\nName of second person: ',empty=False)
print('\n\n'+pers1,'and',pers2,'are just good friends')
input('\nPress <ENTER> to finish')
```

If run in interactive mode this prompts for two names and then outputs a message using the names. To run in batch mode, we could create a text file containing two names (e.g. **Names.txt**):

```
Anthony
Cleopatra
end
```

Note that we also need an additional entry to respond to the 'Press <ENTER> ...' prompt at the end. This could be a simple line feed, but we have added the word 'end' (which will be ignored) here for clarity. If you are only going to run the program in batch mode (or interactively in IDLE), you could dispense with the 'Press <ENTER> ...' line.

The program could be run in batch mode using:

```
> python gossip.py < Names.txt > Scandal.txt
```

This would create a new file called **Scandal.txt** to contain the output message. If you run this example, you will find that the output file includes the prompts, but not the answers supplied by the input file.

Entering Arguments On A Command Line

If there are only a small number of data values to be input, an alternative approach is to design the program to read the data values as arguments on the command line. The program **sum1.py** provides a simple example:

```
import sys
a=sys.argv[1]
b=sys.argv[2]
print('The sum of',a,'and',b,'is:',float(a)+float(b))
```

This adds two numbers using a command such as:

```
> sum.py 45.3 32.5
```

where 45.3 and 32.5 are the two numbers to be added.

So how does it work? A copy of the items on a command line is saved to a list called `sys.argv`, which is provided by the `sys` module (imported in the first line). The first item in this list (i.e. `sys.argv[0]`) is the name of the program (in this case `sum1.py`).[66] The subsequent items in the list are any other items (if any) in the command line separated by spaces – in this case strings representing the numbers '45.3' and '32.5'. All items are read as strings, so if we wish to treat them as numbers we must convert them, in this case using the `float()` function. The program, as currently set up, can only be run from a command line, so there is no need for a 'Press <ENTER> ...' line at the end as the command prompt window will remain open.

Attempts to run **sum1.py** from within IDLE or by double clicking on its name in Windows Explorer will fail because no arguments would have been provided. Also, if the user does not provide exactly two numbers as arguments, then the program will again crash. We can use a `try ...  except` construct to provide feedback on the nature of the problem (**sum2.py**):

```
import sys
try:
    a=float(sys.argv[1])
    b=float(sys.argv[2])
    c=a+b
    print('The sum of',a,'and',b,'is:',c)
except IndexError:
    print('Must be run from command line.')
    print('Two arguments required.')
    input('\nPress <ENTER> to finish')
except ValueError:
    print('Both arguments must be numbers')
```

The `IndexError` exception is raised if the program is not run from a command prompt or if two arguments are not provided, whilst the `ValueError` exception is raised if one of the arguments is not a number. Note that we need to provide a 'Press <ENTER> ...' line to allow the message to be read if caused by double clicking the program's name in Explorer.

The `sys.argv` list can contain any number of items, so we could rewrite the program to accept an unspecified number of arguments (**sum3.py**):

```
import sys
```

---

[66] Even if the program had been run using > `python sum1.py 45.3 32.5`, the value of `sys.argv[0]` would still be `sum1.py`.

```
def sum():
    total = 0.0
    for n in sys.argv[1:]:
        try:
            total+=float(n)
        except Exception as err:
            print('Error - ',err)
            print('Total not calculated')
            return
    print('Total is: '+str(total))

#Main program starts here
if len(sys.argv)>2:
    sum()
else:
    print('Must be run from command line.')
    print('Two or more arguments required.')
    input('\nPress <ENTER> to finish')
```

If fewer than two numbers are supplied (or if the program is not run from a command prompt), a message is displayed by the main program. If there are sufficient arguments, they are summed by the function in a for loop. Because sys.argv[0] is a filename rather than a number, we need to cycle from sys.argv[1].

The arguments in the above examples are simply numbers to be summed. This is a fairly trivial use of sys.argv, but other arguments could be passed in a similar manner (e.g. an indeterminate number of filenames that need to processed by a program similar to **split_lines.py** in Answers, Chaper 15). We could also add a help facility to provide help if the user enters '-h' or '-help' as the first argument, as illustrated by **sum4.py**:

```
import sys

def sum():
    total=0.0
    for n in sys.argv[1:]:
        try:
            total+=float(n)
        except Exception as err:
            print('Error - ',err)
            print('Total not calculated')
            return
    print('Total is: '+str(total))

#Main program starts here
if len(sys.argv)<2:
    print('Must be run from command line.')
    print('Two or more arguments required.')
    input('\nPress <ENTER> to finish')
elif sys.argv[1] in ('-h','-help'):
```

```
    print('\nSum4: Adds numbers together')
    print('\nRequires two or more numbers entered')
    print('as arguments on the command line')
elif len(sys.argv)<3:
    print('Insufficient arguments provided')
else:
    sum()
```

The main thing to watch is the sequence of the `elif` statements: it is necessary to catch the no arguments error before testing for '-h' or '-help'.

Exercises

16.1. Write a command line version of the program **unicode1.py** (Answers, Chapter 14).

16.2. Write a program to print out the contents of one or more text files entered as parameters on a command line.

16.3. The program **sum4.py** issues error messages if the user enters too few or the wrong type of arguments. Modify the program to allow the user to remedy the problems at run-time.

Chapter 17. Project Suggestions

That is more or less all I have to say at this stage, except to emphasise that the best way to learn how to program is to do it. To reinforce what you have learnt, you need plenty of practice. If you have any projects you want to work on, dive into them straight away. You may make mistakes, but you will get there in the end. However, if nothing comes to mind, the following suggestions will give you a chance to practice 'putting the bits together' (or maybe suggest other things you might try for yourself). Solutions are provided, but they are not necessarily the optimal solutions. You may well find that your own solutions are neater and/or more robust.

So, close the book, fire up IDLE, and start programming. Try to avoid looking at my solution until you are either completely flummoxed or have something that works.

Body Mass Index

The body mass index (BMI) provides an indication if a person is over- or under-weight for their height. The BMI is calculated by dividing a person's weight (measured in kilograms) by the square of their height (measured in metres). Many people, however, are more used to pounds and inches. Write a program inviting users to enter their height in inches and weight in pounds, convert the input values to metres (1 metre = 0.0254 inches) and kilograms (1 kg = 0.45359237 pounds), and then calculate their BMI. A BMI of less than 18.5 is regarded as indicating a person is underweight, 18.5 to 25 is normal, 25 to 30 overweight, 30 to 40 as obese, and above 40 as morbidly obese. Print a message indicating what category the person falls within and how much weight they would need to gain or lose to fall within the normal category.

A Solution

See **bmi.py** for my solution. There is little that requires any comment. The `main()` function calls three other functions (`get_data()`, `body_mass_index()` and `print_result()`) which input the data, do the calculations and print out the results respectively.

Possible Enhancement

Modify the program to accept the user's height in feet and inches and their weight in stones and pounds.

Days Calculator

Do you know how many days old you are? You may have a significant event coming up that you were unaware of – the 'big 1-0-0-0-0' or maybe the 'big-2-0-0-0-0'! Write a program to calculate the number of days that have elapsed between two dates (e.g. your date of birth and today's date). Do not forget to allow for leap years - i.e. most years divisible by 4, although bear in mind that years ending '00' are not leap years unless they are also divisible by 400. Thus 1800 and 1900 were not leap years, but 2000 was. Note also that we currently use the Gregorian calendar, originally proposed in a papal decree in 1582 to replace the Julian calendar (initiated by Julius Caesar in 45 BC), resulting in a number of days being 'lost'. The Gregorian calendar was introduced at different times in different countries, so the number of days 'lost' depends on when the change was introduced. For example, it was not introduced into Great Britain (and its possessions at the time, including Ireland and the eastern parts of the United States) until Wednesday 2nd September 1752, which was immediately followed by Thursday 14th September, resulting in a 'loss' of 11 days.

For the sake of simplicity, assume all dates are Gregorian.

A Solution

To view one solution, see **days_calculator.py**. The general strategy is convert each date into the number of days since an arbitrary starting date (selected here as the 31st December in the year 0 AD (or, or if you prefer, 0 CE).[67] The time that elapsed can then be calculated by simply subtracting one from the other. By taking the absolute value of the difference, using the abs() function, it does not matter whether the earlier or later date is entered first.

The main() function makes two calls the get_date() function to input the two dates. The dates are should be entered using a dd-mm-yyyy format (e.g. 21-12-2012),[68] although in practice it does not matter what

---

[67] Strictly speaking there was no year 0 AD. The year before 1 AD was 1 BC, but 0 makes the calculations simpler.

delimiter is used (e.g. 21/12/2012 also works). The `get_date()` function makes various checks to ensure that the date entered is valid, taking account of variations in the number of days per month and between leap years and other years. If the date passes all the tests, `get_date()` makes a call to `days()` to convert the dates to days since 31st December in the year 0 AD. The `main()` function calculates the number of elapsed days by subtracting one converted date from the other.

The trickiest part is calculating the number of days that have elapsed since 31st December in the year 0 AD. This is calculated by counting the number of days to the end of the previous year (assuming 365 days per year), plus the number of days to the end of the previous month, plus the number of days in the specified month. An adjustment is then added for the number of leap years up and including the previous year, plus a further adjust of 1 day is added if the specified year is a leap year and the specified date is after the 29th February.

PS. If you do not have a significant birthday coming up counting in days, maybe you have a significant birthday coming up counting in weeks.

Possible Enhancements

1. Extend the program to accommodate Julian calendar dates.

2. Extend the program to accommodate BC (BCE) dates. For example, the Maya dated the creation of the world to 11th August, 3114 BC in the Gregorian calendar, so you could use the program to count how old the world is in days.

3. Modify the program to calculate the date x days after a specified date. For example, when will you be 25,000 days old?

Perfect Numbers

In mathematics the divisors of an integer number are the integers that can be divided into the number without leaving a remainder. For example, the number 12 has the divisors 1, 2, 3, 4, 6 and 12 because none of these leave a remainder when divided into 12. A **perfect number** is defined as a number whose positive divisors (other than itself) sum to the number, or if the sum of its divisors (including itself) add up to twice the number.

---

[68] This is the day the world is due to end according to one interpretation (hopefully a misinterpretation) of Mayan Long Count calendar.

Thus, for example, 6 is a perfect number because its positive divisors (1, 2 and 3) add up to 6. Write a program to identify the 4 lowest perfect numbers. (N.B. The correct answer is 6, 28, 496 and 8128).

A Solution

There are probably clever mathematical algorithms that arrive at answer much quicker, but **perfect_numbers.py** gets there using a trial and error approach. Starting at 1, each number is examined in turn. The divisors of each number are identified and summed, and the sum is compared with the number times 2. Identified perfect numbers are printed, and the program continues until all four have been identified. Comments are included to help you follow the logic.

It will be noted that the fourth number takes considerably longer to identify than the first three because the number of calculations is increasing exponentially with each iteration. The fifth perfect number is 22,550,336, so it could take quite a while to get there. However, if you want to give it a try, bear in mind that the `try ... except` construct permits a CTRL+C interrupt.

Possible Enhancement

The main program includes a timer. See if you can devise a computationally more efficient solution. (Hint: It is not necessary to test every number up to n as a possible divisor of n – e.g. apart from n itself, no other number greater than n/2 can possibly be a divisor, and if 2 is not a divisor the list of possible divisors that need to be tested becomes even smaller).

CSV File Creator

As explained in Chapter 6, many application programs assume the data to be organised in a tabular format or data matrix in which each row corresponds to an entity (e.g. a person, a household, an area) and each column represents an attribute that can vary between entities (e.g. age, number of children, population density). Each cell in the table contains the attribute value for a particular entity. Data organised in this manner may be transferred between application programs (e.g. spreadsheets, database management systems, statistical packages) using a comma delimited or CSV (Comma Separated Values) file.

One way to create a data matrix is to enter the data into a spreadsheet, using the first row to contain labels to identify the attributes in each column. The data could then be exported as a CSV file and imported into other application programs as required. However, for this project, your objective is to write a program that allows the user to enter labels for as many attributes as they require, and then use these labels to prompt for the data values to be entered for each entity in turn (i.e. row by row). Include a unique identifier for each entity in the first column. Provide an option to save the data and then add additional data (i.e. more rows) on a subsequent run. (Hint: This project has similarities to Exercise 15.11, so you could use your answer to this question as a starting point).

Test the saved file by opening it in a spreadsheet (e.g. Excel).

A Solution

One possible solution is provided by **csv_creator.py**. The `main()` function calls two other functions in sequence: `open_file()` and `get_data()`. The `open_file()` function asks the user to enter a csv filename and then uses an `os.path` call to test whether the file already exists. If the file exists, the `read_names()` function is called to read in the variable names; if it is a new file, the `get_names()` function is called to invite the user to enter the variable names. After the variable names have either been read or entered, the `get_data()` function uses the names to prompt for data values. These are added to the end of the csv file one whole row at a time.

There are a few minor points which maybe deserve mention. The csv file, whether new or a re-opened file needs to be opened for both reading and writing, so the file mode indicator needs to include a '+'. However, when opening the file we need to specify 'a' to append an existing and 'w' to write to a new file.

A CTRL+C interrupt is the method used to allow the user to terminate the input of variable names and also the input of data values. In both situations the CTRL+C generates a KeyboardInterrupt exception which returns control back to the calling routine. The CTRL+C mechanism is also used to exit the program if the user accidentally opens an existing file that they do not want to append to.

The prompt in the `get_data()` function includes the current case number. This is calculated by reading the number of lines of data already in the file and incrementing by one. When working with a new file, the first record containing the variable names was read as part of the data, causing the case number to be erroneously incremented by one, but the line `f.tell()` prevents the file being rewound to the beginning, resulting in a correct case count.

Finally, when a new file is created, an additional field called 'ID' is added. This is used to store the case number. However, as the case number is calculated automatically, we do not want 'ID' to be displayed as one of the prompts when entering data. This is handled using an `if ...` `continue` construct. To maintain consistency, a similar construct is used to hide the 'ID' variable when listing the variables in a reopened file. The ID data field therefore remains completely hidden until the file is opened in a spreadsheet or other application.

Possible Enhancements

1. The file created by **csv_creator.py** are in a CSV format, but the program does not require the user to give the file a .csv extension. As a result, the file will not necessarily open in Excel (or whatever application is associated with csv files) if it has a different extension (or none at all). You could extend the program to ensure that the output file name provided by the user includes a .csv extension.

2. One advantage of using a program like **csv_creator.py**, rather than enter the data directly into a spreadsheet, is that you could build in checks to test the validity of the data values as they are entered. You could either do this by writing the checks required for specific dataset, or you could attempt to generalise the program to enable the using to set minimum and maximum permitted values for each variable that they define.

3. It is a simple matter to add extra cases (i.e. rows) to a data matrix using the program as it stands. You could extend the program to allow the user to enter additional variables (i.e. columns).

4. It is quite possible that the user may discover that they have entered some data values incorrectly. Once the data have been saved, **csv_creator.py** does not provide a mechanism to make corrections (although the necessary corrections could of course be made within a spreadsheet or other application). One possible enhancement would be to provide an editing facility within **csv_creator.py** to permit values already saved to be corrected.

5. The program currently requires the data to be entered case by

case (i.e. row by row). However, in some situations it may be more convenient to enter the data variable by variable (i.e. column by column).

Merging Spreadsheets

Many people find it useful to use a spreadsheet for record keeping purposes. For example, if keeping a record of the marks obtained by students for different modules one might set a data matrix in a spreadsheet using a row for each student and a column for each module. A separate spreadsheet might be created for each year of their studies. This all works smoothly until you need to merge the marks obtained by the students in the different years. At this point you may find that some students who were in the spreadsheet for year 1 have dropped out and are therefore missing from the spreadsheet for year 2, whilst the year 2 spreadsheet may contain some students who decided to take a year out and who do not therefore appear in the spreadsheet for the previous year 1. With only a small number of students, you can probably find and match the students common to both spreadsheets, but if your spreadsheets contain hundreds of students, cutting and pasting their details can be both tedious and error-prone. It is at this point that you will probably wish that you had used a database rather than a simple spreadsheet in the first place!

The objective of this project is to write a Python program to merge two spreadsheets into a single spreadsheet containing a combined record for each student common to both the input spreadsheets, plus two additional spreadsheets for students who appear in the first spreadsheet but not the second, and the second spreadsheet but not the first.[69]

To keep things simple, assume that the each of the spreadsheets contain a unique identifier (e.g. a student ID number) in the first column and that the records have been sorted in ascending order using this identifier. Assume also that both spreadsheets have been exported as comma delimited files. The sample files **year1.csv** and **year2.csv** may be used for testing purposes.

---

[69] Although student records are used as the example here, a similar problem often arises in other contexts. For example, when attempting to match small area census data for different census years, some small areas may be merged for some census years (to preserve confidentiality where the population falls below a threshold value) but not for others.

A Solution

One strategy might be to use the set operations described in Chapter 12, but the approach adopted in **csv_merge.py** is to simply read through both input files record by record and then sort the records depending upon whether the IDs match or not. This approach has the advantage of retaining the output records in sequence. It can also handle very large spreadsheets without any concerns about the amount of memory available.

The `main()` function calls three other functions in turn: `open_files()` which opens two user-specified csv files for input, plus three new files for output; `merge()` which sorts the input data into the output files; and `close_files()` which closes all the files at the end.

The `merge()` function is the key one. After reading the header records from each of the two input files (using `read_rec()`) and writing the variable names to the output files, this reads the first data record in each input file. If the two records have the same ID, the function `output_both()` is called to write the both sets of input data as a combined record to the output file **Common.csv**. The function then reads in the next record from each of the input files, and control is returned to `merge()` to check whether the two IDs are the same. If the ID on the first input file is lower, the function `output_one()` is called to write the record from the first file to the file **Only1.csv** and then read in the next record from the first input file only, before returning control to `merge()`. If the ID on the second input file is lower, `output_two()` is called to write the record from the second file to the file **Only2.csv**.

The procedure continues to sort the data into the three output files until the end of one of the input files is eventually reached. At this point it gets a bit messy. If we reach the end of both input files at the same time (i.e. if the final record on each has the same ID), we simply need to close the files. However, if we reach the end of one file before the other we need to copy the remaining items from the other file to the appropriate output file. The `merge()` function contains three sets of similar code to handle these contingencies. Although this works, I suspect there may be a neater way to do this.

Possible Enhancements

1. Accommodate situations where the identifier field is not in column 1.

2. Allow the user to specify the names for the output files.

3. Extend the program to work with unsorted records.

4. Output all the data to a single file, leaving the appropriate cells blank when a record is not common to both input files.

5. Try writing an alternative solution using sets. Do not forget to sort the records in the output files.

Suduko problem solver

The objective of this project is to write a program to solve Sukoko puzzles. For those who are unfamiliar with Sudoko, play takes place on a grid containing 9 rows and 9 columns. Each row and each column contains 9 cells (or squares), giving a total of 81 cells. The grid is further divided into 9 blocks (regions or boxes), each containing 3 rows and 3 columns or 9 cells - i.e. rows 1 to 3 and columns 1 to 3 represent one block of 9 cells, rows 1 to 3 and columns 4 to 6 form a second block and so forth.

A number of cells are assigned initial starting values and the objective of the puzzle is to fill in the blank cells in such a way that each of the digits 1 to 9 only occur once in each row, once in each column, and once in each block. Most newspapers and magazines provide puzzles with more detailed instructions.

Your program should provide a facility for entering the initial starting values.

Hint 1: The strategy to adopt may not reflect the most efficient method if you were to solve the problem by hand. Bear in mind that computers are very good at doing repetitive tasks very quickly, whereas humans tend to seek out more efficient solutions. If you are stuck, the solution below provides additional hints.

Hint 2: Begin by considering all the possible values for each cell and eliminate those that are not possible. Create a 9x9 matrix, fill each square with the possible numbers 1..9, then eliminate the impossible ones. If only one value remains in a cell, then this must be the value for the cell. This in itself will not necessarily provide a solution, but it will reduce the number of alternatives that need to be tested.

Hint 3: Having eliminated as many wrong possibilities as possible, identify values that occur only once in a row, column or grid. If a value has only one possible location, then that must be where it is located, even if the cell appears to have other possible values.

Hint 4: For difficult problems it may be necessary to resort to trial and error. Select a cell with only two possible values, select one of them and run to see if you get a solution. If not try the other value.

There may be other strategies. For example, if two cells in the same row, column or block have only two possible values that are the same, then no other cells in the same row, column or block cannot have these values.

If you think you have a solution, try it out on the following puzzle.

3	1	5					6	
9								
4	6	2	3		1		7	8
1			5	6		9		
6		4	2	9	7			
	3	9	4	7				6
7		3	8	4	6	5	1	
				3				7
8	4			5		2	3	9

A Solution

The program **sudoko.py** provides a solution. The remainder of this section explains how this was derived.

It is useful to break the project into a number of discrete steps:

1. Decide how the grid is going to be stored.
2. Decide how the grid is going to be displayed.
3. Decide how the initial starting values are to be input.
4. Decide how the puzzle is to be solved.

The fourth step is obviously the key one, but let us consider the other three first.

One solution to the first step is to use a list to store a 9 by 9 matrix, although an alternative would be to create a dictionary with keys called 11, 12, through to 98, 99. One slight drawback with using a list is that Python numbers the rows and columns in the matrix from 0 to 8, whereas the end-user would probably be more comfortable referring to them as rows and columns 1 to 9. One option might be to create a 10 by 10 matrix and just ignore the first row and first column (or, depending upon the method decided upon for step 4, possibly use them to store summary information for each row and column). However, I have opted for a 9 by 9 matrix (see **sudoko1.py**) using Python numbering (although to the user it will appear to number the rows and columns 1 to 9). The createGrid() function sets up a 9 by 9 matrix in which each cell is initially assigned a value 0 (which will be used to indicate that the value of the cell is currently blank or undetermined). The main thing to watch out for is that deepcopy() is used to duplicate the rows (otherwise they would all refer to the same row object and any change made to a row would be replicated in all the other rows). The deepcopy() function requires the copy module to be imported. The print() function at the end is simply to test whether things appear to working correctly and will be improved upon in the second step.

Step 2 displays the grid using a function called printGrid() - see **sudoko2.py**. This prints the grid in a crude but reasonably clear format, but may require some adjustment to the spacing depending upon your output device. Note that the empty cells are displayed as blanks rather than using the digit 0. The appearance of the grid could obviously be improved using graphics modules. This is explained in the companion volume Object Python, but for present we will make do with text output.

Step 3 allows the user to input the starting values and is fairly straightforward (see **sudoko3.py**). The initialise() function prompts the user to enter the row number, column number and value for each known cell. The getValue() function checks that the responses to each of the prompts is a digit in the range 0 to 9, otherwise the user is prompted again. It is assumed that the user will number the rows and columns starting from 1, therefore the return statement subtracts 1 from each answer to convert to Python row and column numbers.

To terminate input, the user may enter a zero for either the row or column number. This will return control to the main program which then calls `printGrid()` to display the current assignments. The `yn()` function is then called to ask whether the grid has been set up correctly. Answering 'n' (or 'N') for 'no' calls the `initialise()` function again, allowing the user to enter any missing values or correct existing values by either inserting the correct value or a zero to indicate a blank cell. Note that the entire table does not need to be entered in one go: by answering the question 'n' the user may input the cell values in smaller amounts (e.g. one row at a time) and display the grid for checking purposes. If a cell contains the wrong value, you can simply overwrite it with the correct value (or 0 if the cell should be blank). When the user answers 'y' or 'Y' to indicate the grid is correctly set up, the program will attempt solve the puzzle.

This brings us to step 4. Most people, when solving a Sudoko problem manually, normally use a combination of strategies. Some strategies entail attempting to identify the only possible locations for a specific number. For example, some people begin by working through the grid identifying the only possible positions of as many 1s as possible, then repeat the process for 2s, and then each of the other numbers. Other strategies proceed by a process of elimination – i.e. invalid responses for each cell are eliminated one by one until one is left with only one possible value. This program adopts the latter strategy – i.e. it proceeds by a process of elimination.

The basic strategy can be broken down into a number of steps as follows:

(a) Identify all the possible values for each cell not already assigned a value – i.e. for each cell eliminate as possibilities all values known to occur elsewhere in the same row, column or block.

(b) Identify any cells which have only one possible value. This value must be the correct value for that cell and therefore forms part of the solution.

(c) Check the cells in each row to see if a possible value occurs only once. For example, if only one cell in a row contains, say, a 3 as one of its possible values, then even if the cell has other possible values the correct value must be 3 as there must be a 3 in every row.

(d) Repeat step (c) for each column – i.e. if a particular value is only found in one cell in a column, then that must be the value for that cell.

(e) Repeat the process for each grid.

If values of any cells are identified in steps (c), (d) or (e), then we need to return to step (a) to update the list of possible values for the remaining cells and then repeat the subsequent steps. Cycling through the above steps will provide a solution to most simple and medium difficulty puzzles, but some of the more difficult puzzles may prove more intransigent and require additional steps. These are discussed later, but we will implement the above first.

Step 4(a) is implemented by the addition of three lines to the main program in **sudoko4.py.** The first makes a call to the `createGrid()` function which was previously used to create the 9 by 9 grid to contain the eventual solution, but on this occasion it creates a second 9 by 9 list called `possibles` to hold the possible values in each cell. Each cell is initially populated by a string containing the digits 1 to 9. Note that the `createGrid()` function was modified slightly to allow the initial values to be passed as an argument.

Once the `possibles` list has been created, the `updatePossibles()` function is called to eliminate values known to be impossible. This searches the `grid` for known values. Each time it finds a cell with a known value, the string containing the possible values in the corresponding cell in the `possibles` list is set to an empty string to indicate that the value of a cell has been determined. The `updatePossibles()` function then calls the `adjustRow()` function to remove the known value from the possible values of each other cell in the same row. If the value is currently recorded as possible in a cell, the `removeValue()` function is called to remove it. The `updatePossibles()` function then calls the `adjustCol()` and the `adjustBlock()` functions to remove the known value from the list of possible values for other cells in the same column or same block in a similar manner.

The final line in **sudoko4.py** simply prints out the `possibles` list in case you wish to check the program is working as intended, but it will be removed in later versions.

Having eliminated some of the values as possibilities for each cell, we may find that some cells have only one possible value remaining. Step 4(b) therefore entails identifying which (if any) of the cells in the list contain only one possible value. If a cell has only one possible value remaining, then that must be the correct value for that cell. We can add these values to the grid of known values, and adjust the possible values in the other cells in the same row, column and block accordingly. This is implemented in **sudoko5.py**.

The `soloCells()` function checks each cell in the `possibles` list. If the string in a cell has a length of 1, meaning there is only one possible value, that value is added to the grid of known values (`grid`), and the string in `possibles` is changed to an empty string.

If we find a cell with only one possible value, then we must also remove that value as a possibility in the other cells in same row, column and block – i.e. we need to call the `updatePossibles()` function again. One way to do this is to place the `updatePossibles()` function and the `soloCells()` function in an indefinite loop in the main program, but use a Boolean variable (`change`) to record whether any changes were made in the call to `soloCells()`. If a change was made, then the main program transfers control back to the beginning of the loop using a `continue` statement and `updatePossibles()` makes the required changes to the list of possible values in the remaining cells. This may create a few more cells with only one possible value, which will then be detected in the next cycle of the loop. If no changes are made by `soloCells()` then we proceed to the remainder of the loop. At present this simply prints out the current list of possible values for checking purposes, but it is where we will locate the code for some additional strategies in the next stage.

If we are lucky the puzzle may be solved simply by looping through the `updatePossibles()` and `soloCells()` functions. However, we need to add some mechanism to tell us whether the puzzle has in fact been solved, otherwise we will keep looping indefinitely. This is implemented by adding a Boolean variable (`complete`) to the `updatePossibles()` function. This returns a value of `True` if all the cells in `grid` have a non-zero value. If complete is `True`, we break out of the loop in the main program and call the `printGrid()` function to print the solution.

The likelihood is that the puzzle will still require some additional strategies to reduce the number of possible values in the remaining cells. In **sudoko6.py** the `thinRow()` function checks whether any of the possible values occurs only once in a row. If so, then that must the correct value for the cell, even if the cell appears to have other possible values. A similar logic is applied in **sudoko7.py**, which adds the `thinCol()` function to check each column; whilst **sudoko8.py** adds the `thinBlock()` function to do the same for each block.

At this stage our program should be capable of solving most Sudoko puzzles. However, a few especially difficult puzzles may prove more resistant. If tackling the puzzle manually, there are various other strategies that could be applied. For example, if two cells in a block have, say 1 and 2 as the only possible values, and two other cells have 1, 2, 3 and 4 as possible values, we can conclude that the values 1 and 2 are not realistic options for the second pair of cells because the first pair of cells must have the values 1 and 2 (although we may not know which one is 1 and which is 2) and therefore the values 1 and 2 are not available to the second pair of cells. However, these rules are difficult to program and do not in general get us very far. We may as well therefore proceed straight to the Sudoko-puzzler's strategy of last resort, namely trial and error.

Programming a trial and error approach is quite complex, but we can break it down into a number of sub-steps:

(a) Identify a cell whose value is currently unknown to be used for the test.

(b) Assign a value to the identified cell from the its list of possible values.

(c) Using the test value, run the problem using the procedures outlined above for step 4 until we can go no further.

(d) Test the result. There are three possible outcomes. First, if we are lucky, the problem may be solved and we can proceed to print out the solution. Second, we may be able to deduce that the test value was incorrect. If so, we need to back-pedal and test a different value for the selected cell. Third, we may have no evidence that the value being tested is wrong, but we may not yet have a solution. In such circumstances, we need to test the values for a second cell, using a similar trial and error approach.

Given that there is a degree of overlap between (c) and the main program, the first thing we need to decide upon is whether to subcontract the trial and error process to a function or try to build it into the existing main program. Although it entails a degree of duplication, the approach adopted here (**sudoko9.py**) is to subcontract the entire trial and error process to a function called explore().[70] This is called from the main program. Control is not returned to the main program until the problem is solved (assuming that it does in fact have a solution) – i.e. the trial and error operations are separate to and subsequent to the other 4 steps.

The explore() function begins by creating three lists to keep track of progress: branches records the location of the test cells and the values to be tested; gStore records the current status of grid at the beginning of a

---

[70] **Sudoko9.py** is the final version, and is the same as **sudoko.py** referred to previously.

test so that we can return to the same point later if need be; and `pStore` does the same for the `possibles` list. After initialising two Boolean variables (`found` and `solved`) to `False`, the remainder of the function is placed in an indefinite loop.

The loop begins by calling the `findBranch()` function to find a suitable test cell (step (a)). In theory any cell containing two or more possibles is an option, but the `findBranch()` function confines it search to cells having exactly two possible values remaining. The reason is that if we can dismiss one of the values as a possibility, then we know that the other value must be correct. The function searches the `possibles` list row by row, until it finds a cell with two possibilities. A list containg the row and column numbers and the two possible values is added to the `branches` list, and a copy of the `grid` and `possibles` lists are added to `gStore` and `pStore` respectively.

It should be noted that if no cells in the `possibles` list contain two possible values, then the problem is aborted without searching further for a solution. However, it is difficult to imagine the circumstances where this might arise (provided the problem has a solution). Indeed extensive testing on even the most difficult problems has so far failed to produce a solution. However, it must be regarded as a remote possibility, and therefore a potential loophole in the program.

Having identified a branch (or 2-value cell), the step (b) is to try one of the values. The `testSetup()` function reads the row and column number of the test cell in `branches` and the higher of the two possible values for the cell. (If the higher value had been tested previously and rejected, then the function would select the lower value). The `grid` and `possibles` lists are reset to the values saved in `gStore` and `pStore` This is unnecessary when running the first test, but a reset is necessary if other values have been tested and rejected. The test value is assigned to the cell in `grid` and the corresponding cell in `possibles` is blanked.

Having assigned the test value, step (c) is to call `workThrough()` to run the problem using the same functions as called by the main program in step 4. When no further possibilities can be eliminated, `explore()` then calls `checkResult()` to test the current status. If the value of some cells has not been established, then an 'incomplete' status is returned; whilst if some cells in `possibles` have no remaining values yet no value has been assigned in `grid`, or if the row and column values in `grid` do not each add up to 45, then there must have been an error and the status is returned as 'deadend'. If the status is neither 'incomplete' or 'deadend' then the puzzle must have been solved and the status is returned as 'solved'.

If a 'solved' status is returned by checkResult(), explore() returns control to the main program which prints out the answer. If an 'incomplete' status is returned, then explore() returns control to the beginning of the loop and the search begins for a second possible branch. If checkResult() returns a 'deadend' status, then we need to eliminate the current test value and back-pedal to test other values. This is where it gets complicated. This is handled by the backpedal() function.

To understand how this works, consider the situation where the first cell to be tested has possible values 1 and 2. Suppose that testing for the value 2 indicates that it is necessary to test a second cell with possible values 3 and 4. This can be shown diagrammatically as:

$$1 \text{ --- } 2$$
$$|$$
$$3 \text{ --- } 4$$

If the test for 4 produces a 'deadend', then we need to consult the branches list, which would contain [[r1,c1,1,2],[r2,c2,3,4]] (where r1,c1 and r2,c2 are the cell row and column numbers). The last top-level element in branches (i.e. [r2,c2,3,4]) contains the information for the cell currently being tested, and the last element within this (i.e. 4) is the value being tested. If 4 produces a 'deadend', then we need to remove it from branches to give [[r1,c1,1,2],[r2,c2,3]]. When control is returned to explore(), found has the value True, so explore() does not search for another branch, but begins to test the value 3 after resetting grid and possibles.

If 3 produces another 'deadend', the backpedal() function deletes the remainder of the last top-level element in branches, along with the last top-level elements in gStore and pStore – i.e. we are back to the first branch. The continue statement causes us to go through the loop a second time, and this time the value 2 is deleted, leaving only the value 1. Having eliminated 2 via its sub-branches, we can deduce that 1 must be the correct value in the first cell. We can now proceed to test the effects of assigning the value 1 to the cell. We may need to explore other sub-branches if checkResult() returns an 'incomplete' status, but this procedure will eventually produce a solution.

Possible Enhancements

1. Although it has not been found necessary, you could extend the program to do trial and error tests for cells with three remaining possible values.

2. Whilst **sudoko.py** works, the code contains an ugly amount of duplication. See if you can streamline the program.

3. Include code to test that the solution is in fact a valid solution.

4. The text-based display is not very attractive. The aesthetics could be improved considerably using the graphics facilities provided by Python. To find out how to do this, you might want to consider buying this book's companion volume – *Object Python*.

Appendix A. Installing And Running Python On Non-Windows Platforms

Chapter 2 provides instructions for downloading and installing Python on Microsoft Windows. This appendix discusses how to install Python on non-Windows platforms, with a particular focus on Unix-like systems, especially Linux, but also BSD and Mac OS X. It also includes some minor addendums to the procedures used to execute Python programs as outlined in Chapter 3.

Initial Checks

It is quite possible that you may already have Python installed, especially if you have a Linux or Mac OS X system. To find out, enter `python` (or possibly `python3`) at a command prompt.[71] If you get some text followed by a >>> prompt then you have a Python interpreter installed. However, check the text carefully for the version number.[72] If you do not have version 3.0 or higher, then you should install the most recent 3.x production version, but do not delete the older version as it may be required by other software on your system. The interpreter may be shut down using CTRL+D.

In some cases the python command may start an older version of Python even if Python 3.x is installed. If so, consult the section below on 'Multiple Versions'.

Installing Python

Package Management Systems

For Linux and other Unix-like operating systems the simplest way to install Python is to use the system's Package Management System. This should take care of the dependencies, but it may not necessarily provide the most recent version of Python. You will normally need to install more

---

[71] The 'command prompt' could be the prompt in a terminal, a console or a shell, or a Run command.

[72] You can also establish the version number by typing 'python –V' at the shell prompt.

---

than one package. For example, in Red Hat / Fedora systems, you will require the *python* package for Python and the *python-tools* for IDLE; for Debian-based systems (e.g. Ubuntu) you will require *python3* and *idle3*. Make sure the packages are version 3.0 or above and then follow the normal installation procedures.

Mac OS X

Mac OS X users should find a Mac Installer Disc Image for the latest version of Python on the download page of the Python web site (http://www.python.org/download/).[73] Select the 64-bit version if you have a 64-bit machine. Just download the appropriate .dmg file and run it following the on-screen instructions. (Note that Python must be installed on the boot drive, even though you may be offered an option to install it elsewhere). The 'Fix system Python' option should probably be disabled as it makes Python 3 the default for all scripts, consequently some programs on your system requiring Python 2 may no longer work.

Python will be installed in a subdirectory of your /Applications directory. Open the Python directory and double-click the IDLE icon to run IDLE.

Macintosh users should also check out the MacPython website at http://homepages.cwi.nl/~jack/macpython/. MacPython integrates Python into the Macintosh environment and provides specially tailored tools and extensions. The MacPython integrated development environment, simply called IDE, is similar to (although different to) IDLE.

Other Platforms

Users of other systems should consult the Python website for further information on platform-specific installers. If an installer is not available for your particular operating system, you can always compile the source code, given a suitable C compiler, using a similar procedure to that described below for Linux.

Installing Python From Source Code (Linux)

If none of the simple solutions work, then you may need to compile Python from source code. These instructions apply to Linux, but should be similar for most other operating systems.

---

[73] You ideally require Mac OS X 10.3 or later, but installers do exist for older versions.

The source code may be downloaded from the official Python website as either a gzipped (.tgz) or a bzipped (.tar.bz2) tarball. The contents are the same, but the bzip2 option is more compact and will therefore download quicker if you have a slow connection. However, it does not make much difference which you download. The **bzip2** utility is provided on most Linux distros, but if it is not available **gzip** almost certainly will be. You will also need **tar** to de-archive the files.

One easy way to test whether the necessary software is installed is to open a terminal window and enter each of the following at a command prompt:[74]

```
> bzip2 --help
> gzip --help
> tar --help
```

If help information is displayed then the utility is installed. If you are missing both gzip and bzip2 then you will need to install at least one of them. Likewise tar will need to be installed if it is not already present.

Having downloaded one of the archive files from the Python website to a suitable 'download' directory (e.g. ~/download), the next step is to decompress and then de-archive the archive file. This could be done in two separate steps using either gzip or bzip2 followed by tar. However, tar may be used with switches to complete the operation in a single step. Navigate to the 'download' directory and then enter one of the following at the command prompt:

```
> tar -xzvf filename.tgz
> tar -xjvf filename.tar.bz2
```

where *filename* is the version-specific name of the downloaded file (e.g. Python-3.3). These commands will unzip the files into a subdirectory of the 'download' directory with the same name as the archive file (e.g. ~/download/Python-3.3). I will refer to this as the 'source' directory.

Having de-archived the files using tar, move to the newly created 'source' subdirectory e.g.

```
> cd ~/download/Python-3.3
```

and look for a file called README, RELNOTES (or similar). This may contain platform-specific installation notes. The 'source' directory contains a number of subdirectories. Many of these contain README

---

[74] A > prompt is used to represent the command prompt, although it may be different on your system. A space is also inserted after the prompt for clarity. Neither the space nor the prompt should be typed.

---

files that explain their contents.

To compile the source code, the **gcc** compiler must be installed. To check, enter:

```
> gcc --help
```

As before, if help information is displayed you are ready to proceed. If not, you will need to install gcc.

Assuming gcc is installed, enter the following commands in sequence at the prompt from the source-code directory:

```
> ./configure
> make
> make test
> sudo make install
```

Some of these can run for several minutes so, unless you want to practice your rapid reading skills as the messages flash past on the screen, now is a good time to make that cup of coffee your frazzled nerves have been crying out for. (N.B. unless you are logged on as the administrator, you will be required to enter the administrator password after you enter the sudo command).

Python should be installed when all the commands have been entered and run their course.

Testing The System

To test the system, enter:

```
> python        or
> python3
```

(all lowercase) at a command prompt. If everything is working correctly, Python will start in interactive mode. Check that the version number in the first line of the text above the >>> prompt is correct. If Python does not start, then you may need to edit the path environment variable (see below). If an older version starts, then you may need to use a different command to run Python 3.x, as explained below in the section on 'Multiple Versions'. If Python is running, you can return to the command prompt by pressing CTRL-D.

You should also test IDLE by entering:

```
> idle
```

at a command prompt.

Although Python usually installs without too many problems, IDLE sometimes gives problems. The problem is usually missing dependencies (often related to Tk/Tcl graphics system). If IDLE fails to work, check the last few lines of the `make` and `make test` output to identify the missing dependencies, install them, and then re-run the installation process.

If you are unable to install IDLE, it is not the end of the world. You can still write, edit and run Python programs using a text editor and the Python interpreter. However, IDLE provides a more user-friendly environment, so it is worth making a little effort to get it to work. A Google search may identify a solution to your problems.

If IDLE is running, exit it by pressing CTRL+D.

Some distros provide other Python IDEs. One of these may serve as an alternative to IDLE, but IDLE has the advantage of being 'standard' and simple to use

Setting The Path

Python and IDLE will probably be installed in a directory that is already in your search path (e.g. /usr/bin or /usr/local/bin in Linux). However, if they do not start up, it may be that they were installed in a location not listed in the path. You can check where they are located using the commands:

```
> whereis -b python
> whereis -b idle
```

Check the current path using:

```
> echo $PATH
```

using capitals as indicated. If the Python 'installation' directory is not in the path then you will need to add it.

To temporarily change the path, you can enter the following at a command prompt (without spaces):

```
> PATH=$PATH:/usr/local/bin
```

assuming the Python 'installation' directory is '/usr/local/bin'. (Note that Linux uses a colon to separate the directories, whereas Windows uses semicolons).

Test whether Python and IDLE run as expected.

To make the changes permanent, you should edit the path in the appropriate startup file in your home directory (e.g. ~/.bashrc or ~/.profile).

Multiple Versions

If an older version of Python starts when you enter `python` at a command prompt, or if Python 3.x starts but some of your application programs fail to work correctly, then you probably have two or more versions of Python installed. As the older version may be required by some applications then the 'python' link file in the 'Python' 'installation' directory (e.g. /usr/bin) should point to the older version. If necessary, replace the current link with a new 'python' link pointing to the older version of the python executable (e.g. /usr/bin/python2.5). Then create a second link called 'python3' pointing to the new python executable (i.e. /usr/bin/python3.1 or whatever). To start the 3.x version, you should now enter:

```
> python3
```

instead of `python` at the command prompt.

Similar considerations apply to IDLE. The 3.x version of IDLE is initiated by a script called 'idle' in the Python 'installation' directory. You should change the first line of the script (e.g. #!/usr/bin/python2.5) to the full path and name of the new 3.x executable (e.g. #!/usr/bin/python3.3).

Most Linux distros provide options for adding a launcher (i.e. shortcut icon) to your desktop or to a panel. Now is probably a good time to create a launcher for IDLE – you do not really need one for the Python interpreter.

Running Scripts

If everything is set up correctly, the Python interpreter can be started in interactive mode by entering:

```
> python (or python3)
```

at a command prompt. Likewise IDLE can be started by entering:

```
> idle
```

Python scripts may be run from within IDLE, either by using IDLE to write the script or by loading a pre-written script into IDLE.

Python scripts may also be run directly from a command prompt by adding the script name as a parameter to the Python interpreter. For example, if you are in the directory containing a HelloWorld program you could enter:

`> python hello_world.py` (or `python3 hello_world.py`)

The program could also be run from any other directory by specifying the full path, for example:

`> python ~/python/hello_world.py`

It is also possible to run the scripts by just entering the script name, although this requires a little more preparation. First, you need to add an additional line (known as a **shebang**) at the beginning of the script, beginning with the characters #! followed by the path and filename of the Python interpreter, in one of two formats. For example:

`#!/usr/bin/python3`

or

`#!/usr/bin/env python3`

where /usr/bin/ is the Python 'installation' directory and python3 is the link to the executable – these should obviously be modified if you have a different filename or location. The second format is generally preferred as it will locate the first python3 interpreter found in the path even if it is in a directory other than /usr/bin (which could arise if the program is run on a different machine).

The shebang must be the very first line within the file. The file **hello_world3.py** provides an example. Because the first character is #, the line is treated as a comment and is therefore ignored by Windows, so there is no harm in including it in scripts which might also be run on Windows. The ! character tells the system that the file is to be interpreted using the interpreter specified in the rest of the line. You can leave a space after the ! for readability if you wish. (N.B. The shebangs are not included in the sample programs (see below) so, if required, you will need to add them yourself.

Second, having saved the file, you need to declare it as executable, for example by entering:

`chmod u+x hello_world.py`

at a command prompt.

You should now be able to run the script from within the directory using:

```
> ./hello_world.py
```

or from elsewhere by including the full path. For example,

```
> ~/python/hello_world.py
```

A Python script can also be run from a Linux file manager in much the same way as from Windows Explorer by clicking or double clicking on its name provided the file is declared as executable and includes a shebang. If asked, indicate that you wish to run the program in a terminal – this book does not cover how to write programs to run in a graphical user interface.

If writing a script to be run in a terminal window, but initiated from a file manager, you may need to include a line similar to:

```
input("\nPress <ENTER> to finish")
```

to keep the terminal window open when the script terminates..

Sample Programs

This book provides a number of sample programs. These have been saved in compressed archive files in three different formats (.zip, .tgz and .tar.bz2). The contents in each archive are the same.

Linux users (and other Unix-like users) should download either the .tgz or tar.bz2 file from http://www.nuim.ie/dpringle/python into their intended 'programs' directory (e.g. ~/python) and then decompress and de-archive it using one of the following commands from the directory where the zip file is located:

```
> tar -xzvf SimplePython.tgz
> tar -xjvf SimplePython.tar.bz2
```

If you intend to run the programs directly from a command prompt or a file manager, you will need to add a shebang and make sure the file is executable (as described in the previous section).

The sample files have been saved using the standard DOS end of file bytes (i.e. CR+LF). However, the UNIX convention is use only LF, whilst the classic Mac convention is to use only CR. If a script does not open correctly (e.g. in IDLE), you may need to adjust the end of line characters. The gedit text editor found on most Linux distros contains a Save As option to save a file using Unix/Linux, Mac OS Classic or Windows formats.

Appendix B. Language Changes In Python 3

The examples in this book conform to the language specifications of Python 3. If you are new to Python, then there is little point in learning older versions of the language. However, there are situations where it may be useful to know a little about how Python 3 differs from earlier specifications. For example, there are many excellent books on programming using Python 2 – with a little knowledge of the changes introduced in Python 3 these books may still prove to be an invaluable source of information. Also, you may come across an old program that you might want to update to Python 3.

Changes

The list below summarises some of the major changes. Whilst the list includes some features not covered in this book, it is by no means a complete list. Emphasis is placed on features within Python 2 which are treated differently in Python 3, but the list also includes a few new features in Python 3 for which there is no Python 2 equivalent. For a more complete list, and a more detailed explanation, you should consult the 'What's New In Python 3.0' page on the official Python website: (http://docs.python.org/3.0/whatsnew/3.0.html).

- The old `print` statement has been replaced by a `print()` function. In most instances the changes can be implemented by simply enclosing the items to be printed in parentheses – e.g. `print x` would become `print(x)`. In some instances this may be all that is required to make a Python 2 program Python 3 compatible. The inclusion of parentheses does not prevent the program being run as a Python 2 program.

- The old `raw_input()` function is the same as the new `input()` function, whilst the old `input()` function is no longer used. To replicate the old `input()` you can use `eval(input())`.

- Previously a number beginning with a zero was treated as an octal number (e.g. 012) unless the zero was followed by a letter b or x to indicate binary or hexadecimal (e.g. 0b1010). Now an octal number must include the letter 'o' (e.g. 0o12).

- All integers are now treated as long integers and have no maximum limit. Previously, unless specified as long integers, they were 32-bit.

- Integer division now returns a float rather than a rounded down integer, even if the numerator is an exact multiple of the denominator. For example, 3/2 now gives 1.5, whereas under Python 2 (and many other languages) it would evaluate to the integer 1.

- Strings are now a sequence of Unicode characters rather than a sequence of bytes (i.e. the old `unicode` type is now `str`). The functionality of the old `str` type is now supported by the new `byte` (immutable) and `bytearray` (mutable) classes. The old `basestring` class has been removed.

- `String1O` and `cString1O` have been superseded by `io.String1O` and `io.bytes1O`.

- The `str.format()` method discussed in Chapter 14 is new; Python 2 used string interpolation with a % operator

- Index numbers in a sequence can now exceed n-1; previously this would have triggered an exception.

- Dictionary comprehensions and set comprehensions (as discussed in Chapter 12) are new to Python 3.

- The dictionary method `has_key()` to test for the presence of a key in a dictionary has been removed. You now need to use the `key in dict` test instead.

- The old dictionary methods `keys()`, `items()` and `values()` have been changed. The new ones return views rather than lists and are equivalent to the old `iteritems()`, `iterkeys()` and `itervalues()` methods. The new `keys()` and `items()` methods cannot return duplicates, but the `values()` method can.

- The `xrange()` function is the same as the new `range()`; the old `range()` function is no longer used.

- Some functions are no longer available. These include `apply()`, `coerce()`, `cmp()`, `execfile()`, `file()` (to open a new file) and

```
reload().
```

- The old `exec` is now a function.

- The old `filter()`, `map()` and `zip()`, functions are now classes. The old `reduce()` function has been moved to the `functools` module.

- `Exception` is now a class, rather than a module.

- The exception handling syntax now requires the use of `as` if the exception's argument is to be printed.

- The syntax for raising an exception `raise exception, args` is now `raise exception(args)`.

- Python 2 had old-style and new-style classes; Python 3 only has new-style classes.

- The comparison operator <> (not equal) may no longer be used - use `!=` instead.

- Python 3 only permits comparisons between items of the same type. Python 2 permitted different types of item to be compared (usually meaninglessly).

- The `repr()` function should now be used instead of backticks e.g. `repr(x)` instead of `` `x` `` to display a string representation.

- The standard library has been reorganised. Several modules that existed previously have been dropped, renamed or merged into other modules.

Converting Python 2 Programs To Python 3

The above, although not complete, should allow you to read most Python 2 programs. It may also be sufficient to enable you to translate a Python 2 program into Python 3. However, tools are provided by Python to ease the process.

If you have an older program, it is recommended that you begin by checking that it is 2.6 compliant. Python 2.6 is backwards compatible with older versions, so all 2.x programs should run without difficulty. Python 2.6 also contains many of the features introduced in 3.0, so these features may be added to ease the transition.

Python 2.6 also includes a useful switch which identifies any features not compatible with Python 3.x. To test a program, simply add -3 to the end of the line when running the interpreter at a command line, i.e.

```
>>> python my.prog -3
```

This will identify any deprecated features.

Python 3 comes supplied with a very useful script called **2to3** that automates the translation from Python 2 to Python 3. It also produces a list of the changes made and flags code that may be problematic but which it cannot fix itself. The script can be run from a command line, using:

```
>>>2to3 my.prog
```

although options are also available to provide more control.

For further details see http://docs.python.org/3.0/library/2to3.html#to3-reference).

Appendix C. Reserved Names

The following are **keywords** in Python. They may not be used as identifiers for an object reference (e.g. a variable name). Attempts to do so will generate an error.

and	as	assert	break	class
continue	def	del	elif	else
except	False	finally	for	from
global	if	import	in	is
lambda	nonlocal	None	not	or
pass	raise	return	True	try
while	with	yield		

Table C.1. Python Keywords

In addition, it is better to avoid using any of Python's pre-defined identifiers. A full list for the current version of Python may be obtained by entering:

```
>>> dir(__builtins__)
```

in interactive mode. Table C.2 lists the pre-defined identifiers in version 3.3.0.

Pre-defined identifiers can be changed without producing an error message. However, this could cause problems if it is not what you intended to do. A simple way to establish whether an identifier is already in use before you use it is to test it using the `type()` function. For example,

```
>>> type (max)
```

would produce a message telling you that 'max' is 'class builtin_function _or_method'. You should therefore avoid using 'max' as a variable name. However,

```
>>> type(maxValue)
```

produces an error message telling you that 'maxValue' is not defined. It would therefore be safe to use 'maxValue' as the name for a variable.

ArithmeticError	AssertionError	AttributeError	BaseException
BufferError	BytesWarning	DeprecationWarning	EOFError
Ellipsis	EnvironmentError	Exception	False
FloatingPointError	FutureWarning	GeneratorExit	IOError
ImportError	ImportWarning	IndentationError	IndexError
KeyError	KeyboardInterrupt	LookupError	MemoryError
NameError	None	NotImplemented	NotImplementedError
OSError	OverflowError	PendingDeprecation	ReferenceError
ResourceWarning	RuntimeError	RuntimeWarning	StopIteration
SyntaxError	SyntaxWarning	SystemError	SystemExit
TabError	True	TypeError	UnboundLocalError
UnicodeDecodeError	UnicodeEncodeError	UnicodeError	UnicodeTranslateError
UnicodeWarning	UserWarning	ValueError	Warning
WindowsError	ZeroDivisionError	__build_class__	__debug__
__doc__	__import__	__name__	__package__
abs	all	any	ascii
bin	bool	bytearray	bytes
callable	chr	classmethod	compile
complex	copyright	credits	delattr
dict	dir	divmod	enumerate
eval	exec	exit	filter
float	format	frozenset	getattr
globals	hasattr	hash	help
hex	id	input	int
isinstance	issubclass	iter	len
license	list	locals	map
max	memoryview	min	next
object	oct	open	ord
pow	print	property	quit
range	repr	reversed	round
set	setattr	slice	sorted
staticmethod	str	sum	super
tuple	type	vars	zip

Table C.2. Pre-Defined Identifiers (Python 3.3.0)

Appendix D. Reference Tables

Although Python uses a smaller vocabulary than most programming languages, beginners are still faced with more details than they can comfortably remember. Many of these details are summarised throughout this book in the tables. To avoid having to thumb through the book looking for the appropriate table, all the tables have been collected in this appendix to form a 'one-stop' reference. You may find it useful to photocopy this appendix and keep it handy as you develop your programming skills.

+	Plus
-	Minus
*	Multiply
/	Divide
**	Exponent
//	Quotient (integer)
%	Modulo (remainder)

Table 4.1. Arithmetic Operators

**	Exponent
+ -	Unary Operator
* / // %	Multiply, Divide, Floor, Modulo
+ -	Plus, Minus

Table 4.2. Operator Precedence (Simplified)

Operator	Example	Equivalent to
+=	x += 5	x = x + 5
-=	x -= 5	x = x - 5
*=	x *= 5	x = x * 5
/=	x /= 5	x = x / 5
**=	x **= 5	x = x**5
//=	x //= 5	x = x // 5
%=	x %= 5	x = x % 5

Table 4.3. Augmented Operators

Function	Role
float(x)	Converts x to float number
int(x)	Converts x to int (rounding down)
round()	Converts x to int (rounding to nearest)
str(n)	Converts number n to a string

Table 4.4. Conversion Functions

Escape sequence	Effect
\\	Backslash \
\'	Single quote
\"	Double quote
\n	New line
\t	Tab

Table 5.1. Some Common Escape Sequences

Function	Use	Sample Syntax
len()	Returns number of items	n = len(aSeq)
min()	Returns the minimum value	item = min(aSeq)
max()	Returns the maximum value	item = max(aSeq)
sorted()	Returns a sorted list	bSeq = sorted(aSeq)

Table 6.1. Some Functions That May Be Used With Sequences

Method	Use	Sample Syntax
append()	Adds 1 item at end of list	aList.append(item)
extend()	Adds multiple items at end of list	aList.extend(sequence)
insert()	Inserts 1 item at specified position	aList.insert(pos,item)
remove()	Removes first occurrence of specified item	aList.remove(item)
pop()	Removes and returns item at specified position	var = aList.pop(pos)
sort()	Sorts the items *in situ*	aList.sort()
reverse()	Reverses the sequence of items in a list *in situ*	aList.reverse()
count()	Counts number of occurrences of item	n = aList.count(item)
index()	Finds first occurrence of item	n = aList.index(item)

Table 7.1. List Methods

Method	Use	Sample Syntax
upper()	Converts all characters in string 'in' to upper case	out=in.upper()
lower()	Converts all characters to lower case	out=in.lower()
capitalize()	First letter is capitalized	out=in.capitalize()
title()	First letter in each word is capitalized	out=in.title()
swapcase()	Swaps case of all characters	out=in.swapcase()
strip()	Removes white spaces at beginning and end	out=in.strip()
find()	Returns index of first occurrence of substring 's'	index=in.find('s')
startswith()	Tests whether the string begins with substring 's'	in.startswith('s')
endswith()	Tests whether the string ends with substring 's'	in.endswith('s')
replace()	Replace 'old' string by 'new'	out=in.replace('old', 'new')
join()	Joins strings in sequence using delimiter 'delim'	out=delim.join(sequence)
split()	Splits a string using a separator sep or whitespace	out=in.split('sep') out=in.split()

Table 7.2. Selected String Methods

Function	Use	Sample Syntax
random.random()	Generates a float number r in range 0.0 to just less than 1.0.	r = random.random()
random.uniform()	Generates a float number r in the range min to just less than max.	r = random.uniform(min,max)
random.randrange()	Generates an integer i in range 0 to max-1, where max is an integer parameter.	i = random.randrange(max)
random.randint()	Generates an integer i in range min to max, where min and max are integer parameters.	i = random.randint(min,max)
random.gauss()	Selects a float number r drawn from a normal distribution with a specified mean and standard deviation passed as parameters.	r = random.gauss(mean,sdev)
random.choice()	Randomly selects one item x from a sequence.	x = random.choice(seq)
random.sample()	Draw a sample of size n from a population without replacement.	aList=random.sample(seq,n)
random.shuffle()	Randomly reorganise items in a list in situ	random.shuffle(aList)
random.seed()	Set the seed used by the generator to specified number x.	random.seed(x)

Table 8.1. Selected Functions In The Random Module

==	Equal to (N.B. two = signs)
!=	Not equal
>	Greater than
<	Less than
>=	Greater than or equal to
<=	Less than or equal to

Table 9.1. Selected Comparison (Conditional) Operators

and	True if both conditions are True
or	True if at least one condition is True
not	Reverses result (i.e. True becomes False)

Table 9.2. Logical Operators

Method	Use	Sample Syntax
add()	Adds item x to set s (if it does not already exist)	s.add(x)
discard()	Removes item x if it is present in s	s.discard(x)
remove()	Removes item x if present in s, or else raises an exception	s.remove(x)
pop()	Returns and removes a random item from s, or raises an exception if s is empty	x=s.pop()
clear()	Removes all items in set s	s.clear()
copy()	Copies s to new set n	n=s.copy()

Table 12.1. Methods For Modifying A Set

Method	Use	Sample Syntax
union()	Creates new set n containing all items in s plus those in t	n=s.union(t)
intersection()	Returns a new set n containing only items in both s and t	n=s.intersection(t)
difference()	Returns items in s not in t as new set n	n=s.difference(t)
symmetric_ difference()	Creates a new set n containing every item in s and t not in both sets	n=s.symmetric_ difference(t)
update()	Adds every item in t to s (if not already present)	s.update(t)
intersection_ update()	As intersection() but result is saved to s	s.intersection_update(t)
difference_ update()	Removes items in t from s	s.difference_update(t)
symmetric_ difference_ update()	Items in s plus items in t, but not items in both, are saved to s	s.symmetric_ difference_update(t)
isdisjoint()	Returns True if s and t have no items in common	if s.isdisjoint(t): ...
issubset()	Returns True if s is a subset or equal to t	if s.issubset(t): ...
issuperset()	Returns True if s is a superset or equal to t	if s.issuperset(t): ...

Table 12.2. Methods For Set Operations

Method	Use	Sample Syntax
get()	Returns a value / tests for presence of key	v=dict.get(key, def)
setdefault()	Returns an existing value or else creates a new item	v=dict.setdefault(key, def)
pop()	Returns a value and deletes the item	v=dict.pop(key)
popitem()	Returns value and deletes the last item in the dictionary	v=dict.popitem()
clear()	Deletes all items	dict.clear()
copy()	Copies a dictionary	new=dict.copy()
update()	Updates a dictionary with the values of another dictionary	dict.update(dict2)
fromkeys()	Creates a new dictionary using keys provided in a sequence	dict={}.fromkeys(seq,val)
items()	Create an iterable view object with all key:value pairs	iter=dict.items()
keys()	Create an iterable view object containing just the keys	iter=dict.keys()
values()	Create an iterable view object containing just the values	iter=dict.values()

Table 12.3. Selected Dictionary Methods

Exception Type	Example
IOError	Attempt to open a non-existent file
IndexError	An index in a sequence is out of range
KeyError	A dictionary key does not exist
NameError	The name of a variable or function does not exist
SyntaxError	Syntax error in program
TypeError	Inappropriate type for a particular operation
ValueError	An argument has an inappropriate value
ZeroDivisionError	Denominator in a division is zero

Table 13.1. Some Common Exception Types

	String	Int	Float
specifier	:	:	:
fill character	anything but }	anything but }	anything but }
alignment	< ^ >	< ^ > =	< ^ > =
sign		- + space	- + space
base prefix		#	#
zero pad		0	0
width	int	int	int
precision	.int		.int
type		b o x X d n c	e E f g G % n

Table 14.1. Format Specifiers

Access Mode	Effect
r	Read from an existing file (default).
w	Write to a new file.
a	Append to a new or existing file.
r+	Read from or write to an existing file.
w+	Write to or read from a new file.
a+	Append to or read from a new or existing file.
t	Text file (default)
b	Binary file
U	Universal newline

Table 15.1. File Access Modes

Method	Use	Sample Syntax
read()	Reads n bytes / whole file	all=f.read()
readline()	Reads n bytes / whole line	line=f.readline(n)
readlines()	Reads lines into a list	aList=f.readlines(n)
write()	Writes string to a file	f.write(s)
writelines()	Writes a list of strings to a file	f.writelines(aList)
tell()	Returns the current position	p=f.tell()
seek()	Sets a new position	f.seek(p)
close()	Closes an open file	f.close()

Table 15.2. Selected File Object Methods

Access Mode	Effect
r	Open existing database for read only.
w	Open existing database for reading or writing.
n	Create a new database for reading or writing.
c	Open a new or existing database for reading or writing (default).

Table 15.3. Shelve Access Modes

Method	Use	Sample Syntax
getcwd()	Get current working directory	d=os.getcwd(
listdir()	List files in directory	aList=os.listdir(d)
chdir()	Set working directory	os.chdir(d)
path.isdir()	Test if a directory exists	t=os.path.isdir(d)
path.isfile()	Test if a file exist	t=os.path.isfile(fname)
stat()	Get information about a file	stat(fname)

Table 15.4. Some Useful os Methods

Attribute	Type	Description
closed	Boolean	Indicates whether a file is closed (True)
mode	String	File mode (as specified in open())
name	String	Name of the file
newlines	String	If U set, indicates the newline codes used
encoding	String	File encoding

Table 15.5. File Object Attributes

Answers To Exercises

The answers to many of the exercises can be checked using IDLE - if your code runs and produces the right answer, then it is 'correct'. The following will work if you get stuck, but are not necessarily the optimal solutions.

Chapter 4

4.2. The variable `ageOfMyWife` would be regarded as acceptable style, although `age_of_my_wife` would be regarded by some as preferable. `x` and `variable2` are also valid, but are not very informative. It is a matter of opinion whether `elvisHasLeftTheBuilding` is preferable to `ElvisHasLeftTheBuilding`. `KEEP_OFF_THE_GRASS` would normally be reserved for a constant. Names beginning with an underscore (`_`, `NOT_OK`) should in general be avoided. However, the only names that are actually invalid are: `2bRnt2b` (begins with a digit) and `i%`, `my_wife's_name`, `myName$`, `(subTotal)` - each contains one or more invalid characters.

4.4. An error message results because ((8+3)//4) evaluates to 2 and therefore ((8+3)//4-2) evaluates to zero. Dividing by zero generates an error.

4.5. The augmented versions are:
```
x += 10
x /= 10
x *= (10+5)
x *= (15/3)
```

4.8. The correct answer, as IDLE will confirm, is 11, but it may not be clear why. As with all expressions we need to start at the centre and work out. Variable `a` refers to the string '2.3e2', `float(a)` converts this to 230.0. Variable `b` refers to the integer 15. Subtracting integer 15 from floating point 230.0 gives the floating point number 215.0. Converting this to an integer gives 215. Dividing this by 20 gives 10.75 – a floating point number even though the numerator and denominator are both integers. Using `round()` to convert this to an integer causes the number to be rounded up to 11.

4.9. The first line gives 116 (i.e. octal 12 raised to the power of binary 10 plus hexadecimal 10, i.e. 10**2+16). The second line causes an error because the augmented operator is applied to a data value rather than to a variable.

Chapter 5

5.1. The first line fails because the apostrophe is not escaped. The last line fails because the double quote after 'what?' should have been a single quote.

5.2. See **baa_baa1.py** and **baa_baa2.py**.

5.3. See **scam1.py** for one solution. The body of the program could in fact be compressed into a single line as in **scam2.py**. Note the use of \n\ in both programs. The '\n' uses an escape sequence to instruct Python to output on a new line, whilst the second \ tells Python that the string is continued on the next line in the program (as explained in Chapter 3).

5.4. See **welcome.py**.

5.5. **average1.py** provides one solution. Note that the numbers (a, b and c) must be converted from strings into a numeric form before they are used in calculations. Although the answer will eventually be an integer, converting the numbers to integers at this stage could result in rounding errors, so the `float()` function is preferable. Finally, having calculated the average it should be converted to an integer using the `round()` function, rather than the `int()` function as `int()` would round down, rather than to the nearest. **average2.py** does the same thing, but in a more condensed manner.

5.6. See **circle1.py** for a solution.

5.7. The program **decimal_degrees.py** provides a solution. This probably expresses the answer to more decimal places than are necessary. We will see how to control the number of places displayed in Chapter 14. Also, there is nothing to stop us entering more than 60 minutes or seconds. We will look at how we can check for invalid input values in later chapters.

5.8. This is a bit trickier than the previous exercise. The program **degrees_minutes_seconds.py** provides a solution using some of the conversion functions introduced in Chapter 4.

5.9. The simplest approach is to draw the board inside a triple quoted long string (**chess1.py**). However, **chess2.py** provides an alternative and shorter approach. This takes advantage of the fact that there is a lot of repetition in the figure we are trying to draw.

Chapter 6

6.2. The following would select the specified sub-lists:

```
aList[0]
aList[9] or aList[-1]
aList[1:4]
aList[6:]
aList[0:7:2] or aList[:7:2]
aList[6::-2] or aList[-4::-2]
aList[:2:-3] or aList[:-8:-3]
```

6.3. See **day_of_the_week2.py** for one solution. The triple-quoted string asking what day it is today is assigned to a variable `prompt`. However, it could have been directly included in the `input()` function. Note that I have labelled the days in the prompt starting at 1, as the user might have found numbering the options from 0 slightly peculiar, but I could have started at 0. However, starting from 1 I must remember to subtract one to get the correct index for the selected day.

6.4. The expression `3*(6+3)` evaluates as 27 because the bit within the parenthesis is treated as an integer number arrived at by addition, rather than an element in a tuple. `'ab' in 'abc, def'` is `True` because `'abc, def'` is a single string, rather than two elements separated by a comma. However, `'ab' in ['abc', 'def']` is `False` because `'ab'` does not match either of the elements within a list. Finally, `'cde' in 'abc, def'` is `False` because the string `'abc, def'` does not contain the sub-string `'cde'`. However, `'c, de'` would have provided a match.

6.5. C has more elements than c because augmented operators change lists *in situ*, whereas tuples are immutable. B is bound to the same object as A, thus A `*=` 2 also changes B, which has twice as many elements as b. C is B `*` 3, so it also has twice the number of items as c.

6.6. This snippet would cause an error message. Although it uses an augmented operator, tuples are immutable, so `a+=b` would create a new object, leaving c to point to the original a. As this only has one element, `c[1]` produces a 'tuple index out of range error'. (Note the inclusion of commas in lines 1 and 2 to ensure a and b became single-element tuples.

What effect would removing the commas have? What would happen if a and b were defined as single-element lists? Use IDLE to check your answers.)

6.7. `[2,3] in a` is `False` because `in` only checks one item. Had a contained the list `[2,3]` as one of its items (e.g. `a=[1,[2,3],3,4,5]`) then the test would have returned `True`. `3 in b` generates an error because you cannot test for an `int` inside a string, but as `'2,3' in a` illustrates you can test for a string inside a list because a string would be a valid list item (although it is not present in this case yielding `False`).

6.8. The statement would evaluate to `False`. The index on the left hand side would evaluate to the number of items minus one, and hence refer to the last item. The index on the right hand side also refers to the last item. The item referred to on both sides is therefore the same, hence `is` would evaluate to `True` and `is not` reverses this to give `False`.

6.9. The error message explains it fairly clearly. The problem is that the `len()` function counts the number of items starting from 1, and therefore returns a value of 5. However, the maximum possible index in this case would be 4. Note, however, that `a[:len(a)]` would not generate an error, even though the second index is out of range.

6.10. Note the second last line returns a list even though a tuple was passed to the function. The last line generates an error message because although the list passed as the argument is valid, the function cannot process mixed string and numeric items. The previous line, however, was able to handle mixed int and float variables.

6.11. The following will produce the desired sequences:

```
a)   s = aList + [6,7,8]
b)   s = tuple(aList)
c)   s = aList[::2]
d)   s = aList * 3
e)   s = aList[::-1]
f)   s = tuple(aList[::-2])
```

6.12. The matrix could be created using:

```
>>> John=['John',34,'Male','Single']
>>> Susan=['Susan',19,'Female','Single']
>>> Mohammed=['Mohammed',45,'Male','Married']
>>> Elizabeth=['Elizabeth',63,'Female','Divorced']
>>> matrix=[John,Susan,Mohammed,Elizabeth]
```

Using the above, the answers are:

```
a)   ['Mohammed', 45, 'Male', 'Married']
b)   'Single'
c)   'John'
d)   'Divorced'
```

6.13. See **month2text.py** for one solution. There is no need to convert the day and year into integers as we are printing them out again as strings. We need to subtract 1 from the month to take account of the silly counting used to index the months tuple.

6.14. Your message should read: 'T g slnhcphelh o eoeaeafwt u'. See **encrypt1.py**.

Chapter 7

7.1. Note that the answer to the first line was converted to a list by the sorted() function. The list() function in the fourth line is redundant for the same reason - this is why the fifth line gives the same result as the fourth. One might expect the sixth line to also give the same result, but instead it generates an error because the sort() method sorts the list *in situ*, but does not return anything (i.e. what is returned is type None).

7.3. The following would do the job:

```
a)  aList.extend([4,5,6])
b)  aList.append([4,5,6])
```

7.4. The even numbers could be removed using:

```
del aList[1]
aList.pop(2)
aList.remove(6)
aList[4:5]=[]
```

7.5. d is True. The second line makes a copy of a in b. b is unaffected by any of the subsequent changes, therefore b[3] in the final line has the value 2. The third line binds c to the same object as a, consequently the a.sort() and c.reverse() methods in the subsequent lines affect both a and c. After these operations c[3] has the value 2, the same as b[3] (although b[3] only happens to be 2 due to the original sequence of the items in a). The final line tests whether these two values are the same object. They are, because the previous operations simply moved the object references contained in the lists around; they did not create any new objects with the value 2. If you got the right answer (for the right reasons), give yourself a pat on the back.

7.6. I trust you did not fall for this. The string at the end is exactly the same as it was at the beginning because the changes were all temporary and not assigned to `aString`. However, if you were to insert `'aString='` at the beginning of each line, the changes would be cumulative. This would bring you back almost to where you started except 'Spain' would now be 'Bahrain'.

7.7. `aString = 'four one three two'` would do it, but it was not really what I was looking for. I was thinking more along the lines of `aString=' '.join(sorted(aString.strip().split()))`. (Do not worry if you did not get this one – it is a totally contrived example which you are very unlikely to meet in the real world.)

7.8. **fox_sort.py** provides an answer. The second line uses a string method to convert the string to upper case – this must be done before the letters are sorted. The third line uses the `sorted()` function from Chapter 6 to sort the characters in the string. The fourth line uses the `join()` function to join the characters into a string without any spaces. (Note that `str(s)` would not have the desired effect). Finally the string `strip()` method is used to remove the white space which would otherwise be at the beginning of the string.

7.9. **lazy_fox.py** provides two answers. The first solution gives the right result by splitting the string into a list of words, but is not very elegant. The second is much neater, using `replace()` methods in a triangular manner.

7.10. See **population.py** for a solution. Each of the countries is represented by a tuple saved in a list. Note that the population is the first item in each tuple because this is the one used as the sort field. The `sorted()` function is used to sort the tuples in ascending population size, then the `reverse()` method is used to sort them in descending size.

Chapter 8

8.1. Although not very elegant, you could use:

```
>>> import random
>>> round(random.gauss(97.8, 7.3))
>>> round(random.gauss(97.8, 7.3))
>>> round(random.gauss(97.8, 7.3))
```

8.2. The following lines would do the necessary:

```
>>> import random
```

```
>>> random.uniform(0.0,30.0)
```

8.3. The function `random.random()` generates a number in the range 0.0 to just less than 1.0. We need to 'amplify' this by a factor of 20 (i.e. 0.0-10.0) and then add 10.0 to change the minimum possible value from 0.0 to 10.0. Hence:

```
>>> import random
>>> 20*random.random()+10.0
```

would do the trick.

8.4. Assuming the random module has not already been imported, enter the following:

```
>>> import random
>>> aList = ['Matthew','Mark','Luke','John','Hamish']
>>> random.sample(aList,3)
```

8.5. To allow replacement, we could use the `random.choice()` function:

```
>>> import random
>>> aList=['Matthew','Mark','Luke','John','Hamish']
>>> x=random.choice(aList)
>>> y=random.choice(aList)
>>> z=random.choice(aList)
>>> x,y,z
```

8.6. There are other ways to do this, but **card_select1.py** provides one solution. (If you had a list containing every single card, you could use `random.shuffle()` to shuffle the cards, then use the list `pop()` method to pick the last card. However, setting up a list of 52 cards would be tedious without using a loop would be tedious. Loops are explained in Chapter 10).

8.7. Two solutions are provided: **recession1.py** and **recession2.py**.

8.8. See **lottery.py**. Note that the output from `random.randrange()` must be incremented by 1 as the method produces a number in the range 0 to 99 inclusive. The `random.randint()` method output does not need to be incremented, but it requires two parameters. To compare the two results the seed must be reset to the same value before each call. In this case the seed `s` is itself randomly generated, but you could have assigned a specific arbitrary value (e.g. 123). Because the seed is randomly generated, a different winning lottery ticket should be selected each time the program is run, although the tickets selected by the two methods should always be the same.

Chapter 9

9.3. See **random_integer.py**.

9.4. If 'number' is an initialised integer, the following will do the job:
```
>>> print('Odd' if number%2 else 'Even')
```

The expression `number%2` will return the remainder after dividing number by 2. 0 is interpreted as `False` and all other values, including 1, as `True`. Although more verbose, `number%2==1` would also work.

9.5. The 6 lines in the `if` ... `elif` ... `else` construct could be replaced by:
```
print('Low' if x<4 else ('Medium' if x<7 else 'High'))
```

This embeds a second conditional expression in place of the `False` outcome of the outer conditional expression.

9.6. See **id_add1.py**. One obvious limitation with this program is that it does not make the changes permanent, but we will see how to save the changes to a file in Chapter 15.

9.7. See **number_guess.py**. This includes an `else` clause to catch unexpected answers, but in fact most invalid answers will cause the program to crash when passed to the `int()` function. We will see ways to handle this in Chapter 13.

9.8. See **yes_no.py**. This solution allows the user to either type 'yes' or 'no' in full or just the first letter.

Chapter 10

10.1. See **ascii.py**.

10.2. See **vowels.py** for a solution. This solution checks whether a letter is in a list of upper case vowels, but lower case vowels could have been used just as easily. The `ord()` function used to specify the arguments in the `range()` function has not been discussed, but it returns the Ascii code of a character – i.e. it is the reverse of the `chr()` function. You could have used the Ascii codes directly (ie. `range (65,90)` for upper case, or `range(97,122)` for lower case) – these codes can be ascertained from the solution to Exercise 10.1.

10.3. See **card_select3.py**. Note that if you use **card_select2.py** as your starting point, all the lines inside the `for` loop need to be indented (or double indented if already indented). If your program fails to work, make sure all your lines are correctly indented. You can indent several lines at the same time in IDLE by selecting the lines to be indented and pressing CTRL +] (right square bracket).

10.4. See **coin_toss2.py**. This program has three levels of indentation, but note how easy it is to follow the structure, especially using the colour coding in IDLE.

10.5. See **repeated_sample.py**.

10.6. See **coin_runs.py**. This program contains one for loop inside another.

10.7. See **green_bottles2.py**. If you detest this song as much as I do, you may prefer **dynamite.py**. This has been written in a particularly opaque style, but see if you can figure out how it works.

10.8. **pangram1.py** provides a solution. This begins by converting all the characters to upper case, then it counts the number of occurrences of each letter in the first for loop. The second for loop checks that each letter has occurred at least once. If not pangram is set to False and the break statement prevents any further checks. If the second loop completes without a break, then pangram remains set as True. The if statement determines the output message. **pangram2.py** provides a neater and more direct solution. This does not count the occurrences of each letter, but simply uses a for loop to test whether each letter appears in the sentence using the in operator.

10.9. See **r_months.py** for a solution. Note that if the letter 'r' is not present the find() method returns -1 (which is True), so we must test if it is >0 to produce False.

10.10. **big_words.py** provides three solutions. The first is the 'verbose' solution, the second uses a list comprehension whilst the third reduces this still further. Note that the list comprehension is provided directly as an argument to the print() function in the third solution, so we do not need to create a named list (similar to BigWords or BigWords2). Also, the text string is split into individual words within the list comprehension in the third solution, rather than depending upon the prior creation of the list words.

10.11. See **reverse_text1.py** for one solution. Note that while n: would not work as the loop would terminate when n was 0 and the first letter in the message (i.e. `text[0]`) would not be added to the output string. **reverse_text2.py** provides an alternative, and arguable neater, solution using a `for` loop.

10.12. **input_check4.py** should catch most problems (although it is still possible to thwart it). This program operates much the same as **input_check3.py** in the text, except the valid range checks are removed and lines 4 and 5 have been added. Line 4 uses a list comprehension to create a list `r` containing only negative signs and the digits 0 to 9. Line 5 checks whether any invalid characters were detected by comparing the length of the new list with the length of the input string (i.e. `reply`). It does not matter that `reply` and `r` are different types – if both sequences have the same number of elements then no invalid characters were detected and we can proceed to convert the string to an integer and then break out of the loop.

One problem (there may be others!) with **input_check4.py** is that it does not distinguish between a negative sign and a minus sign. For example, enter '7-3' as a response to see what happens. See if you can amend **input_check4.py** to fix this loophole.

input_check5.py provides a solution by using another list comprehension to count the number of minus signs after the first character in the input string.

10.13. **number_guess1.py** provides one solution, but it does not attempt to track invalid answers. **number_guess2.py** is more unwieldy, but it traps invalid answers using a similar approach to exercise 10.12.

10.14. See **encrypt2.py** for one possible solution. If correct, your message should read:

'WtoomnT g slnhcph   ue:helh o eoady a eaeafwt u. Tsesoi   h a tntmimnnhgoe. Pa sdo sgipiSmvnlsre umsenlnlbieeenyrea a ooa.'

10.15. See **decrypt.py**. The decrypted text should read: 'Our security has been compromised. That ****** Pringle has gone and told everyone our secrets.' (Slombovian sources inform me there is no direct English translation of the original Slombovian word represented by the asterisks, although 'person of considerable esteem' was suggested as one approximation. Other sources intriguingly suggested that the word might in some way allude to my ancestry, but they declined to elaborate).

10.16. C'mon, get real! If I knew the answer to this, do you think I would be writing books about Python? However, the program **lottery_numbers1.py** does select a possible (albeit highly unlikely) winning combination of numbers after asking the user how many numbers they require and what range they must fall within. It also calculates the odds of winning. Before looking at the answer, see if you can write your own program to do the same things. (N.B. The number of ways of selecting r objects out of a total of n is given by n! / r! (n-r)!, although you may need to think your way around running the risk of overflow if multiplying a large number of numbers together.).[75]

Chapter 11

11.1. See **lazy_fox2.py**. The test program produces one successful and one unsuccessful result.

11.2. See **pangram3.py**. Try changing 'jumps' to 'jumped' in the test program to confirm that the function works correctly. Note that the function returns either `True` or `False`, allowing it to be directly used in an `if` statement.

11.3. See **factorial.py**. Note that if we enter a non-integer the program will crash. We will develop a function to test that the value entered is a valid integer shortly (exercise 11.7).

11.4. If you answered yes, could I interest you in investing in my sure-fire money-making pyramid scheme? As **scam.py** illustrates, you would be out of pocket. However, what would happen in a month with only 30 days?

11.5. See **poker_hand.py**. The selected cards are stored in a list (`cards`). A new card is only added if it does not already exist in the list. Each card has two data items (a value and a suit). These are returned from the function as two separate values, but they are assigned in the main program to a tuple (`card`). The list (`cards`) is therefore a list of tuples.

11.6. **yn.py** provides one solution. The `while` loop is exited by a `return` if the user enters one of the valid answers, otherwise the user is prompted again. Rather than test for every conceivable combination of upper and lower case responses the function converts the response to lower case

---

[75] The ! symbol means factorial. n! is equal to n multiplied by (n-1) multiplied by (n-2) etc. down to 1. For example, 3! is 3x2x1=6.

before testing. The first call statement uses the default prompt, whilst the second supplies a prompt as an argument.

11.7. **get_int.py** provides a possible solution. The `get_int()` function has three parameters. By default the value entered must be zero or higher, but maximum value can be up to 100 digits long - note the use of scientific notation to assign the default value of `max`. The default prompt is an empty string - this allows the user to specify their own prompt. The function checks that the user only enters digits 0 to 9 or a negative sign. If a negative sign is entered, if must be the first character in the response (i.e. 7-4 would be rejected). If it passes the tests, the input string is converted to an integer and tested if it lies in the acceptable range. (N.B. This solution would not permit an integer to be entered in scientific notation, or as a binary, octal or hexadecimal number.) If you think there must be an easier way to do all this, then you are correct. All will be revealed in Chapter 13.

11.8. **get_float.py** provides a solution. It is very similar to **get_int.py**, except it permits a decimal place. However, the function checks that there is only one decimal place. The default minimum is set to a very low value rather than zero.

11.9. See **mylib**. Your functions and docstrings will probably be different, but as long as they work that is all that is required. Do not forget to move your **mylib** module to the 'site-packages' folder to make it available to programs in all folders.

11.10. See **number_guess3.py**. This calls the `get_int()` and `yn()` functions in **mylib**.

11.11. See **lottery_numbers2.py** for a solution. Note that the import statements need to be in the main program (at the beginning), rather than in either the `main()` function or the functions where they are used.

11.12. See **int_mean.py**. Although the numbers entered are all integers, the answer will be a float. You may have thought that the parameter in `average()` should have had an asterisk. The number of values entered is variable, but no matter how many are entered they are passed as a single list so the asterisk in this case an asterisk is unnecessary. In fact, it would cause the program to crash.

11.13. See **slombovia.py** for a module file. **slombovia_test.py** uses the functions to encrypt and decrypt sample text. As a further test, see if you can decrypt the following text in interactive mode (a copy of which may be found in **Slombovia.txt**):

Iagntwtt sot oiert ooa sogorehrtfhbknnyeSmvnw i i ee eo cpdlbi. Hert bsrciiwlbt fctorfeov,hplhslmtodeodfu o-awe euie a u oiiltpord.

Chapter 12

12.1. Did `c&b==a` catch you out? The logical 'and' (`&`) means both must be present, rather than 'add together'. `c.union_update(b)` raises an exception because the method is simply called `update()`.

12.2. See **nato.py**. To list the EU countries not in NATO we need to remove the NATO members using a difference operation. **nato.py** provides two alternative ways to do this.

12.3. See **voters.py**. This uses an intersection to identify the undecided voters. It also uses difference operations to determine the committed supporters for each candidate.

12.4. See **mail_list.py**. This is much the same as **voters.py** except that it uses a union operation.

12.5. **pangram4.py** provides a solution. This enters the test text as a string, converts it to lower case, and then converts it to a set `s`. A second set `alpha` is created containing all the lower case letters of the alphabet using a set comprehension. If `s` is a superset of `alpha` then it must contain all the letters of the alphabet, plus possibly a few extra characters (e.g. spaces, punctuation marks), and is therefore a pangram. If the entered text is not a pangram, the program uses a difference operation to identify the letters that are missing.

The file **Pangram.txt** contains a few sentences you can use to test your program (courtesy of Wikipedia).

12.6. **supporters1.py** provides a solution, although it is far from ideal on a number of levels (not least being that it would have been quicker to answer the questions without writing a program). We can answer the two questions using three sets (i.e. without creating sets for English or the other teams). We need to union the United and Liverpool sets. The first question can be answered by testing if the Irish set is a subset of (i.e. completely contained within) the unioned set. The second question can be answered by testing if the unioned set is equal to the Irish set using an equal to operator. One weakness with the solution is that it assumes that each name is unique.

12.7. See **enter_set_items1.py**. The `set_input()` function should not require much explanation, but the `assign_type()` function may do. This attempts to identify if the string entered by the user is a valid integer or floating point number. The first three `if` statements attempt to eliminate situations where the user entered a dot or a minus by itself; where the user entered more than one dot or minus; or where the user entered a minus that was not the first character. In each instance, the string entered by the user is returned as a string. The next line uses a set comprehension to create a set of valid digits, to which a minus sign is added in the following line. The next two lines create a similar set including a decimal point. Note that `digits` must be copied before adding the decimal point character: `realdigits=digits.add('.')` would have changed `digits` as well. The string entered by the user is converted to a set, which in turn is tested to see if it is a subset of either `digits` or `realdigits`. If so, the appropriate conversion is made.

12.8. See **champions2.py**. In addition to removing the quotes around the keys in the dictionary definition, the `input()` function that asks the user to enter a year, and the `print()` function that displays the champions need minor adjustments.

12.9. If you entered the code (**sorted_view_trap.py**), you will discover that the answer is 5, whereas you might have expected 3. Changes to a dictionary are automatically reflected in a view, but `dview` (despite its cunningly deceptive name) is not a view: when the view created by the `items()` method is passed through a `sorted()` function it is converted to a list. You can confirm this by entering `type(dview)`. This list contains each key-value item as a two-element tuple, so the unpacking in the `for` loop works as it would with a view. Whilst the (unsorted) view would have reflected the changes caused by the two `pop()` methods, the list is totally independent and remains unchanged.

12.10. **supporters2.py** creates a dictionary containing a list as the value for each key (name). An item view is then used in a `for` loop to create the required sets. The final part is similar to exercise 12.6, with a bit of additional information displayed as a bonus. **supporters3.py** provides a neater solution by creating a function `sub` that defines a set using a criterion passed as an argument. The function uses a set comprehension to identify the items which contain the criterion anywhere within the values list – i.e. it no longer matters which sequence nationality and team supported are entered for each individual. The sets are calculated as required by the set operations in the main program. This involves a certain amount of duplication and might become a consideration if working with very large samples. If so, named sets could be created using the function and then used in the set operations.

12.11. **dict_update2.py** provides a solution. Both dictionaries are converted to key views. The updates are applied to items in the intersection of the two views.

12.12. See **letter_count.py**. This creates a list of letters using a list comprehension. This is then used to create a dictionary using a `fromkeys()` method. The letters of the alphabet form the keys, and each is assigned an initial value of zero. The text is then read one character at a time, and the value of the appropriate key is incremented by one. The second `for` loop displays the results using an item view.

12.13. **eurovision2.py** begins by creating a new dictionary `count` using the countries as keys. The value is count of the number of wins, created by cycling through a view of the `eurovision` dictionary and incrementing the count each time a country is mentioned. Note that a simple `count[winner]+1` would not work as it would throw an exception if the country had not been encountered before; using the `get()` method we can assign a default (i.e. 0) on the first occurrence and then increment it.

The second part is more difficult. Whilst dictionaries can be sorted using their keys, they cannot be directly sorted using their values. The ranked table is therefore generated by adding the number of wins and the countries to a list as string items. This list is sorted and printed. The `reverse` key displays the items in reverse order (i.e. highest wins first) – unfortunately this also causes the countries to be displayed in reverse alphabetical order. Further code would be required if you wished the countries to be listed in alphabetical order.

12.14. See **phonebook1.py** for a suggested answer. Note that the key is case sensitive, so the user could find it frustrating if they had to guess the correct combination of upper and lower case letters. However, the line

```
name=name.title()
```

forces the user's response into the correct format.

12.15. See **phonebook2.py** for a suggested answer.

12.16. See **phonebook3.py** for a suggested answer. It will be noted that the program makes extensive use of functions. This is primarily to make the program more readable, but the `mySub` library functions are also used to 'subcontract' repeated operations.

The program does not check whether the phone numbers entered are valid. If required, this could be 'subcontracted' to a function to check that the number of digits is correct, that there are no invalid characters, etc.

The `setup()` function creates a starting dictionary for testing purposes. However, by deleting the two lines after the comment, the program can be initiated with no starting entries.

12.17. **phonebook4.py** is very similar to **phonebook3.py**, but it uses a nested dictionary to store the phone numbers, addresses and emails for each individual. Although lengthy, it does not introduce any other new features.

Chapter 13

13.1. See **zero_divide_fix3.py**. The test for a percentage in the valid range is included as part of the *try_suite*. If the test fails, a `ValueError` exception is raised using `raise`. The other potential problems are trapped in the usual manner.

13.2. See **day_of_the_week3.py**. This not only traps an answer out of range to the first question, but a non-integer answer to either question.

13.3. See **float_test.py**. This is similar to **int_test2.py**.

13.4. See **yes_no_test.py**. Apart from trapping unanticipated errors (which will probably never happen), this `yn()` function adds little to the `yn()` function in Chapter 11.

13.5. The program **string_test.py** contains a function `get_string()` which in truth does little more than the basic `input()` function. However, it traps unanticipated exceptions (although it is difficult to envisage what these might be), but permits a CTRL-C escape. The `strip()` method removes surplus white space. This could be useful if the string was to be used with comparison operators, although it could in other circumstances create problems. The `empty` parameter determines whether empty strings are or are not permitted.

13.6. See **mylib.py**.

13.7. See **safe_pop1.py** for one solution. Although this works, testing for the exception in the function is somewhat cumbersome. A neater alternative, taking advantage of the fact that exceptions propagate upwards, is provided by **safe_pop2.py**.

13.8. See **enter_set_items2.py**. This uses `try … except` in the `getInput()` function to check for unanticipated errors, but the big change is in the `assignType()` function which is considerably simplified. This attempts to convert the input string to either a float or an int depending upon whether the string includes a decimal point. If the conversion raises an exception, the string is returned as a string.

13.9. The program **dictionary_editor.py** contains suitable functions. Some functions take advantage of the fact that a non-existent key will raise an exception, whilst others do explicit checks. Note that the dictionary can be modified within a function because only its object reference is passed as an argument. The file is currently set up as an executable file, but it could be easily converted to a non-executable module by editing the last few lines.

Chapter 14

14.2. The following produce the desired output, but are not necessarily the only solutions:

a) `>>> print('{0:^^8}'.format(' Up '))` – Note that the first ^ is a fill specifier, whilst the second is an alignment specifier.

b) `>>> print('{0:>>15}'.format(' Exit'))` – In this example it would have been simpler to use: `>>> print('>'*10,'Exit')`.

c) `>>> print('{0:25}'.format('Left adjusted'))`

d) `>>> print('{0:>25}'.format('Right adjusted'))`

e) `>>> print('{0:}{1:>21}'.format('Left','Right'))`

f) `>>> print('{0} {1} {0}'.format('ooo','0'*3))` - Note that the second argument uses a different approach to repeat the character three times. You could of course just use `print('ooo000ooo')`!

g) `>>> print('{0:>>20}'.format(' This way >>>'))`

h) `>>> print('{0:~^26}'.format('Don\'t Make Waves'))`

14.4. These will do the job, but are not necessarily the only solution:

a) `>>> print('{0:*^12}'.format(12345678))`

b) `>>> print('{0:=12}'.format(-12345678))`

c) `>>> print('{0:>12}'.format(-12345678))`

d) `>>> print('{0:=+12}'.format(12345678))`

e) `>>> print('{0:<+12}'.format(12345678))`

```
f) >>> print('{0} in hexadecimal is {0:#x}'.format(345))
g) >>> print('{0} in octal is {0:#o}'.format(345))
h) >>> print('{0} in binary is {0:#b}'.format(345))
```

14.6. The following produced the desired results:

```
a) >>> print('{0:.^14.2%}'.format(n))
b) >>> print('{0:^14.2%}'.format(n))
c) >>> print('{0:14.2%}'.format(n))
d) >>> print('{0:^+14.2%}'.format(n))
e) >>> print('{0:=+14.2%}'.format(n))
f) >>> print('{0:<14.2%}'.format(n))
g) >>> print('{0:14.2f}'.format(n))
h) >>> print('{0:<14.4f}'.format(n))
i) >>> print('{0:14.2e}'.format(n))
j) >>> print('{0:^14.2E}'.format(n))
k) >>> print('{0:.>14.2E}'.format(n))
l) >>> print('{0:>> 14.2e}'.format(n))
```

14.7. See **unicode1.py**. This uses the `get_int()` function in the `myLib` module, but the key part of the solution is the use of the two `str.format()` calls. The second of these defines four different formats for the same data value.

14.8. This exercise is more complex than it might first appear. **dictionary_display.py** provides one solution, but it contains a few features that may require comment. First, the keys can be any length, therefore if we want the colons to be vertically aligned we need to know the length of the largest key before we output the results. This is achieved using the variable `max_length`. It is initialised to 3 because even if all the keys have less than 3 characters, the column will still need to be 3 characters wide to accommodate the heading 'Key'. Second, the program will stop prompting for input if the user enters a zero-length key. However, once the user has entered a key, they are not permitted to enter a zero-length definition. It is assumed that if the user has gone to the bother of typing a key, then they would only enter a zero-length definition by accident. However, you may prefer to use this as an indication that they do not wish to enter any more definitions. Third, we are required to print the keys in alphabetical order. This is done using an item view, as explained in Chapter 12. Fourth, when printing the heading we want to pad the word 'Key' with leading blanks. This is handled by a `str.format()` method. Note that `max_length` is assigned to replacement field 2, which in turn forms part of the format specification for replacement field 0. The same specifications are used for body of the table. Finally, the number of dashes below the heading is calculated as `max_length` plus 13 (i.e. `max_length` plus the length of ' : Definition').

Chapter 15

15.1. See **open_read_file2.py**. The function returns either the file handle or the Boolean value `False`. If a file handle is returned, the file is printed then closed. The function checks whether the file exists, and invites the user to try again if it is not found, and also checks for other unanticipated errors.

15.2. **open_read_file3.py** uses a `with` statement. However, this causes the file to be closed when the function returns control to the main program, so the output lines have to be moved inside the function.

15.3. See **id_add2.py** for a possible solution. This opens **Valid.txt** as mode 'r+' (i.e. reading and writing without destroying the original). The current ids are read into a list, and new ids are appended if they do not already exist. When the user finishes adding names, the file pointer is set to 0 and the new list is written out on top of the original contents. The `with` statement ensures the file is closed.

A slightly different approach is used in **id_add3.py**. This opens the file in 'a+' mode. Each time a new id is entered it is appended to the file immediately, rather than waiting to write the entire list at the end. One advantage of this is that if the program crashed for any reason, only the last entry would be lost. Note that the file pointer is set by default to the end of the file, so before reading the existing names it must be set to 0. However, any writes to the file will always be appended at the end of the file irrespective of the pointer's current value.

15.4. See **split_lines.py**. This begins by establishing the length of the longest word in the file; this (plus one for a space) determines the minimum length of line that can be permitted to avoid splitting words between lines. The input file is read in chunks whose length is determined by the maximum line length specified by the user, or (if shorter) by the end of paragraph. Chunks containing only a newline character are discarded to eliminate treble spacing between paragraphs. Each chunk is searched for the last space between words; this defines the end of the line to be output. The pointer for the input file is reset to the first character after this space before reading the next chunk. The process is repeated until the end of file is found.

15.5. See **peek.py**. The file is opened as a binary file. This allows the contents to be read one byte at a time, even if it is a text file. Only the bytes in the printable ASCII character range (plus the special codes 10

<LF> and 13 <CR>) are displayed using the `chr()` function.

15.6. See **phonebook5.py**. This is identical to **phonebook4.py** except that the `setup()` function now reads the phonebook data from a pickle saved in the binary file **Phonebook.dat** and the `main()` function contains a couple of lines to save the current phonebook once the `while` loop is exited. The `pickle` module must of course be imported before it is accessed.

15.7. The program **epl_save.py** saves the information, whilst **epl_read.py** could be used to interrogate it.

15.8. The password file can be created using **password_edit.py**. A `dictionary` provides a very suitable structure for holding userids (as keys) and passwords (as values). Although `shelve` could be used to retain a key structure there is little need as a `dictionary` can be easily pickled as a single object. The program uses a `try` statement to test whether a **Password.dat** already exists and if so it loads the data into a dictionary; if not, it begins with an empty dictionary. Userids and passwords are added until the user indicates they are finished. The `dictionary` is dumped to a file for future editing or to test userid and password combinations.

The **password_edit.py** program contains few frills. It does not, for example, allow you to change the password for a given user nor does it provide an option to remove userids. However, these options could easily be added if required. Also, the userids and passwords are case sensitive – it might be desirable to force the user input into either upper or lower case to make life easier for the user (although mixed case userids and passwords are more secure).

The program **password_check.py** uses the file created by **password_edit.py** to test whether the userid and password entered by a user is a valid combination. The `check_validity()` function is effectively the main function. At present this prints a message indicating whether the userid/password pair is valid, but it also returns either `True` or `False`. This means it could be used to determine whether the user should get access to the remainder of the program using a call statement taking the form:[76]

---

[76] Whilst the programs in this exercise demonstrate the basic principles, they provide very little security. Because the source code is visible to everyone, anyone running **password_check.py** could simply edit the source code to set `valid()` to `True` or

```
if valid():
    permit access
else:
    terminate program
```

15.9. See **open_read_file4.py**. The program opens by displaying the contents of the current directory. Subdirectories are prefaced by the letter 'D'. The list omits files whose names begin with a '.' or end with a '~' to simplify the list for Linux users by omitting hidden files and backup files, but this should not affect Windows users. To display a text file enter its name – binary files raise an exception which is handled by displaying an error message. To change folders, enter 'cd `dirname`' where `dirname` is the name of the folder you wish to move to. You can use 'cd ..' to move to the parent folder. To exit the program enter CTRL+C.

15.10. See **filesize.py**. The program contains three functions. The first (`get_folder()`) gets the name of the folder to be interrogated. This uses the `os.path.isdir()` method to check whether the folder specified by the user exists. If not, the user is invited to try again or abort (by pressing CTRL+C. The second function (`get_files()`) reads the files in the specified folder. The size of each file is determined and the information is stored in a dictionary using the filenames as keys. The tricky bit is to sort the filenames by filesize. This is done using the `dict_sort()` function. This creates a list of the key:value pairs stored as tuples, but with the values (filesize) and keys (filename) in reverse order. The tuples are sorted by filesize using the `sort()` method and the sequence is then reversed to put the items in descending filesize. The list is then returned with the original key:value order restored. The final few lines of the `get_files()` function displays the information using the `str.format()` method described in Chapter 14.

15.11. See **csv_create.py**. The `open_file()` function tests whether the file to be opened for output already exists. If it does, the user is offered the choice of overwriting it or aborting. After the output file is opened, the `get_data()` function prints out a header line (placing the variable names in quotes) and then inputs data from the user and writes it out line by line until the user terminates the input by pressing CTRL+C instead of entering a data value. All the data (including 'age') are output as strings, but are interpreted as data or strings as appropriate by the application program.

alternatively could access the **Password.dat** file to get everyone's userid and password. If you want to keep your credit cards safe, you would be better off just sending the details to me.

15.12. **csv_read.py** does the job. The `main()` function calls three functions: `open_file()` opens a CSV file for input; `read_data()` reads the file, discards the first (header) line, and converts each subsequent line to a list (`new_row`), which is added as an item to a list for the entire dataset (`dset`); whilst `process()` performs the required calculations using the data in `dset`. The key line in `read_data()` is `new_row=` `line.replace('\n','').split(',')-` this removes the newline characters and splits the string into separate list items. Note the use of the `strip()` method in `process()` – this removes the surplus spaces at the beginning of the list items.

Chapter 16

16.1. See **unicode2.py**.

16.2. See **read_text_files.py.** This contains few frills, but should cope with most contingencies. If not, the `try` … `except` block should indicate the problem. Using `with` ensures the files are closed. The `print()` functions at the beginning of the loop help identify which file is which – note the use of the * operator to provide 'underlining'.

16.3. See **sum5.py.** This traps all the wrong responses. Non-numeric parameters are trapped and the function `fix()` is called to allow the user fix the problem. Likewise the problem is trapped and remedied if only one number is entered. However, if no parameters are entered on the command line the program terminates as this situation cannot be distinguished from running the program from IDLE or Explorer (which cannot be fixed by the `fix()` function).

Index

www.ingramcontent.com/pod-product-compliance
Lightning Source LLC
Chambersburg PA
CBHW060822170526
45158CB00001B/60